The Press
and the
Suburbs

The Press
and the
Suburbs

The Daily Newspapers
of New Jersey

David Sachsman
Warren Sloat

CENTER
FOR URBAN
POLICY   RESEARCH

Copyright 1985, Rutgers, The State University of New Jersey
All rights reserved.
Published in the United States of America
by the Center for Urban Policy Research
Building 4051 — Kilmer Campus
New Brunswick, New Jersey 08903

Library of Congress Cataloging in Publication Data

Sachsman, David B.
    The press and the suburbs.

    1. American newspapers—New Jersey. 2. Community newspapers—
New Jersey. I. Sloat, Warren. II. Rutgers University. Center for Urban
Policy Research. III. Title.
PN4897.N49S23 1985   071'.49   85-5934
ISBN 0-88285-108-X

Contents

Foreword

The historic definition of newspapers-USA was linked to the city. There are few children of a generation ago unfamiliar with the Hollywood platitude of high-speed presses whirling out the crime stories of the metropolis while their parents chuckled over Ben Hecht's and Charles MacArthur's *Front Page*. The reporters were the epitome of "Big-City Slickers," and their bosses and advertising departments were closely associated with — if not prisoners of —the major downtown emporiums.

The changing economic and demographic patterns of the United States have many measurements; few of them, however, are more comprehensive than the new circulation realities of the press. The "hole-in-the-doughnut" phenomenon has afflicted practically all major central city newspapers. The decline in population counts, changes in socioeconomic characteristics and, in many cases, shrinkage of business activity in core areas have caused a desperate areal expansion of the classic major urban newspapers. In an intense effort to keep pace with the changing location of their readers — and most particularly with the upscale consumers — the shift to the suburbs has been marked by changes in news coverage, advertising, and promotion. This dynamic has been symbolized by the frequent dropping of the founding city from the masthead. The *Plainfield Courier* gave way to the *Courier*, and the *Newark Star Ledger* became the *Star Ledger*. This is a process repeated throughout the country and is a true reflection of the new targeting. But this centrifugal shift has necessitated a new merchandising orientation and a capacity to overcome an increased diversity of competition. Many of the new suburbs — and even more tellingly the high-growth exurbs — already have local "small town" newspapers with strong local franchises. Retailing, long the undisputed major source of advertising revenue, is now far more dispersed than was true in the days of central city hegemony; the problem of servicing it now is equally complex. One of the fastest growing forms of print media, for example, is the so-called "give away" which provides saturation in selected areas and is completely dependent upon advertising for its revenues.

Overarching all of these phenomena is the arrival of new graphic media. Television increasingly has come to dominate the dissemination of the news categories which once commanded the front pages of the press. The fight for consumer attention, given the flood of new alternatives, is nearly overwhelming.

Yet, the major newspapers always have occupied a unique status as guides, mentors, and sometimes infuriators (and frequently as entertainers as well) of the broad masses of middle America. They still possess a level of acceptance and authority which is rivaled by "the tube" but is far from completely subordinated by it.

The adaptation process has been an uneasy one, and it is certainly not over. It is epitomized in the most suburban of states — New Jersey. With perhaps the greatest saturation of television alternatives in the United States, with major cities of relatively small scale, New Jersey is subject to all of the competitive pressures. It thus provides a true test of the capacity of newspapers not only to survive — but to do so while maintaining credibility and a public function.

The authors are ideally suited to their task. Sachsman is chair of the Department of Journalism and Mass Media at Rutgers University, and former president of the New Jersey chapter of the Society of Professional Journalists, Sigma Delta Chi. He is the coauthor of *Media: An Introductory Analysis of American Mass Communications*, which is now in its third edition. Sloat, a free-lance writer, has had a long and distinguished career as a reporter for several New Jersey newspapers. He is the author of *1929: America Before the Crash.*

The Center for Urban Policy Research of Rutgers is delighted with the book — and we hope you are too.

George Sternlieb
Director, CUPR

Preface

This book examines the phenomenon of suburban journalism by telling the story of the daily newspapers of New Jersey. It is newspaper research, press criticism, and, we hope, good journalism.

If we have succeeded in our task, it is due to the efforts of many people besides ourselves. Much of the credit belongs to our sources, the scores of reporters, editors, and publishers who spoke to us freely, telling us the inside stories of their newspapers. Many were willing to speak on the record, and their names can be found throughout the book. Others asked not to be identified. In dealing with information from confidential sources, we followed the now standard journalistic practice of obtaining confirmation from a second source. Everything in this book either comes from a named individual or was confirmed by a second party.

Thanks also go to George Sternlieb of the Rutgers Center for Urban Policy Research and James Hughes of the Department of Urban Planning and Policy Development, who had faith in this project from start to finish and who helped obtain the two small, seed-money grants needed to begin the initial content analysis of daily newspapers. These grants were provided by the Rutgers University Research Council and the Fund for New Jersey in East Orange. We hope C.F. Main of Rutgers and Gordon A. MacInnes, Jr., who then directed the Fund, are pleased with the results.

Credit for the actual production of this book belongs to Mary Picarella of the Center for Urban Policy Research, and we would also like to thank Joe Perone who worked on the content analysis when he was a graduate student at Rutgers.

Since this is a book about newspapers, it was written in a style that is unusual in normal book publication. It was written the way journalists write, according to the bible of American newspapers, the *Associated Press Stylebook,* which was completely revised under the direction of editor Howard Angione and was published by the Associated Press in New York in 1977. At first, the reader of this book may notice the differences, such as the way numbers like 14 and decades like the 1970s are presented. But the reader will soon fall in step with this simpler form of writing, the style used by virtually all newspapers and many magazines.

We are convinced that the story of the press and the suburbs is the story of the future of American newspapers. If this book contributes to an understanding of suburban journalism, then the years of effort that went into it will have been worthwhile.

David Sachsman
Warren Sloat

The Press
and the
Suburbs

Introduction

New Jersey in 1950 was a state of cities and vast rural areas. While more than one-quarter of its residents lived in the six biggest cities (then Newark, Jersey City, Paterson, Elizabeth, Trenton, and Camden), New Jersey's 26,900 farms and 1.8 million acres of farmlands made it truly the Garden State.

But America's lifestyle was changing. On Long Island, William J. Levitt had decided to build an entire town of identical, low-cost, single-family homes. His new concept of affordable suburban life would be copied throughout the 1950s and 1960s as Levittowns of every size and shape filled the areas surrounding America's cities. A vast network of highways was being constructed, and the white middle class was buying automobiles and moving to the suburbs.

All this was especially true in the 90-mile stretch between New York and Philadelphia, and the near suburbs of New Jersey were filled to the brim by the end of the 1960s. Then corporate America moved to previously rural locations along the highways, and suburban areas developed far from the cities. As the price of single-family houses increased, commuting distances grew longer and longer, and suburban developments of attached homes became commonplace.

New Jersey today is a state where even the suburbs have suburbs. Only about one-eighth of its 7.3 million residents live in the six cities that were once population centers, and only 9,100 farms still exist on the state's remaining one million acres of farmland.

3

More than 50 billion miles now are driven annually in New Jersey, compared to 16.7 billion miles in 1950. And there are actually more vehicles registered in the state than the number of licensed drivers. Parking is a key to success in the suburbs, where enormous shopping centers circled by giant parking lots have replaced downtown shopping areas, and highway restaurants and movie houses showing as many as six different films provide an evening's entertainment.

The Suburbs and the Press

No one on Long Island benefited more from the growth of suburbia than did *Newsday*. Founded in 1940, it now sells more than 525,000 copies a day, and pages and pages of advertising space. *Newsday* is also a very good newspaper, considered by many the best suburban paper in America.

New Jersey has similar success stories, most notably those of the Bergen *Record* and the *Asbury Park Press*. The *Record* grew with affluent, educated Bergen County in the post-World War II era, and while its circulation of around 149,000 daily and 216,000 on Sundays is no longer on the increase, its advertising revenues are enormous. The construction of the Garden State Parkway carried suburbia to Monmouth and Ocean counties, transforming the territory of the *Asbury Park Press* into an advertising and circulation gold mine. The newspaper's circulation has grown from 27,000 in 1956 to more than 121,000 daily and 177,000 on Sundays in 1983—and the numbers continue to increase as the shore communities continue to grow.

In the period from 1963 to 1983, the circulations of 17 New Jersey daily newspapers increased, and three new dailies were created. To a greater or lesser degree, all these papers gained from the suburbanization of New Jersey. Some did so by physically moving their complete operations or their printing plants to the suburbs. Others simply were able to expand their suburban territories. For many of these newspapers, the years of significant circulation growth ended in the late 1970s, either because their suburbs had filled or because of competition from other papers.

Six newspapers suffered circulation losses from 1963 to 1983, and four dailies that existed in 1963 did not survive the suburbanization of New Jersey. The *Newark News*, the best newspaper in the state, might be alive today if in the 1960s it had built its new printing plant in the suburbs instead of in Newark. The Paterson *Call* fell to the Paterson *News*, which itself lost circulation during the period. The Bayonne *Times* fell to the Jersey City newspaper, the *Jersey Journal*, another circulation loser. And the Long Branch *Record* did not survive the stiff competition of suburban Monmouth County. Other papers suffering circulation losses were the Elizabeth *Daily Journal*, the Passaic-Clifton *Herald-News*, the *Trenton Times*, and the Hudson *Dispatch*.

The list of the dead and the circulation losers is almost exclusively a list of urban newspapers unable to gain from the suburbanization of the state and unable to compete in a changing environment. When the population and economic base of New Jersey moved to the suburbs, the newspapers left behind in the cities had to change to survive. The *Courier-Post* moved from Camden to nearby Cherry Hill, and became a regional suburban newspaper. The *News Tribune* moved fom Perth Amboy to Woodbridge, with its giant shopping center. The *Courier-News* moved from Plainfield to Bridgewater, and the *Star-Ledger* built its new printing plant on Route 287 in Middlesex County instead of in Newark. The urban newspapers that died or lost circulation either failed to adjust to the changing circumstances or were hemmed in by the competition and unable to expand into the suburbs.

Suburban Journalism

Five of the 12 largest newspapers in America are published in New York and Philadelphia and widely circulated in New Jersey. All but the business-oriented *Wall Street Journal* are classic metropolitan newspapers, filled with pages and pages of news from the big city, national and international reports, extensive coverage of major sports, endless "lifestyle" stories, and at least a spattering of regional news. All but the *New York Post* are great newspapers, doing what they do extremely well. The *New York Times* is still the nation's newspaper of record, while the *Wall Street Journal* is now a truly national newspaper. The New York *Daily News* is the best tabloid in America, and the Philadelphia *Inquirer*, with its solid regional coverage, may be the best all-around newspaper of the bunch. No New Jersey newspaper can compete in terms of coverage with the great New York and Philadelphia metropolitan newspapers, and none really tries.

Instead, the newspapers of New Jersey offer a form of countercoverage, emphasizing those areas of news coverage that are virtually ignored by the New York and Philadelphia papers. Local and regional coverage is given top priority, statehouse reporting is a serious matter, and "lifestyle" coverage centers on suburban family living. Every Wednesday, for example, the *Courier-News* publishes a 12-page Family section, complete with neighbor notes, wedding and birth announcements, and news of activities such as the Readington Reformed Church's annual Harvest Home and Roast Beef

The Courier-News *Family* Edition

A Gannett Newspaper Serving Central Jersey   Bridgewater, Wednesday, August 29, 1984   722-8800   News of your friends and neighbors reported every Wednesday by The Courier-News

Patty and Sue Connor, left to right, sell local produce during the Harvest Home festival.

Julian Gengler, Sue Blood, Lee Pascadlo and Doris Johnson, left to right, put the finishing touches on a quilt to be offered for sale during the Harvest Home festival at Readington Reformed Church.

Harvest Home

They keep coming back year after year

By ROBIN GABY
Courier-News Staff Writer

The Readington Reformed Church held its annual Harvest Home and Roast Beef Dinner recently — a day full of fun, friendship, and wonderful food.

Although the year of the first Harvest Home cannot be specifically determined, Horace Brokaw of Readington said that "it has been going on since before I was born and that was 80 years ago." He said he has been attending ever since he was old enough to go to church.

Mabel Case of Somerville said she has come every year for the past 50 years, while Catherine Atkinson of Jacksonville, Fla., claims she attended her first Harvest Home in 1922.

"I'm glad I'm still around to come," said Atkinson.

Vegetable stands set up on the church grounds offered local produce, and a variety of items for sale — from knitted baby blankets to jewelry — made and donated by church members were displayed in a craft room. An antique room held a collec-

tion of mourning clothes and baptismal outfits from the late 1800s from the collection of Lorena Cole Vincent and Charlotte Cole.

A puppet show performed by the Sunday school children was the favorite of 9-year-old Merry Kreen and her brother, Doug, 5. Doug said he especially liked the singing and dancing of "Praises in Puppetry."

A quilt show and sale boasted dozens of magnificent handmade quilts, some more than 100 years old and others made throughout the year by a group of churchwomen. The women meet once a week at the church for a quilting session, working on two or three quilts at a time. Lee Pascadlo, a member of the quilting group, calls Readington "the hot bed of quilting."

"Quilting is an original American art," Pascadlo said, "and quilts are very 'in' right now."

The highlight of the day, and a sellout, was the roast beef dinner. Between 3 and 8 p.m., 800 dinners were prepared and served by 25 kitchen volunteers who cooked 450 pounds of roast beef and peeled 350 pounds of potatoes. Homemade applesauce and green beans added to

the meal, which was topped off with the locally renowned "Harvest Home Cake." This culinary delight was originated by a former church member, Bertha Force, according to Roger Tharp, a church member since 1957.

"The dinner is always well-attended," said Tharp, with Katherine Dorsey, a kitchen volunteer, adding "They come from all over."

When asked what their favorite part of the day was, Matt Terhune, 11, and Paul Stransky, 14, both of

Readington, called out in unison "the food!"

The Rev. Donald McCabe, pastor of the church, said that "people just bubble" preparing for and participating in the affair, while his wife, Betty, added that it "really brings

Jenny Kang, 9, of Bridgewater admires crafts offered for sale during the Readington Reformed Church's Harvest Home festival.

Courier-News Photos
By Fred Keesing

Rosemarie Manzo removes the meat from the oven for the roast beef dinner at Readington Reformed Church.

people together."

The annual event is planned, organized and staffed by parishioners who donate their time, talent and ideas year-round. Proceeds go to the church treasury for continued restoration of the 283-year-old church.

Neighbor notes

Ruth E. Conover is treated to a birthday balloon ride.

Conover celebrates 80th

Ruth E. Conover of James Street, Whitehouse Station, wife of the late John Russell Conover, celebrated her 80th birthday on July 22. A dinner party was held at Perryville Inn, Clinton, with four generations of her family attending.

After dinner, Conover was treated to an impromptu hot-air balloon ride when a balloon sponsored by N.J. Monthly landed at Brown-Ingram field across the street from her home. The balloon was participating in the New Jersey Festival of Ballooning being held that weekend.

Conover, the former Ruth Mc-Catharn, was born and lived in Tewksbury most of her life. She has six children, 18 grandchildren, 19 great-grandchildren and one great-great-grandson.

Rosenblum to serve

Professor Peter Rosenblum of Short Hills, a member of the marketing art and design faculty at Middlesex County College, Edison, has been elected to serve on the board of directors and as treasurer of the Association for Computer Art and Design Education.

The group is a non-profit, professional association of educators and industry representatives dedicated to the advancement of computer-assisted graphic design and fine arts curricula.

Rosenblum has been a member of the college's faculty for 12 years. He holds a bachelor of fine arts degree and a certificate in industrial design from the Parsons School of Design, The New York School, N.Y. and a master of arts degree from Kean College. In addition to teaching commercial art, Rosenblum designs jewelry and is a silversmith. He is also a member of the board of directors of

the Children's Institute in South Orange and a member of the board of directors of the Millburn/Short Hills Little League.

Opdyke is runner-up

Barry Opdyke of Somerset, a floral designer for Henning's Flower Fair in Somerset, was chosen as first runner-up at the 1984 FTD Americas Cup, a prestigious floral design contest sponsored by the Florist Transworld Delivery Association, at the national convention held recently in Montreal, Canada. He was awarded $1,000 and a silver trophy.

Opdyke was required to produce five designs before five judges and an audience of 1,000. Each contestant was given 30 minutes to complete each of the arrangements, which included a dinner-table setting, a wedding bouquet, a design representing the convention's theme of "FTD—A Family Celebration," a designer's choice arrangement, and a "surprise" design.

Prior to working at Henning's, Opdyke was assistant chief respiratory therapist at Somerset Medical Center, Somerville. He is also a Vietnam veteran.

All decked out

Students of the Matheny School in Peapack-Gladstone join Bob Regan, standing in foreground, past president of the E.J. Hall Chapter Telephone Pioneers of America, on the school's new "Pioneer Deck" during a recent dedication ceremony. The deck was built by the E.J. Hall Chapter and measures 24 by 30 feet. The project, which began in May, was spearheaded by Pioneers members Frank Herzberg, Walter Buczek, Mike McGowan and Foster Vestal. The Pioneers who worked on the deck are employees of AT&T Communications in the Somerset County area.

Dinner. The *Courier-News* is so proud of this section that it mails it free to non-subscribers in its circulation area. This is suburban journalism in New Jersey, and the New York and Philadelphia papers cannot duplicate it.

The *Star-Ledger* is the closest thing to a metropolitan newspaper in the state. But unlike true metropolitan papers, it offers relatively little coverage of its home city. The *Ledger* is, in fact, a regional newspaper, with aspirations of being a statewide newspaper. It publishes more than enough national and international news for most readers, and about three times as much state news as any other paper in New Jersey. With about 432,000 copies sold daily and 631,000 on Sundays, the *Ledger* must be doing something right—especially considering the fact that newspapers in the United States reach an average of 2.2 readers.

The *Star-Ledger* is unique in New Jersey in that it deemphasizes local news. The other large regional newspapers in the state are true suburban papers, with many pages of local stories covering everything from government meetings to chicken (or roast beef) dinners. The *Asbury Park Press* and the *Courier-Post* lead the state in local coverage with about 30 such stories a day—three times as many as the *Star-Ledger*.

The circulation areas of New Jersey suburban newspapers often include dozens of different municipalities in two or more counties. Thus, providing adequate local coverage in the suburbs is a much more difficult task than in an urban environment, where there is a centralized city government. Suburban reporters must spend a good deal of their time driving from town to town and meeting to meeting just to find out what is going on. Solid suburban journalism requires large news staffs and large news holes, and while a surprising number of New Jersey newspapers get the job done, even 30 local stories a day does not necessarily mean a daily story for each municipality.

Although elements of suburban journalism have long existed in small-town and urban reporting, modern suburban journalism is a relatively recent phenomenon, a product of the post-World War II era. It is a phenomenon so new that it is still in a period of constant change—witness the continuous changes in the layout and design of suburban papers. It is a nationwide phenomenon, and if the suburbs are the future of America, suburban journalism is the future of American newspapers. Even in a United States of Broadcasting, Cable, and Computers, local news will be delivered by suburban newspapers.

The story of the 26 daily newspapers of New Jersey is, for the most part, the story of the press and the suburbs. As urban and rural New Jersey became suburban New Jersey, every newspaper in the state was faced with a changing environment. Some newspapers were successful, while others failed or were unable to meet the challenge. There are, in fact, 26 very different stories of daily journalism in New Jersey.

1

Evaluating a State's Daily Newspapers

The story of the press and the suburbs is the story of today's newspapers. Is suburban journalism good journalism? Are New Jersey's newspapers good newspapers? Is it possible to judge newspapers the way reviewers rate restaurants, with three stars going to the best?

Newpapers are brand new every day. Every story and every picture is a premiere performance—there are no reruns on the newspaper page. But good newspapers, like good restaurants, are usually consistent. Their reliability is, in fact, a measure of their quality. Ordinary newspapers are somewhat less consistent. A new editor, like a new chef, can turn things around. Unfortunately, such occurrences are not commonplace. And where there is no history of quality, the changes made by a new editor are likely to disappear when that editor moves on.

The best way to judge a newspaper is to follow it over time, evaluating it on several different occasions from as many different perspectives as possible. The same holds true for restaurant reviews, which should be based on several visits over time and are enhanced by an interview with the chef and an inspection of the kitchen.

9

This study of New Jersey's daily newspapers is based on just such an approach. The study began in 1977 and continued until 1983. It started by measuring exactly what was in New Jersey newspapers in 1977. This established a base line, a starting point for what would be a long-term examination of the state's daily papers.

It was like putting together the pieces of 26 different puzzles. At the end, a profile was written for each newspaper, including historical background, the results of previous studies, the base-line measurements, the examinations of papers over time, and interviews with reporters, editors, and publishers. At the end it was also possible to make an evaluation of the quality of each newspaper, and this evaluation was included in each profile.

These are the stories of New Jersey's daily newspapers, and taken together they say a great deal about the press and the suburbs.

This chapter provides the background for the telling of these stories. It begins with a short history of press criticism and newspaper research in America, including the previous studies similar to this one. It then explains this study, and presents the methodology of the 1977 base-line measurements. The rest of the chapter is devoted to a detailed report of this content analysis.

The chapter was written after the long-term study was completed. Thus it includes circulation figures for 1983 as well as 1977, and it is able to compare the reputation of New Jersey newspapers today with the measurements taken in 1977. But while the content analysis is presented in perspective, it remains essentially the base-line background for the meat of the book, the profiles of New Jersey's daily newspapers.

The Anatomy of Newspapers in America

Press criticism in America has been based largely on qualitative analyses. The critic, usually an experienced journalist, reads a newspaper carefully, interviews many of its editors and reporters, and then provides a subjective analysis of the quality of the newspaper, supporting each argument with detailed examples.

Most press critics openly admit the subjectivity of their judgments, acknowledging that they are based on personal standards of press quality such as objective reporting, interpretive reporting, and news judgment as reflected in the selection and emphasis of news stories in newspaper layout. Press critics have an ideal newspaper in mind, and they evaluate the press in terms of their own ideal standards.

Newspaper research in America today is based largely on quantitative analyses. Anything and everything can be counted, from the number of news pages and advertising pages to the number of sportswriters and political reporters. A complete content analysis of a newspaper counts and labels every item found within the pages of a newspaper in an attempt to describe the press in quantitative terms.

There are subjective judgments in newspaper research as well. The labels used to describe the contents of a newspaper are themselves highly subjective, and the evaluation of quantitative data can be just as subjective as qualitative press criticism. The very nature of newspaper content analysis implies that more is better than less, that more news pages are better than fewer news pages, that a newspaper with five international news stories is doing a better job than a paper with only two such stories. If counting is of value, the implication is that numbers can be used for evaluating the performance of the press.

Evaluating even a single newspaper, either qualitatively or quantitatively, is sufficiently difficult that few attempts have been made at systematically evaluating the press of an entire region. To do this requires not only an analysis of each individual newspaper, but also a means of comparing each newspaper with the others.

One such study of a region's press was conceived in the late 1960s by the Institute of Governmental Studies at the University of California, Berkeley. Stanford University Professor William L. Rivers and graduate student David M. Rubin analyzed San Francisco Bay Area newspapers, with special reference to the treatment of public policies and community affairs. In their 1971 report, *A Region's Press: Anatomy of Newspapers in the San Francisco Bay Area*, Rivers and Rubin made it clear that they saw themselves as press critics with ideal standards of newspaper quality, and that they also saw the need to use quantitative measures to provide a more solid foundation for their subjective judgments. Rivers and Rubin found content analyses particularly useful for making comparisons among newspapers.

The 1973 New England daily newspaper survey, *Evaluating the Press*, headed and edited by Loren Ghiglione, editor and publisher of the Southbridge (Mass.) *News*, viewed comparability as a major problem—probably because it did not use quantitative content analyses. Instead, the study depended on 13 journalists serving as press critics to evaluate the daily newspapers of six states. The evaluators and staff met to review the standards to be applied, which took into account six ideal criteria, and the survey included 24 standardized questions that were asked of each newspaper's editors or publisher. The study achieved some comparability in the responses to the standardized questions, although an editor's report of the number of columns of news space may not be as reliable as an independent content analysis.

John Kolesar, now night news editor of the *Record*, gives an assignment.

The New England survey did not ask the editors to compare their newspapers to others, to rank the newspapers in their state in terms of quality, for example. This rather common measure of excellence was used in 1974 by the Center for Analysis of Public Issues in Princeton, N.J., when it asked New Jersey reporters and editors which daily newspaper was the best in the state, overall and in seven specific categories (local news, statehouse coverage, national news, political coverage, investigative reporting, editorials, and writing/editing). The results of the poll were reported by center director John Kolesar in an article titled "The *Record* and *Star Ledger* Rated Tops by News Pros," in the center's September 1974 issue of *Public Issues*. Fifty-eight journalists responded to the poll, and their evaluations are a measure of newspaper quality as well as reputation.

The key to evaluating a region's press may be the use of multiple measures, rather than a dependence on any single evaluative technique. Rivers and Rubin used both qualitative and quantitative measures, while the New England survey was weak in quantitative terms. The Center for Analysis of

Public Issues, in addition to polling journalists, conducted a five-day content analysis of 1974 New Jersey daily newspapers. The study, "The Daily Press: News By The Yard," measured the number of pages of advertising and news and the number of columns of foreign, national, state, and local news per day in every daily newspaper in the state. The December 1974 issue of *Public Issues* was devoted entirely to the report of the study, written by Kolesar. In the report, the center director acknowledged the limitations of quantitative measurements—that sheet quantity can be a sign of loose writing and editing rather than thoroughness—while making the case for the use of content analyses in evaluating newspaper quality. Quantitative measures allow for systematic comparisons, and more can indeed mean better. "Sheer quantity of news in itself is not a negligible quality in a newspaper. It can be a sign of diligence, thoroughness and diversified content, of a serious intention to inform," Kolesar argued.

As it turned out, the December 1974 report of the study contained many incorrect numbers, the result of miscalculations. In January 1975 *Public Issues* carried the correct figures in a chart titled, "A Slight Recalculation."

The results of the poll of journalists and the content analysis did not always agree. While the journalists rated the Bergen *Record* first and the *Asbury Park Press* second in local news coverage, the content analysis found the *Asbury Park Press* first and the *Record* seventh in the amount of local news. And where the poll placed the Newark *Star-Ledger* first and the *Record* second in national news, the content analysis listed the *Star-Ledger* first, the *Asbury Park Press* second, and the *Record* fifth in the number of columns of national coverage. The disagreements can be explained by two factors. Quality and quantity are not always identical. The 1974 Bergen *Record* may have been as good as the journalists said it was, despite its somewhat lower ratings in quantitative terms. But polls are a measure of reputation as well as quality, and the 1974 *Asbury Park Press* may have been as good as the content analysis suggests, despite its slightly lower reputation at that time.

The journalists rated the Bergen *Record* the best all-around newspaper in New Jersey, the *Star-Ledger* second, and the Camden *Courier-Post* third. The report of the content analysis did not attempt to evaluate overall newspaper quality. Nevertheless, in terms of the sheer quantity of news pages, it ranked the *Asbury Park Press* first, the *Star-Ledger* second, the Paterson *News* third, the Bergen *Record* fourth, and the Camden *Courier-Post* fifth. The 1974 Paterson *News*, which was 17th in national news coverage, was not as good a newspaper as its total number of news pages suggests, and the 1974 *Asbury Park Press* was a better newspaper than its reputation. The fact that three of the top five newspapers in terms of the number of news pages were rated by journalists as the three best newspapers in New Jersey lends substantial support to the argument that quantity is a measure of newspaper quality.

The research conducted by the Center for Analysis of Public Issues examined newspapers within a limited time frame. The New England survey also was limited to a single year, although some of the evaluators included meaningful historical discussions in their essays. Rivers and Rubin, though limited by time in their quantitative measures, did not restrict themselves by time in their qualitative sketches of newspapers.

The New Jersey Newspaper Study

This study evaluated the quality of New Jersey's daily newspapers from 1977 to 1983. In addition, because the 1960s and early 1970s were important years in terms of the development of New Jersey newspapers, this period was examined from a historical perspective.

The study began with a content analysis of 1977 New Jersey daily newspapers. This content analysis provided a quantitative base line for the qualitative analyses, which continued until 1983.

The quality of the newspapers first was evaluated in quantitative terms, using the findings of the content analysis. The newspapers then were examined qualitatively over time, and reporters, editors, and publishers were interviewed concerning each newspaper. Finally, the quantitative findings and qualitative findings were combined, and each newspaper was evaluated individually.

A profile was written for each newspaper, including historical background, the results of previous studies, the findings of the content analysis, the findings of the qualitative examination, and the evaluation of the quality of the newspaper.

The quantitative findings of the content analysis made it possible for the evaluation of New Jersey daily newspapers to include meaningful comparisons of nine measures of quality, and to divide the newspapers into four groups in terms of quality.

Content Analysis: Method

A content analysis of the coverage offered by the 26 New Jersey daily newspapers was performed for the weeks of October 31 through November 4, 1977, and November 14 through November 18, 1977.

The time period included one week when pre-election political coverage was expected to be present, and a second week after the statewide elections, but still in the same month.

All non-advertising newspaper content was examined that was 5½ column inches or more in length, not including headlines. Thus a newspaper item of substance was defined as any non-advertising content 5½ column inches or more in length. Fillers, letters to the editor, and obituaries therefore were eliminated from the content analysis unless they were substantial enough to be at least 5½ inches long. Comics were coded as a single item.

All newspaper items of substance were coded as to whether they concerned local, state, national, or international matters, or whether they concerned other matters of general interest such as hobbies, comics, puzzles, and horoscopes. All were coded as to whether they were locally originated stories or wire service and syndicate stories. Longer stories were defined as stories running 15 column inches or more in length, and were coded in two categories: those 15 column inches or more, but less than 30 inches, and those 30 inches or more in length. The use of photographs was measured by coding stories with photographs and photographs standing alone. Finally, the total number of newspaper pages was counted along with the number of pages of advertising and the number of pages of news and other editorial content.

Five coders analyzed newspaper content, recording their findings on daily coding sheets for each newspaper. The definitions and coding sheets stood up to tests of validity and reliability, meaning that they measured what they were supposed to measure, and that the results came out pretty much the same no matter which person was doing the coding. In a pretest in which the coders analyzed identical newspapers, the average intercoder reliability or average percentage of agreement was 80 percent. The pretest was done using $C.R. = 2M / N_1 + N_2$, meaning that the coefficient of reliability or percentage of agreement equaled two times the total number of agreements or identical decisions made by two coders divided by the sum of the total number of decisions made by each of the coders. In subsequent checks, the intercoder reliability was always more than 80 percent.

The findings concerning the 10 weekday editions of each newspaper were combined and averaged in order to record each newspaper's average daily number of total pages, pages of advertising, pages of news and other editorial content, total news and feature items of substance, local news and feature stories, state stories, national stories, international stories, other items of general interest, locally originated stories, wire service and syndicate stories, longer stories, stories with photographs, and photographs standing alone.

Since newspaper size often is related to newspaper circulation, the 1977 daily circulation of each newspaper was recorded. Because the qualitative analyses continued into 1983, a comparison was made between the 1977 and 1983 daily circulation figures (see Table 1).

Table 1
Daily Circulation of New Jersey Newspapers

	1977	1983
The Star-Ledger (m)	411,443	432,110
The Bergen Record (e)	153,235	149,281
Asbury Park Press (e)	96,092	121,394
Camden Courier-Post (e)	123,653	117,927
Atlantic City Press (m)	71,409	79,629
The Trentonian (m)	60,108	(66,477 in 1982)
The Trenton Times (m) (was e)	73,632	(65,047 in 1982)
Passaic Herald-News (e)	80,964	64,682
The Jersey Journal (e)	73,151	63,618
Morristown Daily Record (m) (was e)	49,702	60,245
The Home News (e)	57,319	56,406
The Courier-News (e)	58,777	55,619
The News Tribune (e)	51,845	51,597
Paterson News (m) (m & e in 1977)	61,587	48,114
Burlington County Times (e)	39,929	43,152
Elizabeth Daily Journal (e)	52,090	39,303
The Hudson Dispatch (m)	45,239	36,388
The Daily Register (e)	31,219	30,137
The Gloucester County Times (e)	24,824	28,234
Ocean County Times-Observer (m) (was Observer)	24,637	23,948
New Jersey Herald (e)	15,857	17,748
Vineland Times Journal (e)	17,032	17,441
The Daily Advance (m) (was e)	19,632	13,082
Bridgeton Evening News (e)	11,833	(12,419 in 1982)
Today's Sunbeam (m)	9,683	(10,685 in 1982)
The Millville Daily (e)	7,126	(6,915 in 1982)

m=morning newspaper
e=evening newspaper

Sources: Audit Bureau of Circulations (ABC) Sept. 30, 1977. *1978 Editor & Publisher International Year Book* (New York: Editor & Publisher, 1978). pp. 1-144-9.

   ABC Sept. 30,1982. 1983 Editor & Publisher International Year Book (New York: Editor & Publisher, 1983). pp. 1-193-200.

   New Jersey ABC FAS-FAX September 1983.

Content Analysis: Findings

New Jersey newspapers ranged in daily circulation from more than 400,000 to less than 10,000, and in size from 74 pages to 16 pages (see Table 2). Since the differences among newspapers are so great, it is not meaningful to think in terms of a typical New Jersey daily newspaper. But it is useful to categorize the state's daily newspapers by circulation and size.

The *Star-Ledger* stands alone with a daily circulation of more than 400,000. The Bergen *Record*'s circulation of around 150,000 makes it a far-distant second, and only two other newspapers can be classified as having more than 90,000 subscribers. Thirteen daily newspapers had circulations ranging from 35,000 to 80,000, and nine had fewer than 35,000 subscribers.

The content analysis findings did not show differences among the four large-circulation daily newspapers comparable to their disparities in readership. They were the four largest papers (62 to 74 pages), they carried the greatest numbers of stories (91 to 118), and their news holes ranged from 24 to 29 pages. Only one other newspaper, the tabloid *Trentonian*, offered as many as 24 pages of news and other editorial matter.

Twelve of the 13 medium-circulation newspapers ran more than 30 pages daily, though none carried more than 52 pages. Ten of the 13 offered from 61 to 82 stories daily in news holes ranging from 16 to 21 pages. The *Trentonian* ran more—84 stories in the equivalent of 24 standard-size news pages—while two medium-circulation newspapers carried less. The Hudson *Dispatch*, with only 28 total pages, and the Elizabeth *Journal*, with 33, ran fewer than 60 stories daily in 15-page news holes.

Seven of the nine small-circulation newspapers ran fewer than 30 pages per day during the coding period. Six carried fewer than 60 stories daily, and a slightly different six offered news holes ranging from eight to 13 pages. The two newspapers with the highest circulations in the group, the *Daily Register* and the *Gloucester County Times*, were larger than 30 pages and carried more than 60 stories daily in 16-page news holes.

New Jersey newspapers have a reputation for solid local news coverage, a reputation supported by the content analysis findings (see Table 3). Twenty-one newspapers carried 15 or more local news and feature stories daily, and 12 of these newspapers offered 20 or more local stories per day. The Bergen *Record*, though known for its local coverage, ranked 16th in the number of local stories during the coding period. This was partly due to the fact that the *Record* replates its local news pages, changing the local stories for various delivery areas. Thus the newspaper maintains a small local news hole, but actually produces many local news stories. The *Star-Ledger*'s last-place showing in local coverage was also partly due to the replating of local news pages,

Table 2
Size of New Jersey Daily Newspapers

	News	Ads	Total
The Star-Ledger	27 pages	47 pages	74 pages
The Bergen Record	24	49	73
Camden Courier-Post	29	43	72
Asbury Park Press	25	37	62
Burlington County Times	20	32	52
The Trentonian (tabloid)	24 (39)*	22 (35)*	46 (74)*
The Trenton Times	19	25	44
The Home News	20	23	43
Paterson News	21	21	42
Atlantic City Press	17	24	41
The News Tribune	17	22	39
Passaic Herald-News	19	18	37
The Courier-News	16	21	37
The Jersey Journal	18	18	36
Morristown Daily Record	17	19	36
The Gloucester County Times	16	17	33
Elizabeth Daily Journal	15	18	33
The Daily Register	16	15	31
Bridgeton Evening News	16	12	28
The Hudson Dispatch	15	13	28
Ocean County Times-Observer (was Observer)	13	13	26
Vineland Times Journal	11	15	26
New Jersey Herald	12	11	23
Today's Sunbeam	12	10	22
The Daily Advance	11	10	21
The Millville Daily	8	8	16

*Numbers in parentheses indicate tabloid pages.

These measurements of space are average weekday figures from newspapers for the weeks of Oct. 31 through Nov. 4, 1977, and Nov. 14 through Nov. 18, 1977. Space was measured both in pages and in column inches, but since newspapers differ (even on their own pages) as to the number of words per column inch, these results are reported in terms of pages. The typical New Jersey daily newspaper was six columns by 21 inches. The Daily Register, the Bridgeton News, and the New Jersey Herald were eight-column newspapers, and it might be argued that their eight-column size allowed them to publish more words per page than a six-column paper. Only one daily newspaper in the state was a tabloid. Thus the space measurements for the Trentonian are given in terms of standard 21-inch pages as well as tabloid pages.

Table 3
Number of News and Feature Stories
Carried by New Jersey Daily Newspapers

	Local	State	National	Inter-national	Other	Total
The Star-Ledger	8	37	48	7	18	118
Camden Courier-Post	30	12	35	7	20	104
Asbury Park Press	30	9	35	3	25	102
The Bergen Record	18	8	38	4	23	91
The Trentonian	16	11	37	4	16	84
Burlington County Times	15	7	35	5	20	82
The Home News	22	9	26	4	17	78
The Jersey Journal	20	5	27	2	22	76
The Daily Register	28	9	17	1	20	75
Paterson News	21	6	22	3	22	74
The Trenton Times	14	10	29	5	16	74
Passaic Herald-News	21	8	20	1	22	72
Morristown Daily Record	23	9	20	2	16	70
Gloucester County Times	19	6	24	2	16	67
The News Tribune	24	9	16	2	15	66
The Courier-News	24	5	23	3	11	66
Times-Observer (was Observer)	22	7	16	4	14	63
Atlantic City Press	24	4	17	3	13	61
The Hudson Dispatch	13	8	21	2	13	57
Bridgeton Evening News	17	3	18	2	14	54
New Jersey Herald	19	5	14	1	15	54
Elizabeth Daily Journal	15	7	14	0(0.3)	17	53
Today's Sunbeam	19	3	13	2	16	53
The Daily Advance	13	4	11	1	17	46
Vineland Times Journal	16	6	9	1	12	44
The Millville Daily	12	3	7	1	8	31

These are the average daily numbers of stories of at least 5½ column inches in length from newspapers for the weeks of Oct. 31 through Nov. 4, 1977, and Nov. 14 through Nov. 18, 1977.

but even when this factor is taken into account, local coverage is not the *Ledger*'s long suit.

New Jersey newspapers are not known for their national coverage, almost all of which is supplied by the wire services. Nevertheless, the coders found large numbers of news and feature stories on national issues. Twenty newspapers carried more than 15 national stories daily, and 15 of these newspapers offered 20 or more. Six of the newspapers actually carried 35 or more national stories per day, a remarkably high level of performance.

The *Star-Ledger*'s specialty is state coverage, a fact documented by the content analysis. No other New Jersey newspaper came close to the *Ledger*'s 37 state news and feature stories per day. Fourteen newspapers carried seven to 12 state stories daily, while the rest carried six or less. The *Star-Ledger* also led in the number of international news and feature stories, along with the *Courier-Post*. But New Jersey newspaper coverage of international issues was minimal, and even the leaders carried only seven international stories per day.

Newspapers are often judged by the number of locally originated stories they carry, since it is a relatively easy matter to fill a news hole with wire service and syndicate stories. Twenty New Jersey newspapers offered 25 or more locally originated news and feature stories daily during the coding period, and 12 of these newspapers carried more than 30 (see Table 4). Five of the newspapers offered 40 or more locally originated stories each day. These results were not surprising considering the solid local news and feature coverage offered by New Jersey newspapers, and the locally originated state coverage produced by newspapers with statehouse and political correspondents.

The number of longer stories also is a measure of newspaper quality. While long stories may be due to poor editing or a large news hole, they are an indication of in-depth coverage. When a newspaper regularly carries large numbers of longer stories, it is generally a sign of thorough coverage. Ten New Jersey newspapers offered 20 or more longer stories daily during the coding period (see Table 5). The four large-circulation newspapers excelled in this area, carrying from 29 to 32 longer stories per day.

Finally, the content analysis determined the number of stories with photographs and the number of photographs standing alone in order to measure the use of photographs by New Jersey daily newspapers during the coding period (see Table 6). Fourteen newspapers used 25 or more photographs per day, and four of these papers used more than 35 photographs. The *Courier-Post*, with 55 photographs, and the *Record*, with 45, led the list, while the *Star-Ledger*, with a similar news hole, tied for 13th with 25 photographs. The *Ledger* was indeed a gray, non-visual newspaper during the coding period.

Evaluating New Jersey's Daily Newspapers

The content analysis provided an accurate description of the composition of New Jersey's daily newspapers for a single slice of time. The differences among newspapers were real differences during the given time period. Thus the rank

Table 4
Number of Locally Originated Stories Carried
by New Jersey Daily Newspapers

	Wire Service and Syndicate Stories	Locally Originated Stories
The Star-Ledger	57	61
Camden Courier-Post	55	49
Asbury Park Press	53	49
The Bergen Record	46	45
Passaic Herald-News	32	40
The Daily Register	37	38
Paterson News	36	38
The Jersey Journal	42	34
The Home News	45	33
The News Tribune	33	33
Morristown Daily Record	39	31
Atlantic City Press	30	31
The Trenton Times	46	28
Today's Sunbeam	25	28
Burlington County Times	55	27
The Gloucester County Times	40	27
The Courier-News	39	27
Bridgeton Evening News	28	26
Elizabeth Daily Journal	27	26
The Trentonian	59	25
Ocean County Times-Observer (was Observer)	40	23
The Hudson Dispatch	35	22
New Jersey Herald	32	22
The Daily Advance	26	20
Vineland Times Journal	24	20
The Millville Daily	15	16

These are the average daily numbers of stories of at least 5½ column inches in length from newspapers for the weeks of Oct. 31 through Nov. 4, 1977, and Nov. 14 through Nov. 18, 1977. The newspapers are rank ordered in terms of the number of locally originated stories (stories written by newspaper staff writers or stringers, etc.) as contrasted to stories supplied by wire services and feature syndicates.

Table 5
Number of Longer Stories Carried by New Jersey Daily Newspapers

| | Longer Stories | |
	15"-29½"	30"+
Camden Courier-Post	27	5
The Star-Ledger	29	3
Asbury Park Press	27	3
The Bergen Record	25	4
The Daily Register (8-column format)	32*	4*
The Home News	20	3
The Hudson Dispatch	18	4
The Trentonian (tabloid)	24*	4*
Paterson News	19	2
Burlington County Times	17	3
The Trenton Times	16	3
Passaic Herald-News	15	3
Morristown Daily Record	14	2
The Gloucester County Times	13	2
Atlantic City Press	13	2
Today's Sunbeam	13	2
Elizabeth Daily Journal	13	2
Ocean County Times-Observer (some 8-column)	16*	2*
The Jersey Journal	11	3
The Courier-News	11	2
Vineland Times Journal	11	2
New Jersey Herald (8-column format)	14*	2*
The News Tribune	9	2
The Daily Advance	9	2
Bridgeton Evening News (8-column format)	9*	3*
Millville Daily	8	2

These are the average daily numbers of longer stories carried during the 1977 coding period. Longer stories are defined as stories running 15 column inches or more in length, and are presented in two categories: those 15 column inches or more, but less than 30 inches, and those 30 inches or more in length. The newspapers are rank ordered in terms of the total number of longer stories, with ties being broken only when one newspaper has more 30"+ stories than the other. Because the 8-column and tabloid newspapers ran fewer words per column inch than standard newspapers, their positions in the rank order have been adjusted to approximate equivalence with 6-column newspapers. But while the rankings have been adjusted, the actual numbers of 8-column and tabloid stories are presented with asterisks.

Table 6
Use of Photographs by New Jersey Daily Newspapers

	Stories with photographs	Photograph standing alone
Camden Courier-Post	40	15
The Bergen Record	32	13
The Gloucester County Times	23	15
The Trentonian	20	17
Today's Sunbeam	18	16
Asbury Park Press	18	15
The Daily Register	24	9
Burlington County Times	22	10
Morristown Daily Record	22	10
The Home News	19	12
The Daily Advance	12	15
Paterson News	12	14
The Star-Ledger	18	7
The News Tribune	13	12
The Trenton Times	16	7
The Jersey Journal	8	15
The Courier-News	13	9
New Jersey Herald	13	9
Passaic Herald-News	14	7
Atlantic City Press	14	7
Elizabeth Daily Journal	9	11
Ocean County Times-Observer (was Observer)	13	7
The Hudson Dispatch	8	10
Bridgeton Evening News	7	10
Vineland Times Journal	11	5
The Millville Daily	6	6

These are the average daily numbers of stories containing photographs and of photographs run separately from any stories that were carried by newspapers during the weeks of Oct. 31 through Nov. 4, 1977, and Nov. 14 through Nov. 18, 1977. The newspapers are rank ordered in terms of the combined numbers of stories with photographs and photographs standing alone.

orders of newspapers in the various categories could be used to make base-line comparisons of the state's daily newspapers.

Nine of the categories could be considered quantitative measures of excellence: the size of the news hole, the total number of news and feature stories, the number of local stories, state stories, national stories, and international stories, the number of locally originated stories, the number of longer stories, and the number of photographs used per day. By combining the nine rankings for each newspaper and then dividing by the number of measures (nine), it was possible to arrive at an average ranking for each newspaper, and thus to compare or rank order the 26 newspapers using all nine measures of excellence (see Table 7).

The four large-circulation newspapers came out on top, but not in the order that would have been predicted by either circulation or reputation. The Camden *Courier-Post* was first and the *Asbury Park Press* second because of their high rankings across all nine measures of quality. The *Star-Ledger*, which was weak in local coverage and the use of photographs, was third. The Bergen *Record* was fourth because of its low ranking in the number of local stories. Since this was partly due to the fact that the *Record* replates its local pages, it could be argued that the *Record* deserved to be ranked third or even second overall.

Two medium-circulation newspapers, the New Brunswick *Home News* and the *Trentonian*, stood apart from the others. The *Home News* had high rankings across the board, while the *Trentonian* earned its place despite weaknesses in the number of local stories and locally originated stories.

Eleven newspapers fell in the middle of the pack. Nine were medium-circulation papers, while the other two, the *Daily Register* and the *Gloucester County Times*, were small-circulation papers. The *Daily Register* not only outperformed all other newspapers with comparable readerships, but most medium-circulation papers as well.

Nine newspapers formed the rest of the pack, including two medium-circulation papers, the Hudson *Dispatch* and the Elizabeth *Journal*. None of these could be considered solid all-purpose newspapers, although some small-circulation papers that adequately covered their local areas could be considered acceptable.

The quantitative findings of the content analysis allowed for the comparisons among newspapers and provided a base line for the long-term study of New Jersey's daily newspapers. The key to evaluating a region's press appears to be the use of multiple measures—quantitative measures for a base-line time period and qualitative measures over time.

Table 7
Comparison of New Jersey Daily Newspapers
Using Nine Quantitative Measures

THE FOUR BEST NEWSPAPERS:	Camden Courier-Post	(1.67 average rank)
	Asbury Park Press	(4.0)
	The Star-Ledger	(5.33)
	The Bergen Record	(5.67)
TWO THAT STOOD APART:	The Home News	(7.33)
	The Trentonian	(7.78)
THE MIDDLE OF THE PACK:	Burlington County Times	(9.56)
	The Daily Register	(9.56)
	Paterson News	(10.0)
	The Trenton Times	(10.44)
	Morristown Daily Record	(10.67)
	Passaic Herald-News	(12.33)
	The News Tribune	(12.56)
	The Jersey Journal	(12.56)
	The Gloucester County Times	(12.56)
	The Courier-News	(13.89)
	Atlantic City Press	(14.0)
THE REST OF THE PACK:	Ocean County Times-Observer	(15.89)
	The Hudson Dispatch	(16.56)
	Today's Sunbeam	(16.56)
	Bridgeton Evening News	(19.11)
	Elizabeth Daily Journal	(19.33)
	New Jersey Herald	(19.56)
	The Daily Advance	(21.67)
	Vineland Times Journal	(21.89)
	The Millville Daily	(25.0)

The content analysis of 1977 New Jersey daily newspapers rank ordered the newspapers in terms of nine quantitative measures of excellence: the size of the news hole, the total number of news and feature stories, the number of local stories, state stories, national stories, and international stories, the number of locally originated stories, the number of longer stories, and the number of photographs used per day. By combining the nine rankings for each newspaper and then dividing by the number of measures (nine), it was possible to arrive at an average ranking for each newspaper, and thus to compare or rank order the 26 newspapers using all nine measures of excellence.

2

The Big Fish

Four New Jersey daily newspapers tower over the others in the state in readership and in the quality of their news products. The *Star-Ledger*, the *Record* of Hackensack, the *Asbury Park Press*, and the Camden *Courier-Post* are the biggest newspapers in New Jersey and the best.

Together they account for nearly 48 percent of the daily newspaper circulation in the state and a solid majority of Sunday sales. Although all but the *Ledger* are small fish compared to the major newspapers of New York City and Philadelphia, they are the big fish of the state of New Jersey.

All four cover vast regions consisting of dozens of municipalities, and thus, like almost all New Jersey newspapers, they are essentially suburban rather than metropolitan dailies. They are parochial compared to the *New York Times* and the *Philadelphia Inquirer*—as well they must be to provide alternatives to the major metropolitan dailies in what is a very competitive marketplace. All but the *Ledger* provide excellent local coverage, and at their best their parishes encompass the entire state of New Jersey.

Two of the four are owned by large newspaper chains. The *Ledger* is one of 27 Newhouse daily newspapers with a 1983 combined circulation of 3.2

27

million. The Newhouse family companies also include a string of national magazines, Random House books, and extensive cable television holdings. The *Courier-Post* is owned by the Gannett Company, whose more than 80 daily newspapers had a total circulation of about 4.8 million in 1983. Gannett also owns weekly newspapers, television and radio stations, and subsidiaries in news, marketing, research, television production, and satellite information.

The owners of the *Record* and the *Asbury Park Press* have other properties as well, but unlike Newhouse and Gannett, their primary business is New Jersey newspapers. Today's *Record* is very much the product of owner Malcolm Borg, and the success of the *Asbury Park Press* is due in large part to decisions made by its owners, the Plangere and Lass families.

The *Record* is the best-written newspaper in New Jersey. The *Star-Ledger* is the most complete. The *Asbury Park Press* and the *Courier-Post* offer the most local news coverage and some of the best. The four are clearly the leading newspapers in the state today, but all four must compare themselves to one other, a newspaper that no longer exists. And the ghost of the *Newark News* lives on in the memories of New Jersey's journalists.

The Ghost of the *Newark News*

The best newspaper in New Jersey has been dead for more than a decade. It was a big-city evening newspaper that refused to follow its readers to the suburbs. Its trucks were stuck in afternoon traffic when a massive strike put it out of its misery.

On January 23, 1972, during the strike, John McLaughlin wrote in the *Trenton Times:*

> The *Newark News* was a New Jersey institution, like Princeton University and weekends at the shore. It was in its own way a powerful political force—not always evenhanded, but then who is?
>
> It was New Jersey's paper of record, covering the news from Atlantic City to Morristown. It was a bit stodgy perhaps, and it probably told its readers more about government and politics than they really cared to know, but it was required reading for anyone who wanted to keep up on what was happening in New Jersey, and do it in one easy sitting.
>
> It was, for my money, the best big afternoon paper in the East north of Washington. And like hundreds of thousands of other people in this state, I find life a little less liveable without it.

The *Newark News* was called "The *New York Times* of New Jersey," and no

New Jersey newspaper has taken its place. Though the public has forgotten the *Newark News*, journalists remember. The ghost of the *News* remains the standard against which all New Jersey newspapers are measured.

Was it really that good a newspaper? Its arts coverage was corny and provincial. It loved animal stories, and would play "lost dog" stories on the front page. It belonged to an era in which highway accidents were considered big news.

Its personnel policies were cavalier; it made little attempt to keep the many superior reporters who went on to better conditions elsewhere.

To understand the aura of the *News*, one must see it not against the background of the 1980s, but against the time in which it flourished. The *News* had bureaus in Montclair, Elizabeth, Metuchen, Morristown, Plainfield, Kearny, and even Belmar when most other newspapers in the state had none, or just one. Long before the computer era, teletype machines connected the *News* bureaus to Newark, and the news poured in 18 to 24 hours a day.

The *News* offered saturation coverage, and seemed to have battalions of reporters everywhere. The paper loved spectacular spot news stories, especially disasters, and was ready and able to dispatch teams of reporters and photographers at any hour. An airplane crash in Elizabeth or a train wreck in Woodbridge would set the *News* in motion, and if 40 people were killed, the *News* would go to press with 40 obituaries.

The *News* was a complete daily and Sunday paper, with five editorial writers, an editorial cartoonist, a military writer, an aviation writer, theater, movie and book reviewers, New York and United Nations reporters, and even a Sunday magazine.

The *News* had a Trenton bureau, with two statehouse reporters, at a time when solid state government coverage was a rarity. By the mid-1960s, many newspapers were opening bureaus in Trenton, but the *News* regulars were solidly entrenched, and readers who wanted to keep up with state government were best served by the *News*.

The *News* also maintained a Washington bureau, and regularly dispatched reporters to cover important national and even international stories. Its reporters covered World War II with the cry, "Anybody here from New Jersey?" *News* reporters were on the scene in Korea and Vietnam as well. When President Kennedy landed in Dallas on November 22, 1963, William May of the *Newark News* was a member of the press corps. Bob Thompson covered the funeral of Martin Luther King. And when National Guardsmen fired on students at Kent State, John Farmer was on the scene within hours; he had been covering an Ohio primary election for the *Newark News*.

Most of all, the newspaper covered politics. "The *Newark News* had more interest in politics than any other newspaper I ever saw," said Angelo Baglivo, who covered politics for the *News* from Trenton to Miami and Chicago. "We

TRI-COUNTY
ESSEX-UNION

Newark Evening News

STOCK MARKET PRICES
(Page 31)

Clearing tonight, fair tomorrow.

No. 24,883   NEWARK, N.J., WEDNESDAY, JULY 29, 1964   TELEPHONE MARKET 4-1000   SEVEN CENTS

Negro Principal Appointed

Dr. Flagg 2nd in Exam

By ROBERT F. PALMER

The Newark Board of Education last night appointed nine new principals including the first Negro to head a Newark school in more than half a century.

Dr. E. Alma Flagg, who was named principal of Hawkins Street School, is the first Negro in the history of the system to gain appointment to a regular principalship. The only other Negro to head a Newark school was James M. Baxter who was principal of the city's old Colored School for 45 years until he retired in 1909 shortly before his death.

In commenting on Dr. Flagg's appointment, Ronald Owens, a member of the board and himself a Negro, said: "This action represents the first step in appointing Negro principals within our system. A Negro principal will have eligibility but created from be very encouraging to the Negro students and to the Negro community. I'm happy to be a member of the board at this historic time."

DR. E. ALMA FLAGG
Named Principal

Board Names 8 Others

and the top six candidates were appointed to principal posts by the board last night.

The three other principal appointments were in the special education field, for which a separate examination had been held.

Other Appointments

Besides naming the nine principals, the board appointed 12 vice principals and approved the transfer of four elementary principals.

All the appointments and transfers were made effective Sept. 1. The unusually great number of administrative changes was necessitated by heavy retirements last month. Many of the school administrators who retired did so to take advantage of special state legislation granting older public employees both pension and Social Security benefits if they retired before July 1.

Besides Dr. Flagg, the new

Truck Rams Buses, 38 Hurt on Turnpike

Commuters Shaken in Edison

By WARREN SLOAT
Staff Correspondent

EDISON — A tractor-trailer truck and two New York-bound commuter buses were involved in a chain-reaction crash today in the New Jersey Turnpike. At least 38 persons were injured, four of them seriously enough to be hospitalized.

The crash in clear weather occurred at 7:30 a.m. in the northbound lanes of the toll highway about five miles north of the Raritan River.

Two of the three northbound lanes were closed for two hours while the injured were rushed to hospitals by ambulances from eight rescue squads and the buses were towed away.

Traffic was backed up for several miles. The lanes were reopened at 9:30 a.m.

The hospitals said most of the injuries were minor cuts and bruises. All the injured are from the New Brunswick area.

List of injured on Page 2.

The four hospitalized persons are:

Richard Teitelzweig, 21, of 140 Montgomery St., Highland Park, in Middlesex General Hospital, New Brunswick, with a concussion and a broken nose. He is in fair condition.

DAMAGED VEHICLES—One of two commuter buses (left) hit in New Jersey Turnpike crash today and tractor-trailer which hit them and was towed from scene in Edison Township. Trucker, 33 aboard buses were hurt.

Newark Group Plans Steps To Assure Race Harmony

Mayor's Parley to Reconvene

By ANGELO BAGLIVO

A cross-section of civic, religious and political leaders agreed last night to work together to promote racial harmony in Newark.

Immediate apprehension over a rally scheduled tonight in the Central Ward drew the leaders to a hastily called, two-hour private conference with Mayor Hugh J. Addonizio at City Hall.

However, Addonizio announced that, going beyond the rally itself, longer-range plans to preserve law and order in Newark came out of the session.

Addonizio reported that the sponsor of the rally, the Negro Nationalist, had changed its purpose to the promotion of racy registration among Negroes. The mayor said the

sponsors also had given assurances there would be no violence.

Monthly Meeting Set

One major result of the meeting, Addonizio said, was a decision to have a representative group of the leaders present meet at least once a month with Police Director Dominick A. Spina. The mayor reported that the suggestion came from Spina, who attended the meeting.

"It will give an opportunity for the civil rights leaders to discuss problems with Director Spina," the mayor declared, "and will give him a chance to convey the problems he faces as police director."

Addonizio said he would select the smaller committee to meet with Spina and would announce the makeup at another meeting of the over-all group to be held in two weeks.

There also was agreement that the mayor will consider

Turner Deplores 'Militancy'

Councilman Irvine I. Turner today said he deplored the dangerous militancy being preached by many of the "Johnny-comelately" Negro leaders who are scrambling among themselves for power.

They ran flames by mentioning short patience and violence show inflammatory remarks? Who are we kidding?"

Turner, Newark's first and only Negro councilman, said in a longtime member of the Newark NAACP, said he disagreed strongly with the remarks made Monday night by James Farmer, national director of CORE, in a political lecture at Seth Hall University.

Farmer told Newark an enemy of the Negro glories along with Harlem and Chicago, which he claimed have become "underscores of frustrations, alienation, isolation and anger . . ."

Turner ridiculed any comparison between Newark and Harlem.

This city's Negro population is still under the 90 per cent mark while Harlem is almost all Negro, he said. "To holler ghetto here is clear out of proportion. Newark is not a riotous city or violent type city—and never

Seek Federal Aid

King, Wagner to Reveal Proposals

By GUY SAVINO
N.Y. Staff Correspondent

NEW YORK—Stepped-up federal aid for the city and assistance of a more sympathetic City Hall are our charges of police brutality were mapped today by Mayor Robert F. Wagner and Dr. Martin Luther King, Negro rights leader, to firm up peace in the Negro community.

Saigon Unit Change Near

Report Says Duty Term of Special Forces Will Be Doubled

SAIGON, Viet Nam (UPI)—Green-bereted, guerrilla-trained U.S. Special Forces troops are expected to have their six-month duty tours lengthened to the one year that other American soldiers serve in Viet Nam.

Wagner, after conferring with White House aides yesterday, said to be ready to reveal details of the federal assistance plan.

King is expected to summon a summit meeting of Negro leaders to reveal what he has been discussing with Wagner at drawn-out conferences at Gracie Mansion, Wagner's mayoral home.

Both Wagner and King are said to recognize that the grand jury report on the shooting of a 15-year-old Negro schoolboy by a white police officer presents a problem to which they must address themselves.

Jury in Session

The jury panel met again yesterday to hear additional testimony on the fatal shooting of James M. Powell, a summer student at Robert F. Wagner Junior High School, by Police Lt. Thomas R. Gilligan.

Radio Scramble Delays Council

WALDWICK (AP) — A ham radio operator unknowingly delayed the start of a Borough Council meeting here until he finished his transmission last night.

When the council assembled, it plugged in a tape recorder to listen to the minutes of a previous meeting. Instead it heard the voice of ham operator Edward Kubinski, broadcasting from his home on Grove Street three blocks away.

Book Mystery

Village Library Loss Is Uncertain

By ELIZABETH FLANAGAN

Hughes' View

Legislators Seen For Med School

By BRUCE BARRENBURG
Trenton Bureau

TRENTON—Gov. Hughes believes legislative sentiment favors the state taking over the Seton Hall Medical and Dental School at an initial cost of $4 million.

However, Assembly Speaker Alfred N. Beadleston

Drug Tie Minor

Newark Not Figuring in Senate Quiz

By GEORGE KENTERA
Washington Bureau

WASHINGTON — Not much is being heard, or is likely to be heard, about Newark during the current hearings by Senate investigators into the illegal narcotics traffic.

Red Soldiers Ask Asylum

Two Russians Who Fled East Germany in American Hands

HEIDELBERG, Germany (UPI)—Two Russian soldiers who defected to the West Germans have asked for political asylum, the U.S. Army revealed today.

Error Is Blamed For Air Crashes

TAIPEI, Formosa (AP) — The Chinese Nationalist air force said a navigational error by the lead plane apparently caused the crash of three military transport planes into a mountain in south Formosa.

Lunar Shot Zeroing In

Ranger 7 Flight Path Revision Puts It 'On the Nose'

CAPE KENNEDY (UPI) — America's Ranger 7 television spacecraft overcame its biggest obstacle in space today by kicking in a crucial turning maneuver that aimed it for its picture-taking target on the moon.

Ocean Temperature

Fresh Air Fund

Cramped Living

Connie, 3, Needs Outdoor Space

The Market

Stocks' Tone Is Steadier

NEW YORK (AP)—The stock market gained low end, of each index, with prices mixed and trading moderate.

In The News:

Page
Bridge 8
Classified Ads ..... 29 & 30
Comics ....
Community News 20, 50

Scott Carpenter Leaves Hospital

would cover primary elections in other states if they had some national significance."

The paper's interest in politics went beyond coverage. It had enormous influence. Its enemies were the Democratic bosses, notably Dennis Carey of Essex County, and Frank Hague and John V. Kenny of Hudson County. Although essentially Republican, the *News* backed many Democrats who opposed the bosses. The *News* played a major role in the election of Democrat Robert B. Meyner as governor to the chagrin of the Hudson County machine.

At its high point in the 1960s, "The Little Old Lady of Market Street" sold 300,000 copies daily, 420,000 on Sundays, and carried nearly 40 million lines of advertising annually. Its news staff numbered 250. Though not truly a statewide paper, it had influence in 11 northern and central New Jersey counties, and was sold as far away as Atlantic City. The heart of its audience was solid Republican suburbia—towns like Westfield, Short Hills, and Chatham. It outsold the Morristown *Daily Record* in Morris County.

By the early 1960s the *News* had outgrown its plant in downtown Newark, and it spent $12 million for a new one next door to the old. "That was the single most critical business decision they made that helped to finish them," Baglivo said. "Look what they did to themselves. They couldn't get their trucks out. They were at one of the busiest corners in the world. If the *Newark News* had moved to Livingston it might have come out differently."

A move to the west might have changed the history of the *Newark News*. Not only was its influence great in Essex, Morris, Union, Sussex, and the Somerset hills, but even then it was clear that the suburbs were to be the growth areas of the future. Instead it stayed in Newark, a city that was rapidly changing. Newark Mayor Ken Gibson has said that what happens to American cities happens to Newark first, and Newark in the early 1960s was becoming what other cities were to become later—a city of a black majority and of high unemployment. The downtown department stores, once the shopping mecca for northern New Jersey, would fall on hard times, faced with stiff competition from the suburban shopping malls. By 1967 the *Newark News* would recognize where the advertising was, and change its name to *The Evening News*.

The late 1960s were difficult years for the *News*. Circulation within the city had dropped, and although it still had a large suburban audience, the morning *Star-Ledger* was nipping at its heels. By the end of 1969, the *News* led the *Star-Ledger* in circulation 258,000 to 245,000 daily, and 419,000 to 397,000 on Sundays. In 1970, the Sunday *Star-Ledger* passed the Sunday *News* 402,000 to 370,000, and in March 1971 the *Star-Ledger* passed the *News* in daily circulation as well.

Many afternoon metropolitan newspapers have lost to competing morning papers in recent years. Reading habits have changed. Because afternoon delivery through rush-hour traffic is difficult, afternoon papers are really published in the morning, with deadlines only a few hours later than those of morning newspapers. And by evening, an afternoon newspaper can seem stale compared to the immediacy of television news. Suburban readers have increasingly turned to local newspapers at the expense of metropolitan evening papers. And advertisers have gone suburban as well, though still filling the pages of whichever metropolitan newspaper holds the lead in circulation. The *News* was already in deep trouble when the newsroom walked out on strike in May 1971.

The Scudder family, which had owned the newspaper since Wallace Scudder founded it in 1883, had tried to sell it to Time Inc. in 1968, but the deal had fallen through. In 1970, Media General, a conglomerate operating out of Richmond, Virginia, purchased the paper and immediately sought ways to cut back on overhead.

The base pay at the *News* was low, but overtime had been easy, and expense vouchers rarely challenged. Media General took away the overtime and questioned expenses, leaving many reporters unable to keep up on their base salaries. The newsroom, which had never been organized, voted in February 1971 to join the Newspaper Guild, and struck the paper three months later.

The *News* never recovered from the strike. Although the newsroom dispute was settled within four months, other unions had to negotiate new contracts as well, and the paper was not published again until April 1972. By then the Sunday *News* was already gone, sold along with its presses to the *Star-Ledger*. The presses for the daily *News* had been shipped to Media General's newspapers in Tampa, Florida, and the six-day *News* was to be printed by the *Ledger*. The *News* had lost its advertising, its readers, and many of its staffers—it was no longer a quality product.

The *News* died on August 31, 1972, a shell of its former self. The ghost that is remembered was robust and influential. In its heyday it could send out teams of reporters, and when aroused it could shake the state. Even if it was only a big fish compared to those swimming alongside, it was the best newspaper in New Jersey and deserves to be remembered.

The *Star-Ledger*: To the Survivor Go the Spoils

The morning newspaper that survived the battle of Newark has become the 18th largest daily and 12th largest Sunday paper in America. The *Star-Ledger*'s 1983 circulation—432,110 daily and 631,735 on Sundays—was nearly three times that of its nearest competitor, the *Record* of Hackensack.

One of every four daily newspapers and one of every three Sunday papers published in New Jersey is a *Star-Ledger*.

The *Ledger* dropped "Newark" from its name two decades ago, and building from its base in Essex and Union counties, it has expanded its coverage and circulation area to include Morris, Middlesex, Somerset, and Monmouth. It moved quickly into Morris County to fill the void left by the death of the *Newark News*, and now sells almost as many papers there as the Morristown-Parsippany *Daily Record*. In Middlesex County, it outsells the Woodbridge *News Tribune* and the New Brunswick *Home News*—a success story beyond the dreams of the *Newark News*. It is gaining steadily in Somerset County, and apparently is setting its sights for Sussex as well.

The *Star-Ledger* is clearly doing some things right. At a time when metropolitan newspapers generally are losing circulation, it maintains stable total sales by increasing its reach in the suburbs. In an era where morning newspapers appear to have a competitive edge, it is a morning paper competing against suburban evening newspapers.

The *Star-Ledger* holds its readers by providing a thick newspaper that consistently undersells its rivals. With a 1983 price of 15 cents on weekdays, and 35 cents on Sundays, it is a newsprint bargain. While other newspapers have been willing to risk a loss in circulation in exchange for a higher cover price, the *Ledger* has sought the highest circulation possible, and has made its money selling its enormous number of readers to advertisers. The Tuesday Dec. 14, 1982 edition, for example, was 88 pages long, with 54 pages of ads. The Sunday Dec. 19, 1982 issue ran 236 pages, with 168 pages of ads plus five advertising inserts.

The downfall of the *Newark News* can be dated to its decision to house all its printing operations in downtown Newark, trapping its delivery trucks in inner-city traffic. In 1980, the *Star-Ledger* opened a satellite plant not in Newark but in Piscataway, a suburban community in Middlesex County. Located just off Route 287, the site offers easy access to Union, Monmouth, Somerset, and Middlesex counties. Radio signals carry stories and page layouts from the Newark home office to the satellite facility, but the newspaper printed in Piscataway is not exactly the same as the one produced in Newark. Pages are replated in Piscataway to provide local news sections designed solely for distribution to the suburban areas served by the satellite plant. Thus the *Ledger* hopes to be thought of not only as a regional newspaper, but as a local paper as well. The satellite plant is equipped to handle advertising inserts, and an advertiser in Middlesex County, for example, might very well be attracted by the distribution provided by the Piscataway version of the *Star-Ledger*.

The Japanese-made presses in Piscataway also allow the *Ledger* to print more pages. The paper's normal press time is 11:30 p.m., but before the satellite plant opened, the press run had to be moved up two hours whenever the newspaper went over 96 pages, and the maximum limit was 112 pages. The Piscataway plant now makes it possible for the *Star-Ledger* to produce a 144-page daily newspaper.

The goal of the *Star-Ledger* is to be thought of as *the* state newspaper, the role once played by the *Newark News*. "We want to inculcate the feeling that you need the paper if you live in New Jersey," explained Editor Mort Pye. The strategy has been to expand statehouse coverage, now the heart of the newspaper.

On that summer day in 1972 when the *Newark News* died, the *Star-Ledger* statehouse crew walked down the corridor and took over its office. "We thought it was bigger than ours," said reporter Dan Weissman. "Maybe it isn't. But it's a busy corner, the prestige spot in the building." Weissman recalls that he was writing a story at the time. He picked up his typewriter, carried it to what was to become his new office, sat down, and finished the story.

So many reporters were added to the statehouse crew during the first term of Governor Brendan T. Byrne that space became a problem. The *Ledger* left a small contingent in the old *News* office inside the statehouse, and moved the rest of its Trenton staff to rented quarters across the street. "There were days when each of us would be working on three to five big stories," remembers Weissman. "I would walk out at the end of the day completely drained." Under such pressure, the statehouse crew continued to grow.

Strangely enough, the *Ledger*'s chief competition in Trenton in the 1970s was to be the *New York Times* and the *Daily News*, which moved into the state with special New Jersey editions. John McLaughlin of the *Daily News* was a veteran of state affairs with excellent sources and a knack for quality prose. The *Times* staff was small but aggressive, and included Joe Sullivan, who had come over from the *Newark News* when it folded. Although the *Star-Ledger* crew outnumbered the New York reporters, many Trenton sources apparently preferred to break their stories in the prestigious New York papers. Finally, the *Daily News* and the *Times* decided to cut back on their New Jersey efforts, and the good stories came to the *Ledger*, left without any strong competition. Eventually McLaughlin moved to the *Ledger* as well.

"The *Record* is a fine paper," Weissman said. "But it circulates in Bergen County, and that's it." No newspaper even tries to approach the *Ledger*'s depth of coverage. No other paper has more than three reporters in Trenton, and many still depend on the equally understaffed Associated Press.

The *Ledger*'s 11-member bureau is so large that its reporters can afford to specialize in various departments and fields of expertise. Dan Weissman covers the governor, Vincent Zarate writes on insurance and banking, and Linda Lamendola does stories on human services. The most recently assigned specialist covers the appellate division of the state courts and the third circuit

WEATHER
Hot, late thundershowers today and tomorrow
(Details on Page Two)

The Star-Ledger

FINAL EDITION ★★★★

Vol. 71, No. 155 | The Newspaper for New Jersey | Newark, N.J. Thursday, August 2, 1984 | Price: 15 cents

Big wheels . . .

U.S. gold medal cyclist Steve Hegg, center, winner of the 4,000-meter individual pursuit competition, acknowledges the applause on the Olympic victory stand, with silver medalist Rolf Golz of West Germany, left, and bronze medalist Leonard Nitz, Hegg's teammate. The cyclist's effort increased the U.S. total of gold medals to 17 and a total of 27 medals in the first four days of competition. Today, 13 gold medals are slated to be awarded in 17 events, highlighted by men's gymnastics and swimming. Complete coverage of the Olympic summer games is in the Sports Section.

United Press International

Jersey Bell asks 64% hike in rates for basic service

By TED SHERMAN

New Jersey Bell Telephone Co., which was just granted a $46.4 million rate boost in May, yesterday requested an additional $260 million increase in revenues.

The rate filing with the state Board of Public Utilities (BPU) would raise the average cost of basic monthly exchange service by nearly 64 percent.

Under the company's proposed rates, the cost of unlimited local basic monthly service—which went up as a result of the increase in May from $7.15 to an average of $7.41—will go to $12.15; a jump of $4.74, or 63.9 percent.

Bell serves three million customers throughout most of the state.

Company officials said Bell was not earning its authorized rate of return under current rates, as a result of higher operating expenses not included in the last rate award. The May increase was first filed in 1982, although it was updated last August.

Other reasons cited for the request included the costs of negotiated wage increases with employes, higher interest rates, and lost revenues resulting from the divestiture of American Telephone & Telegraph Co. which took away Bell's telephone equipment business.

Bell President Anton J. Campanella said the company must also align its prices for services more reasonably with actual costs.

"No business likes to raise prices and we filed today's request only after we had demonstrated to ourselves—as we will to the BPU—that it is absolutely essential," Campanella said in a prepared statement.

However, the state Public Advocate called the request "clearly exorbitant."

Deputy Public Advocate Roger L. Camacho, who heads the Office of Rate Counsel, said the $260 million figure was extremely high, especially coming on the heels of the May rate case.

"We feel that $260 million is a tremendous amount to be asking from ratepayers in such a short period of time," Camacho commented.

He noted that at least $100 million of the request was due to profit alone, adding, "We will be battling over what is an appropriate level of profit for this company."

Besides the rate increase request for unlimited local basic monthly service, the rates for lower-priced measured service are also going up under Bell's plan. Moderate use service, which costs less

(Please turn to Page 7)

Embattled Burford bows out

By J. SCOTT ORR
Star-Ledger Washington Bureau

WASHINGTON—Former Environmental Protection Agency (EPA) Administrator Anne Burford, bowing to pressure from Congress and environmentalists, yesterday withdrew as President Reagan's choice to head the National Advisory Committee on Oceans and Atmospheres (NACOA).

Burford's resignation, delivered in a letter to Reagan yesterday, came one day after the House voted 363-51 to ask the President to withdraw the appointment and just over a week after the Senate passed an identical resolution by a 74-9 vote.

The resignation came a day before she was set to be sworn in as the NACOA chairwoman, an unsalaried position. Today's scheduled meeting of the NACOA was canceled.

Burford was ousted as EPA administrator last year amid charges of political favoritism and mismanagement in the administration of the agency's superfund hazardous waste cleanup program.

The appointment has been cited by both Democrats and Republicans as a political liability to the President in this election year and Burford, in her letter of resignation, said she did not wish to divert attention from Reagan's "outstanding record on the environment."

"In recent weeks, there has been an unwarranted furor created around my appointment . . . The people of the United States must be given the opportunity to make a fair and objective analysis of your accomplishments," she

(Please turn to Page 11)

Unity for Israel?

Israeli Prime Minister Yitzhak Shamir, right, of the ruling Likud bloc, shakes hands with Shimon Peres, leader of the opposition Labor Party, as they meet in Jerusalem's King David Hotel to discuss the possibility of forming a 'national unity' government. Story on Page 4.

United Press International

State charges Caesars on embezzler-gambler

By ROBERT SCHWANEBERG

Attorney General Irwin Kimmelman charged yesterday that Caesars casino violated gaming regulations in catering to a high-rolling Canadian, who lost $10 million he had embezzled.

The 75-page civil complaint charges Caesars violated state regulations in 1982 by devising a procedure to allow Brian Molony, who was 27 at the time, to transfer millions of dollars to Caesars while preserving his anonymity. It also outlines the lengths Caesars went to, including flying executives to Toronto to get a needed signature, so Molony could gamble at Caesars' tables.

Kimmelman said Caesars executives never questioned where Molony got his money or where he worked. In March, Molony pleaded guilty to embezzling the money from the Canadian Imperial Bank of Commerce of Toronto where he worked as an assistant bank manager.

The complaint, filed with the Casino Control Commission, names Caesars Boardwalk Regency in Atlantic City and nine executives, including casino president Peter Boynton. It is the first time the state Division of Gaming Enforcement (DGE), an arm of the Attorney General's Office, has brought charges against a casino executive of that rank.

Caesars officials had no comment on the charges yesterday.

State gaming officials, while conceding the casino had no duty to ask Molony where he got his money, said the case has implications going beyond the "technical" charges of improperly accepting $2.7 million in deposits.

Kimmelman said the casino industry has "an affirmative obligation to the people of New Jersey and to the image of this state to conduct and self-police its operations so that it will not ease the way for chronic gamblers to commit crimes, to embezzle and to

(Please turn to Page 15)

Mondale, Ferraro open fall drive to Mississippi cheers and snubs

Star-Ledger Wire Services

JACKSON, Miss.—Walter Mondale and Geraldine Ferraro opened their Democratic presidential campaign in Ronald Reagan's Southern stronghold before a large, enthusiastic crowd yesterday, but two top state Democrats gave them the brushoff.

Mondale, who has asked for six debates with the President, needled his opponent for saying the public would be bored by more than two.

"I don't think President Reagan is worried people will be bored," Mondale said. "I think he's afraid they might leave the television set on and learn something."

Mondale called the rally the official kickoff for the fall campaign, recalling that he has visited Mississippi five times in the past two years and it was in Jackson that he launched his campaign for the Democratic nomination.

"Mississippi is my lucky state," he told the crowd, which chanted, "We want Fritz."

The former vice president said if yesterday's reception is any indication, "I'm going to carry Mississippi and I'm going to carry the South. And I'm going to be elected president of the United States."

The Democratic candidates were introduced to the crowd of thousands, jamming the street in front of the governor's mansion, by former state Gov. William Winter, now a Democratic candidate for the Senate.

Winter predicted victory for the presidential ticket in November and said, "Democrats don't mind being the underdog."

Sharing the speaker's platform were Lt. Gov. Brad Dye; state Rep. Robert Clark, a candidate for Congress; former Mississippi Rep. David Bowen; and state Democratic Chairman Steve Patterson.

But other statewide elected officials stayed away.

Gov. Bill Allain, a Democrat, had not returned from the National Governors' Conference—which ended 24 hours earlier in neighboring Tennessee. And another Democrat, state House Speaker C.B. Buddy Newman, welcomed the candidates at the airport but did not attend the rally and told

(Please turn to Page 12)

Suits allowed on birth-defect child if faulty diagnosis halted abortion

By ROBERT G. SEIDENSTEIN

The New Jersey Supreme Court ruled yesterday that infants born with severe health defects, whose lives could have been aborted if their parents had received accurate information from their doctors, may sue those physicians for lifelong "extraordinary medical expenses."

An infant may not sue, however, for the emotional distress of having to live his life with severe handicaps. Justice Stewart Pollock, writing for the court, said there simply was no way to measure the value of an "impaired life" versus "nonexistence."

The court's decision extended rulings issued within the past five years that allowed parents to maintain medical malpractice suits for their own emotional suffering and for the extraordinary medical expenses associated with the birth and support of a severely handicapped child.

In the particular case decided yesterday, however, the parents had been barred from suing. Their court action was begun after the expiration of the legal period for bringing a malpractice complaint.

According to Pollock, the highest courts in only two other states, California and Washington, have gone as far as

Quoting the California case, Pollock said, "The right to recover the often crushing burden of extraordinary expenses visited by an act of medical malpractice should not depend on the 'wholly fortuitous circumstance of whether the parents are available to sue.'"

The justice said, "The present case proves the point. Here, the parents' claim is barred by the statute of limitations. Does this mean that Peter must forego medical treatment for his blindness, deafness and retardation? We think not.

"His claim for the medical expenses attributable to his birth defects is reasonably certain, readily calculable, and of a kind daily determined by

(Please turn to Page 11)

Reagan, Pope's envoy confer on Poland curbs

RANCHO DEL CIELO, Calif. (AP)-President Reagan took a break from ranch chores yesterday to confer with a Vatican representative in preparation for removal of some of the economic sanctions the United States imposed against Poland to protest martial law.

On a flawless summer day, the President and his wife Nancy posed for pictures with Archbishop Pio Laghi, the Vatican's ambassador to the United States, near the President's century-old white adobe ranch house.

Asked whether the amnesty under which Poland agreed to free 632 political prisoners had gone far enough to enable him to lift some of the sanctions, the President replied: "These are things we'll discuss today."

But, a White House official, who spoke on condition of anonymity, had said earlier that some of the sanctions will be lifted and that an announcement could occur later this week.

After the picture-taking session, Reagan escorted his guest to a table on a covered patio for lunch of cold cucumber soup, turkey salad, angel food cake and iced tea.

The archbishop wore clerical garb, including a Roman Catholic collar. Reagan wore cowboy boots and a western shirt.

It was only the third time in Reagan's presidency that reporters—in this case a small pool representing the entire White House press corps—were allowed to visit the President's secluded, well-guarded ranch. The first time occurred in August 1981, when Reagan signed legislation cutting income tax rates. The second occurred in March 1983, when Queen Elizabeth II came to lunch.

NJ Transit takes over Newark Penn Station

By GUY T. BAEHR

With an air of confidence and celebration, NJ Transit yesterday formally took over operation of Newark's Penn Station from Amtrak and promised an even safer, cleaner and livelier station in the future.

Jerome C. Premo, executive director of the agency, told officials and travelers gathered in the restored

is dirty, we're the ones responsible for cleaning it."

Minutes later, evidence of the transit agency's apparent determination to do just that appeared in the form of a blue-uniformed NJ Transit maintenance worker moving through the crowd, sweeping up stray cigarette butts and gum wrappers from the freshly mopped floor.

In a notice to station users,

NJ Transit Executive Director Jerome C. Premo speaks at takeover ceremonies in Newark's Penn Station as Mayor Kenneth A. Gibson, right, and State Transportation Commissioner John P. Sheridan Jr. listen.

Photo by John A. Gibson Jr.

of the federal courts—and that is in addition to the reporter who covers the state supreme court. "I have to assume," said Editor Pye, "that anyone who reads us has more than a passing interest in state government."

The *Star-Ledger* features specialized reporting in other areas as well. Herb Jaffe covers the legal scene, Gordon Bishop covers the environment, and Robert Braun writes on education. Mary Jo Patterson and Arthur Lenehan are high-gloss quality writers who have been given the freedom to develop long-term special enterprise articles. The newspaper has full-time movie critics, a rock 'n' roll writer, a jazz/pop writer, and a classical music writer. "Nobody else covers the arts on a statewide basis except us," said Editor Pye.

The *Ledger* also bases reporters in bureaus throughout most of northern and central New Jersey. Some bureaus have large staffs, such as the six-person Morris County office, while others have only one or two full-time reporters. Bureau staffers generally cover stories of countywide interest, leaving normal municipal meetings to be handled to a considerable extent by stringers provided by an outside contracting service.

This is all part of the *Ledger*'s strategy for success. Sports coverage of schools and colleges is extensive, localizing the newspaper for readers throughout the large circulation area. Court coverage is heavy because of its effect on people's lives. Jaffe's legal pieces attract jurists and lawyers, and Braun's education articles are written with teachers in mind. For commuters, the paper offers transportation stories. "The people interested in these situations," explained Editor Pye, "should get enough so that they feel the paper is worth reading—even though they may not read everything. A lot of people have the same feeling about the [*New York*] *Times.* In all modesty, I should like people to feel about our paper that it's all there."

A great deal *is* there. But it tends, at times, to be there in the form of segmented stories. The paper's intense specialization tends to inhibit a more integrated view of social questions. "Politics is a game that Dave Wald covers," said Stephen Salmore, then chairman of the Rutgers Department of Political Science, "and I think he does a pretty good job. But he doesn't cover the substance of politics. I think they've missed the connection between politics and government. They tend to compartmentalize. Zarate covers one thing, Jaffe covers law, and Bishop covers environment—but who covers the politics of environment?"

Prestige is a matter of importance for Pye and the *Star-Ledger*, and when the quality of the paper is measured by objective standards, many of its scores are high. The study of 1974 New Jersey newspapers conducted by John Kolesar of the Center for Analysis of Public Issues in Princeton showed the *Star-Ledger*'s strengths. At that time, the paper offered 25 pages of news and 50 pages of ads daily—more than any other newspaper. The *Ledger* carried nearly three times as much state news as any other paper, and was ranked first in national news and second in the amount of foreign news. In the category of specialized news (editorials, business, family, amusements, comics, and sports), the *Ledger* ranked fourth on a percentage basis. Fifty-nine percent of its news hole consisted of such specialized news, with 21 percent of the news hole devoted to sports. But the study also showed the *Ledger*'s weakness—it carried less local news than any other newspaper, less even than the smallest newspaper with the smallest news hole. Where was the news of Newark and the suburbs?

The content analysis of 1977 New Jersey newspapers conducted by David Sachsman for this project presents a similar picture. With 27 pages of news, the *Ledger*'s news hole was still three pages larger than its nearest competitor, the *Record* of Hackensack, but its 47 pages of advertising were two pages less than the *Record*. Its state coverage remained three times the size of that offered by any other newspaper, it was first in national news, and tied for first in the number of international news stories. It ranked first in the use of wire service and syndicate stories, first in the number of locally originated stories, and second in the number of longer stories. But it was only 13th in the use of photographs, and it was last in local news coverage, averaging only eight local news stories daily. Since the time of this study, the *Ledger* has beefed up its suburban bureaus, and has opened the Piscataway printing plant, where pages are replated to provide local suburban news. And the *Ledger* publishes a pull-out section called "Newark This Week: A Special Monday section devoted to Newarkers and their neighborhoods."

Officially the *Star-Ledger* has always loved Newark, but one would never guess from looking at its front page that it is published in Newark. Both the *Ledger* and the *Newark News* failed to recognize the conditions and events that led to the riot in 1967. And during the civil disturbance, both newspapers relied almost exclusively on police accounts of the events. In 1968, the special state committee investigating the riot reported wide-ranging excesses on the part of law enforcement forces, and found that many of Newark's problems were due to an atmosphere of corruption surrounding the administration of Mayor Hugh J. Addonizio.

The Addonizio regime began to crumble the following year under the investigation of U.S. Attorney Frederick B. Lacey. Addonizio and a number of other city officials were eventually convicted, and federal authorities contended that the city had really been under the influence of organized crime. None of this was uncovered by either the *Ledger* or the *News*. Both newspapers flubbed the two most important Newark stories of the 1960s, the riot and city corruption, supporting the argument that the two dailies lacked interest in what was happening in the city, an argument pressed by Ron Porambo in *No Cause for Indictment: An Autopsy of Newark*, (Holt, Rinehart and Winston, 1971). As U.S. Attorney Lacey said during a speaking engagement (quoted by

Porambo), "I, for one, found it difficult to understand how blatant, arrogant corruption can exist as long as it did in Newark without devastating exposures by the press."

The *Star-Ledger*'s weekly pull-out section on Newark is evidence that it has become increasingly sensitive to criticism of its coverage of the city. Editor Pye said the section demonstrates that "we want to be both the Newark paper *and* the state paper." Nevertheless, the section is not circulated outside the city, and the people of Newark have been buying the newspaper in steadily decreasing numbers. The paper is making efforts to be thought of as a local newspaper, but it is not a good one. It is a thick, regional paper that is the closest thing to a state newspaper in New Jersey.

Editors and reporters in the state have mixed feelings about the quality of the *Star-Ledger*. In the 1974 poll conducted by the Center for Analysis of Public Issues, they ranked the *Ledger* second best overall, well behind the *Record* of Hackensack. While they ranked the *Ledger* first in state, national, and political coverage, they did not put it among the leaders in writing, editing, editorials, or local coverage.

Editors and reporters interviewed for this project often spoke positively of the *Ledger*'s quantity rather than its quality. They respect it for its size, but many do not think much of its writing and editing, and one managing editor of a suburban daily went so far as to call it a bad newspaper.

Even some *Star-Ledger* reporters find the writing and editing to be major weaknesses of the paper. One reporter insists that in some bureaus a story is expected every day, with the emphasis on quantity rather than quality. The reporter said, "I've seen raw copy come in that an editor has cleaned up a little—when he should have said, 'This stinks, do it over.' "

The *Ledger*'s basic style can be characterized as populist with a touch of blue-collar. It likes to hammer away at state agency problems, court delays, transportation foul-ups, and the like. One former newspaperman suggested that the *Ledger* tries to draw attention to itself whenever possible. Sometimes the style seems reminiscent of early Hearst or Pulitzer crusades for "the people."

These campaigns are more often reflected in the paper's news columns than in its limp and generally undistinguished editorials. The most renowned example remains the *Ledger*'s relentless crusade for a sports complex in the Meadowlands. The paper began running articles promoting the concept of a major league stadium in 1967, and never swerved from its course. When the sports authority ran into difficulty selling its bonds in 1973, the *Ledger* radiated optimism, blaming many of the problems on a "New York conspiracy."

The sports complex crusade was typical in its New Jersey chauvinism, but unusual in that it was directed by the paper's top editors. More often, writers are simply granted carte blanche, supported by copy editors who rarely perform any radical surgery, and the seemingly bottomless news hole. Robert Braun's campaign to rid the state of Education Commissioner Fred Burke went on for years.

The *Star Ledger*'s style has also been called "tacky" by some of its staffers. One reporter noted that the Sunday travel section persists in getting many of its stories by interviewing New Jersey residents who have recently returned from trips, resulting in headlines like "Teen Finds Study a Pleasure on St. Croix" (June 21, 1981), and "Aussie Wonders Amaze Jerseyan" (July 26, 1981). "It's not done just to be cheap," the reporter said, "but because the paper believes the general reader is interested in having somebody to relate to. Once I saw a note on the travel desk that said, 'My husband and I are going to Honolulu and when we return would be happy to be interviewed.' That's what I call the 'home movies' section."

Newsroom people are disturbed by the circulation department's long-standing method of telephoning for new subscriptions "on behalf of the Cerebral Palsy Drive." It is explained that part of the introductory subscription will be donated to the charity campaign. "It really bothers me," a reporter said, "that a newspaper that has so much quality has to resort to such gimmicks."

Many editors and reporters in the state also remember the old stories about *Star-Ledger* reporters who had side jobs doing public relations for news sources. In those days, they say, the *Ledger* asked few questions, and overlooked apparent conflicts of interest.

For all these reasons, and despite its size, the *Star-Ledger* is not considered the best newspaper in New Jersey. But it has become a force in the state and it is respected. "The *Star-Ledger is* the *Newark News*," says John McLaughlin. "It has become what the *News* was. Its devotion to state news is impressive, and it has become a very respectable American newspaper." McLaughlin's position is highly debatable, but today's *Ledger* is better than it once was, and if it is not the best newspaper in the state, it is one of the best.

The Slick, Rich *Record* of Hackensack

Bergen County is a model of affluent, educated suburbia. With an average family income of $28,000 in 1980, it leads the state in effective buying power and retail sales. It is a land of college graduates, multiple-car owners, and cable-television subscribers. They have the money and they spend it.

"The people in Bergen County seem to spend all their time shopping," said

John Kolesar, night news editor at the *Record.* "It's unbelievable. I've gone to a shopping center on a Wednesday morning and found the stores packed with shoppers. That's the *slow* time. At busy times you can't get onto the highway."

Tucked in the middle of this retailing paradise is the *Record* of Hackensack, a newspaper that gives its readers and advertisers precisely what they want. For the readers it provides a sophisticated evening magazine in newspaper form, and for the advertisers it has the perfect up-scale audience—149,281 strong on weekdays and 216,440 on Sundays in 1983.

The *Record* is a suburban regional newspaper that covers 70 Bergen County municipalities, Passaic County, and small portions of Hudson County and New York's Rockland County. It is published basically as a single edition, with five replatings. The local news is contained in one section of the news-paper and is changed for various delivery areas. The best of the local news is published on the section's front page ("North Jersey Today") and remains unchanged.

The Bergen Evening Record Corporation is owned by Malcolm Borg, and his stamp on the paper is indelible. But while he makes the crucial personnel decisions that determine newsroom leadership, he generally leaves the news operation to the editors. He has newsroom experience himself, having started as an obituary writer in 1959. His grandfather, Wall Street financier John Borg, acquired complete control of the newspaper in 1930, having bought out a series of partners one by one. Nowadays, the Bergen Evening Record Corporation also owns an advertising agency, Magna Media Inc., and Gate-way Communications Inc., which operates four television stations in New York, Pennsylvania, and West Virginia.

Many professionals regard the *Record* as the best newspaper in New Jersey, citing in particular the quality of its writing. In the 1974 survey conducted by the Center for Analysis of Public Issues, editors and reporters ranked the *Record* first overall, first in writing and editing, first in local news coverage, first in investigative reporting, second in editorials and national news, and tied for third in statehouse coverage.

News staffers interviewed for this project consistently praised the *Record.* Robert Windrem, a former New Jersey reporter who is now a producer for NBC Network News, called the *Record* the second best regional newspaper in the United States, behind only Long Island's *Newsday.* The *Record* wins the awards, and garners the prestige in New Jersey journalism.

It is the happiest of newspaper cycles. The advertisers supply the money, lots of it (49 pages of ads a day). The newspaper spends the money freely to produce a solid product, employing 198 full-time news staffers and 81 part-timers to fill a 24-page news hole. The high-income audience centered in towns like Ho-Ho-Kus, Wyckoff, Franklin Lakes, and Rivervale buys the news-paper and goes shopping, pleasing the advertisers, who buy more ads.

Mets are exceeding expectations at midpoint of season.

High-rise residents say town sees them as only a tax shelter. B-1

The Record

BERGEN   NORTHERN NEW JERSEY   MONDAY,   JULY 9, 1984   25¢

Figuring trash costs over the long haul

By Joan Verdon
Staff Writer

In North Jersey, it seems, garbage collection always looks better on the other side of the fence.

Plagued for years by sharply increasing costs for private garbage collectors, and having suffered through a week's strike, a number of communities are looking at public collection as the answer to their problems.

The strike created two problems for the approximately two dozen North Jersey towns that collect their own trash, and those communities are being eyed enviously by neighboring towns where garbage piled up last week.

But officials in charge of municipal collection are quick to warn that doing it yourself isn't the perfect answer to every town's garbage woes.

"When there is peace and quiet in private collection, I'm jealous of them," said Louis Goetting, administrator of Bergenfield, which has collected its own garbage for many years.

Though the borough thinks municipal collection is cheaper and better, Goetting notes that doing it yourself brings personnel and management headaches."

The strike, and the number of private garbage haulers in recent years — has forced attention on how towns get rid of their trash. A growing number of small New Jersey communities are including the costs of private garbage collection and wondering if they can save money by doing it themselves.

One of David Moldia's first decisions after he became mayor of Montvale in January was to appoint a committee to study whether there is a better and cheaper way to dispose of the borough's garbage. Montvale is paying a private contractor $230,000 this year.

Moldia says only dollars and cents, rather than the temporary inconvenience of a strike, would persuade...

See TRASH, Page A-4

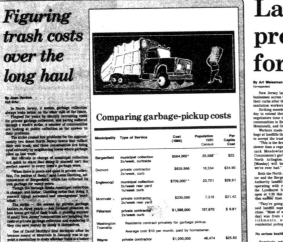

Comparing garbage-pickup costs

Municipality	Type of Service	Cost (1984)	Population 1980 Census	Per Capita Cost
Bergenfield	municipal collection 2x/week, curbside	$564,000*	25,568*	$22.
Dumont	private contractor 2x/week, curb	$639,996	18,334	$34.90
Englewood	municipal collection 2x/week rear yard 1x/week curb	$709,000**	23,701	$29.91
Montvale	private contractor 2x/week rear yard	$230,000	7,316	$31.42
Paterson	private contractor 2x/week curb	$1,368,000	137,970	$ 9.91
Washington Township	Residents contract privately for garbage pickup. Average cost $10 per month, paid by homeowner.			
Wayne	private contractor 2x/week, curb	$1,200,000	46,474	$25.82

* 1983 figures.
** Operating costs only. Does not include capital and other significant costs.

Landfills preparing for deluge

By Art Weissman
Correspondent

New Jersey landfills braced for record volume today as residents and businesses across the northern half of the state hauled bags of garbage to their curbs after the end, at least temporarily, of a one-week strike by 1,400 sanitation workers.

Striking members of Teamsters Local 945 voted overwhelmingly Saturday to extend their contract expires June 30, for 30 days to give negotiators time to reach a settlement with 70 waste haulers serving 200 communities in Bergen, Passaic, Hudson, Morris, Essex, Union, Middlesex, Monmouth, and Ocean counties.

Workers made limited collections yesterday, dumping mounds of garbage at landfills that, although normally closed on weekends, remained open to accept the trash.

"This is the first time I ever recall being open on a Sunday, but it's been slower than a regular day," said Tom Hickey, weigh master at the Hackensack Meadowlands Development Commission's garbage compactor in North Arlington. "But tomorrow [Monday] will be the biggest day we've ever had."

Both the North Arlington compactor and the Bergen County Utilities Authority landfill in Lyndhurst are operating with regular staffs. But the Lyndhurst facility was to be open at 4:30 this morning, 90 minutes earlier than usual.

"They're going to kill us today," said landfill supervisor Peter Bachino. "Most of what came in [Sunday] was from commercial establishments, not much from residential pickups."

No serious health problems

Regularly scheduled residential collections were to start early this morning in most communities. But municipal officials and representatives of the garbage haulers warned that collection schedules would not be accelerated and that some residents...

See DUMPS, Page A-6

Inside

Clear, mild tonight; mostly sunny, warmer tomorrow. Detailed forecast, Page B-20.

Three Sections   54 Pages

Mondale elevates 3 long shots to contender ranks

By Dan Balz
Washington Post News Service

NORTH OAKS, Minn. — After nearly a month, Walter F. Mondale's often-criticized search for a running mate has produced some surprising results, including the transformation of several long shots into serious contenders.

Three mayors, Tom Bradley of Los Angeles, Dianne Feinstein of San Francisco, and Henry Cisneros of San Antonio, by virtue of their performances during the interviewing, have impressed Mondale and his advisers and appear to have kept themselves in the running along with several others.

Mondale's search is a combination of public ritual and private reflection. He says he has not begun to make a final decision. No list of candidates has been released, nor will there be an official end to the likely Democratic nominee's interviews.

More is known about his choices than about any other vice-presidential candidates in the past. Mondale argues, but he and his top aides have refused to provide much information about what is happening beyond news conferences after the interviews at his Minnesota home.

Still, in the last week the process has taken on a form that is likely to influence the decision, which Mondale may announce before the Democratic convention in San Francisco that begins July 16.

While saying the choice is still "wide open," Mondale has begun to provide clues to his thinking, both in public comments about what he seeks for the office and in his response to the way prospective candidates have handled themselves publicly when they have come to see Mondale about the job.

He appears to be operating from a list of about 10 candidates. They include the seven persons he has interviewed formally and three others.

The seven are two black mayors, Bradley and W. Wilson Goode of Philadelphia; a Hispanic, Cisneros; three women, Feinstein, Rep. Geraldine A. Ferraro of New York, and Gov. Martha Layne Collins of Kentucky; and one white male, Sen. Lloyd Bentsen of Texas, whose grasp of economics issues and depth of experience have impressed Mondale.

The other three are Sen. Gary Hart of Colorado, Mondale's chief rival for the Democratic nomination; Sen. Dale Bumpers of Arkansas, and perhaps Gov. Michael S. Dukakis of Massachusetts.

Mondale has laid out what he is seeking: a compatible person fully qualified to be vice-president — and president.

See MAYORS, Page A-2

U.S. envoy to pope draws reprimand

By Ronald J. Ostrow
and Don A. Schanche
Los Angeles Times News Service

WASHINGTON, D.C. — The ambassador to the Vatican has been chastised by the Department of Justice and has alarmed his superiors at the State Department because of his personal intervention in two highly sensitive and widely publicized international criminal investigations, administration officials say.

Ambassador William A. Wilson is a close friend of President Reagan. The nature of the two cases — those of fugitive financier Marc Rich and Vatican banker Archbishop Paul C. Marcinkus — have raised fears among administration officials that Wilson's actions could be viewed as an improper use of his position and thus become an embarrassment.

Administration sources say that Wilson's actions are being examined by the State Department's Bureau of European Affairs, but department spokesmen declined to discuss the inquiry.

In the Marcinkus case, administration officials said that in 1982, Wilson wrote a letter on Archbishop Marcinkus's behalf to Attorney-General William French Smith, a longtime friend and fellow member of Reagan's "kitchen cabinet" of close advisers. Wilson, a Los Angeles developer and rancher, has been co-trustee of the legal trust that manages Reagan's private assets since 1973.

At the time he wrote the letter, Wilson was the president's unpaid personal envoy to the Holy See. Reagan named Wilson ambassador to the Vatican in January and the Senate confirmed him in March when the United States established full diplomatic relations with the Vatican.

See ENVOY, Page A-6

Urban art
In Paterson, some graffiti vandals can be legitimate artists. See story, Page B-1.

Staff photo by Al Paglione

Karcher sees Kean riding high

By Mark S. Herr
United Press International

NEW YORK — New Jersey Assembly Speaker Alan J. Karcher says it will be extremely difficult for the Democrats to defeat Governor Kean if he runs for reelection next year.

"The governor is riding very high, there's no doubt about that," Karcher said on WCBS-TV's "Newsmakers" program yesterday. "It is a very uphill battle for any Democratic candidate."

The combative Middlesex County lawmaker also said it's unlikely that he himself will run for governor, even though he is often mentioned as a potential Democratic candidate. He said he is more concerned with strengthening the Democrats' hold

See KARCHER, Page A-2

The cycle has not only made the *Record* rich, but it has allowed it to become a truly excellent suburban newspaper. Nevertheless, although studies of New Jersey newspapers conducted in the 1970s ranked the *Record* among the state's leaders, they did not find the newspaper to be the best in the state in quantitative terms.

The study of 1974 New Jersey newspapers conducted by the Center for Analysis of Public Issues found the *Record* to be a 68-page daily with 46 pages of ads and 22 pages of news. Thus it ranked a rich second in advertising, but three other newspapers in the state offered larger news holes. The *Record* was second best in the quantity of state news, third in the amount of foreign news, fifth in national news, and seventh in local news coverage.

The content analysis of 1977 New Jersey newspapers conducted by David Sachsman for this project presents a similar picture. The *Record's* 49 pages of ads a day gave it first place in advertising, but its 24 pages of news put it in a fourth-place tie for the size of its news hole. The *Record* ranked fourth in the total number of news and feature stories, second in the amount of national news, tied for fifth place in foreign news, tied for 10th in state news, and was 16th in the number of local news stories. This low score in local news is partly due to the fact that the *Record* replates its local news pages, changing the local stories for various delivery areas. Thus the newspaper maintains a small local news hole, but actually produces many local news stories.

The analysis of 1977 newspapers also ranked the *Record* second in its use of photographs, fourth in its presentation of both locally originated stories and longer news and feature stories, and in a fifth-place tie for wire service and syndicate coverage.

All in all, the content analysis places the *Record* among the top four newspapers in the state, along with the *Star-Ledger*, the *Camden Courier-Post*, and the *Asbury Park Press*. In quantitative terms, the *Record* is an excellent newspaper, but not the best in the state. Why then do journalists rate it number one?

The *Record* is a highly distinctive product that looks like a newspaper but reads like a magazine. Its approach to the news is interpretive, thematic, and encyclopedic. The centerpiece of the *Record's* front page is a major, in-depth story called "The Patch," an investigative or background piece on a topic such as the Moral Majority or teenage alcoholism in Bergen County. "The Patch" takes precedence over breaking stories, and many view it as the cornerstone of the paper. "If you have a patch for every day, the paper has been planned," said Michael Hoyt, a former reporter. "You can always fill in the rest."

The *Record's* free-flowing, interpretive style even appears when it rewrites its wire sources, as in its lead story on July 15, 1981, a second-day follow-up of the resignation of a CIA spy chief:

Max Hugel was an outsider from the start—a millionaire from New Hampshire whose intelligence experience was limited to some postwar work with the Army in Japan. His appointment as chief of the CIA's spy network irked career intelligence officers and surprised some White House officials; but it stood, largely because agency director William J. Casey's closeness with President Reagan allowed him the freedom to pick his own man.

The *Record* looks at the big picture and tries to explain the world. When children threw rocks at a school bus, the paper began putting together a series on dissatisfaction in the school system. On another occasion, the newspaper called upon its local beat reporters to audit the records of all 70 Bergen municipalities—and won a major award for the effort. Computers were used in 1982 to examine the criminal justice systems in Bergen and Passaic counties, and in 1983 reporter Chris Mondies used census data to put together a four-part series analyzing the changing trends in Bergen County.

In-depth interpretive and investigative pieces win journalism awards, and are considered by many the hallmark of quality journalism. This is the *Record*'s strength, and journalists across the state value it highly. But shooting for the big story does have its problems. "One of our editors once said when he heard a story idea that it sounded more like a subject for a term paper," night editor Kolesar said. "Once in a dozen times that stuff turns out to be terrific, but 11 out of 12 times it's dull and gassy. We're never satisfied with telling people what happened yesterday; we're always concerned with and looking for ultimate truth, and there isn't much of it to go around."

Quantitative measurements cannot evaluate the quality of individual stories or the quality of the writing, itself. And the *Record* not only contains many excellent stories, it is a newspaper noted for the high quality of its writing. But can a newspaper be *too* slick?

"Sometimes when I read it," Kolesar said, "I am amazed that a newspaper can be so good from front to back. Our copy is so honed and polished and overpolished that it's *too* shiny—it's lost a little of that frayed edge of a newspaper story. *Star-Ledger* stories are incomplete, but the paper will have another story about it the next day, and the next. Not in the *Record*: it's all there, all squared off. Very often the *Record* story is the best one on the subject, but it's written on the declining side."

The *Record*'s slick, magazine style of reporting makes economic sense. The newspaper sits across the river from New York. Many of its up-scale readers are used to the *New York Times* and the *Wall Street Journal*. They do not ask for page after page of local or statehouse news; they like the *Record*'s approach to the news. "An awful lot of what we do would be much too slick and highbrow elsewhere," said Kolesar, "but it has to be done here."

The paper's approach to the news comes from its editors, and the *Record* is clearly an editor's newspaper. "All the ideas come out of the news meetings rather than from reporters who are out there nosing around," said Hoyt, observing that the editors' ideas sometimes come from *Newsweek*, *Omni*, or *Harper's* magazine. When a big story breaks—such as happened with the first leak on Abscam—reporters sit around, losing valuable time, waiting for the news meeting to end and assignments to be handed out.

The *Record's* large editorial staff is divided into recognizable categories: municipal reporters, statehouse reporters, and specialized reporters in areas such as business, sports, entertainment, and lifestyle. The *Record* differs from other newspapers, however, in its use of general assignment reporters. At most newspapers, general assignment denotes hole-pluggers and trouble-shooters thrown into breaking news situations. At the *Record*, general assignment translates into house generalists, and is the assignment to which many municipal reporters aspire.

Many of the *Record's* big stories have been written by general assignment reporters, but Kolesar feels the system has had its problems. Generalists tend to write their stories and then move on to other stories on different topics. Thus these reporters often did not develop regular territories or sources for continuing news tips.

Even the specialized reporters, Kolesar said, have not been responsible for coverage in any comprehensive way. The education writer (Mary Ellen Schoonmaker at the time of the interview) does not cover education in the way that the *Star-Ledger's* writer (Robert Braun) covers it. "So when the education writer calls an assistant commissioner of education," Kolesar said, "and says 'I'm the education writer for the Bergen *Record*,' the commissioner says, 'I didn't know the *Record had* an education writer.' "

Kolesar and others have been pressing for the traditional beat system of reporting, and the result has been a compromise called the "mini-beat." Many general assignment reporters now spend part of their time covering specialized areas. "It's an effort to tighten things up around here," said Daniel Lazare, whose mini-beat is transportation.

As recently as 1981, the Sunday *Record* front page carried few breaking hard news stories. For example, the May 24, 1981 front page contained six stories, only one of which concerned breaking news. Today about half the articles on the Sunday *Record* front page involve breaking news, but virtually all of them are second-day follow-up stories. The *Record* system is simply not geared to covering breaking news. "A lot of bureaucrats would like to talk to the *Record*," Kolesar said. "Unlike the *Star-Ledger* it has no axes to grind. But if they give a story to us it doesn't get into print until four days later. The *Record* lacks the urgency that I'd like to see."

Schoonmaker says that some reporters miss the adrenaline effect of competition and deadlines, neither of which is highly valued in the *Record* newsroom system.

The three-member statehouse crew, for example, does not compete with the *Ledger's* exhaustive coverage. And unlike other regional papers, it does not concentrate on what hometown legislators have to say. Instead, it focuses on issues believed important to its reader, and provides analytical reports on the statehouse scene. The key to the success of the *Record's* statehouse

The Scoop That Pooped

Just because a newspaper is not known for its coverage of breaking news stories, that does not mean it will ignore a possible scoop.

Back in 1977, Bill Soiffer, then a 24-year-old *Record* reporter, thought he had a hot story, and his editors agreed. At a Paramus Chamber of Commerce luncheon, he had heard—or thought he had heard—state Supreme Court Justice Morris Pashman say that the court was about to release a decision placing a five-year statute of limitations on murder.

It was too late to get a story in that day's paper, but the editors figured the *Record* could still get credit for the scoop by giving a copyrighted story to the wire services and television stations.

When Soiffer got back to Justice Pashman, however, the judge insisted that Soiffer had not heard him correctly. But Justice Pashman did not tell Soiffer that the story was wrong—had he done so he would have revealed the court's actual decision—and so Soiffer and the editors discounted the denial.

The editors gave out the story while it was still being checked. When other people who had attended the luncheon confirmed Justice Pashman's version, the *Record* decided not to run the story, and the wire services were informed that although Soiffer stood by his story, serious questions had been raised.

By 9:30 the next morning, the paper had a copy of the decision. Soiffer had heard wrong. The wire services were notified immediately but it was too late. Some newspapers had already gone to press quoting the copyrighted *Record* story.

"They just went gung ho and made this monumental mistake of trying to show off," said reporter Bruce Rosen, who wrote a story on the foul-up at the time. "Being in the shadow of the *Times* constantly, they get a real complex, and when they finally got a big story, that little c with the circle on it, they were calling all the newspapers."

Record Publisher Malcolm Borg standing on the deck of his pride and joy, the new TKS printing press system.

coverage is the excellence of its personnel. Jon Shure is widely regarded as the best political reporter in New Jersey. Bureau Chief Peter Yerkes writes thoughtfully and incisively, and Harvey Fisher, a go-getter, asks the toughest questions in Trenton. The *Record* has a tradition of excellent statehouse reporters dating back to Robert Comstock, the newspaper's current executive editor.

The *Record's* system clearly works. The newspaper has recently completed a $60 million expansion—an incredible sum when compared to the $10-12 million price paid for the *Trenton Times*, lock, stock, and barrel, in 1981. The new TKS (Tokyo Kikai Seisakusho) presses give the paper, in Borg's words, "a color capability no other American newspaper has," and the new Ferag inserting equipment enables the paper to process 40,000 copies per hour with up to eight inserts. The *Record* has become a six-section newspaper on Wednesdays, Thursdays, and Fridays, and the Sunday edition now consists of 10 sections. There is also a new morning edition distributed to newsstands and coin boxes.

The *Record's* new hardware has been mounted for a major drive into selected areas that demographically look just like upscale Bergen County, such as suburban Wayne Township in Passaic County, where the paper has a 12-member Passaic County bureau. Circulation in Bergen is static, and any future growth must come from such outlying areas. "We'll move into areas where we feel the daily and weekly newspapers may be vulnerable," Borg said.

The *Record* has also gone into television production in a number of ways. It has produced a half-hour news program for three cable outlets, election night coverage for a cable channel, a commercial for a local dance studio, an orientation tape for new employees, and a feature on a Dumont man who collects Snoopy paraphernalia, which has been sold to NBC.

The *Record's* product is "class": advertisements for Saks Fifth Avenue; highly professional entertainment reviews; literate, well-researched and logically developed editorials; and a well-designed and informative op-ed page. The editorial staff of six, headed by David Corcoran, is the best in the state, and the Lifestyle section is equally distinguished. The nine-member art department, which includes artist Bill Hogan, dresses up the paper with fine drawings and graphics. It is a newspaper of integrity, with editorials that are more liberal than its readership, and with a newsroom unafraid of advertisers, as shown by articles on issues such as unsafe conditions in shopping malls. Best of all is the consistently high quality of the writing. It is a very classy product indeed.

The *Record's* use of art enlivens its pages. This artwork by Bill Hogan was designed to illustrate an interpretive piece on retirement.

Retirement is an outdated notion

By Jarold A. Kieffer

The dream of retirement — of a dignified period of ease after a lifetime of work — is so deeply ingrained in the American psyche that any suggestion that the dream is outmoded and economically impractical invariably invites protest.

But we will soon have to radically alter our traditional views of a working life. The majority of us probably will find it desirable and perhaps necessary to delay retirement and work many years longer than most people do now.

Widespread doubts are developing about the long-term solvency of Social Security and of some government and private pension systems. Pressure is growing to scale back pension benefits of future federal-government retirees — and some state and local retirees as well. Labor unions, fighting to save jobs, have had to give back future pension benefits won earlier.

Many Americans already sense correctly that they may not have adequate income to support themselves in retirement and will need to to stay on their jobs longer or learn skills for other jobs. Before the end of the century, many more people will want or need to continue working to 70 and beyond.

The issue is whether we can change the policies of government, private employers, and labor unions to respond to these needs.

Instead of pretending that there's no conflict between the promise and the reality of retirement, the federal government, with the help of private industry, labor unions, and the U.S. education system, should be looking for ways to help older people voluntarily remain in the work force.

Retraining, the abolition of mandatory retirement laws, provision of enough jobs, and the removal of disincentives to working longer will enable the vast majority of future workers to have economic security once they finally do retire.

A policy of encouraging longer work lives may sound hard-hearted. But it can be helpful and give hope to many people who look to their economic future with anxiety.

We have been reacting to longer life and the huge expansion of the older population almost as a calamity. We focus on the huge retirement-income and health-care costs, on the loneliness and ailments of the aged, and on growing burdens placed on families of the elderly. We completely miss the opportunities arising from a healthier, active older population.

Too many employers, educators, and government policy makers still write off older people as a productive resource. Even as we struggle to assure the solvency of our retirement and health-care systems, we fail to take into account how longer work lives could help ease these demands on the system.

In 1977 and again in 1983, Congress and the president had to act to prevent the insolvency of the Social Security retirement and survivors' insurance trust fund. They had to increase the amount of wages subject to the payroll tax each year, borrow from other Social Security funds, tax (for the first time) benefits of many retirees, speed up future payroll-tax increases, cut benefits for some future retirees, and delay cost-of-living adjustments for people already retired.

Staff illustration by William B. Hogan

Originally, Social Security was only meant to provide an income floor for retirees. The expectation was that recipients would have other sources of income. Some do. But according to a 1981 Louis Harris survey:

● Two thirds of people 65 or older were receiving no interest from a savings account.

● Seventy-eight percent had no investment income.

● Sixty-eight percent received no pension income.

● Eighty-seven percent had no wages.

● Ninety-five percent received no money from their children.

Today, a quarter of all Social Security beneficiaries 65 or over get 90 percent of their total income from their Social Security checks. Even those with the highest benefits under Social Security are hardly well off, unless they also have good pensions and other retirement income.

A worker turning 65 last January and eligible for a maximum Social Security benefit could get $8,436 a year (or $12,648, if the benefits of a non-working spouse also over 65 are counted).

While the number of people getting the maximum benefit is increasing, and more working wives are earning their own benefits, most retirees get less than the maximum. The average annual benefit paid to a couple is $8,865. This is less than $3,000 above the official poverty-level income for an elderly couple.

Neither the economy nor political realities are likely to allow a significant hike in Social Security benefits in the foreseeable future.

The economic outlook for workers not yet retired is also not reassuring. Of

Americans currently in the work force, slightly more than half are not covered by a private pension plan. And many of those who are covered will never get the benefits, because they'll change employers, lose jobs, or see their company go out of business before qualifying.

Pensions and Social Security checks are, of course, not the only resources that people have to fall back on when they quit work. There are also savings, homes, insurance policies, stocks, and bonds.

The evidence, however, is that most people 65 and over don't have substantial holdings of these kinds. Census Bureau data for 1982 show that of the 25.7 million people 65 or over in that year, nearly 18 million had an annual income of less than $10,000 from all sources.

Since 1981, millions of Americans have become eligible to open individual-retirement accounts (IRA's). But for many in their late fifties, this has come too late to enable them to build up a substantial nest egg by age 65.

And despite the encouragement that Congress and the president have given to retirement savings, most low-income workers and young families simply don't have enough money to set aside for retirement.

The transition to acceptance of longer work lives will require a radical change in attitudes. Since the end of World War II, this nation has induced older people to leave the work force prematurely. Government, industry, and unions all encouraged early retirement.

Under the Social Security Act of 1935, age 65 was enshrined as the "normal" retirement age, with repercussions that we still feel today. After World War II, jobs had to be found for large numbers of young workers, and the practice of mandatory retirement at age 65 and even younger became pervasive. (Federal Civil Service did not require individuals to retire until 70, but only rarely did workers stay that long.)

State and federal laws sanctioned these mandatory practices in business and industry. In 1967, Congress passed the Age Discrimination in Employment Act, which said employers could require employees to retire, provided no worker be retired for age alone before turning 65.

In 1978, Congress raised the minimum age for mandatory retirement to 70 and eliminated mandatory retirement entirely for most classes of federal workers. In 1983, Congress, by then concerned about the solvency of the Social Security system, passed another law that will gradually raise the age for receiving full Social Security benefits from 65 to 67 after the year 2000.

But in taking these steps, policy makers failed to address the powerful disincentives to delaying retirement that have been built into the system. Older workers are still under pressure to retire rather than work longer. Most employers refuse to retrain workers after they reach their mid-fifties. And in 1983, nearly 60 percent of pension plans did not allow an employee who works beyond 65 to build up additional retirement benefits.

Most retired workers stay retired. Many people over 50, once out of work, often experience major problems getting jobs of interest to them. Social Security and some private pension systems reduce the benefits of retirees who return to work and earn more than certain minimum amounts.

See FORGET, Page O-4

Underground regrets

I was a regular New York subway rider, day and night, for 35 years, from the time I was 3 years old. Like millions of New Yorkers, our family didn't own an auto. Going to work meant using the subway. So did shopping for items you couldn't find in the neighborhood, like furniture. To go to Radio City Music Hall, the theater, museums, or concert and lecture halls meant using the subway.

My family and I, at one time or another, rode almost the entire 231 miles in the system, from Woodlawn to New Lots, from Coney Island to the

Marking Time

Mark A.
Stuart

Wish you were here

EDGARTOWN, Mass. — Where did everybody go? Or, afterthoughts of a resident ghoul on Martha's Vinyard when summer is over and the wind is fumbling in the flues and there isn't much to do but watch the sunrises retreat down the horizon and count the 27 varieties of audible silence.

One morning not so long ago, on my way home from the post office, I stopped to pick up a couple of young men. A young woman scurried up.

"Can I come too?" she said, and in my conscious violation of an established principle — name-

Simeon Stylites

William A.
Caldwell

The Right Paper in the Right Place
at the Right Time: The *Asbury Park Press*

The Garden State Parkway has transformed the New Jersey shore from a strip
of summer colonies to a year-round suburban sprawl. Monmouth and Ocean
counties have grown rapidly over the last generation, filled with commuters
who head north every morning but do their shopping near home in the malls
that have been built to serve them. This is the world of the *Asbury Park Press*,
a distinctly local newspaper that has not only grown and prospered but has
become one of the best papers in the state.

Si Liberman remembers the *Press* as it was in 1956 when he became Sunday
editor. Its circulation was 27,000, and its Sunday staff consisted of "the garden
page writer and me."

Nowadays the newsroom holds 140 full-time editors and reporters and 30
part-timers, including a Sunday staff of 14 full-time people and two part-
timers. With a 1983 circulation of 121,394 daily and 177,171 on Sundays, it is
the state's third largest daily and Sunday newspaper.

The *Press* was in the right place at the right time. "During a critical time in
our growth," said Thomas Jobson, who has been managing editor for more
than two decades, "we weren't faced with much competition, and when the
three big shopping malls opened [Eatontown, Ocean Township, and Dover
Township] we were able to get a bigger bite of the apple." The *Press* was sitting
on an advertising and circulation gold mine.

But the *Press* was also the *right* newspaper. Jobson and Liberman credit the
owners, the Plangere and Lass families, for reinvesting revenues back into the
plant and taking great interest in the improvement of the newspaper. "I have
never been told that I spent too much for a story," said Liberman, who is
authorized to spend up to $7800 annually for free-lance articles for the Sunday
edition, not counting regular features. The Sunday news hole of the *Press* is
one of the largest in the nation, with two news sections, and sections on Arts
and Leisure, Sports, Impact (commentary plus education news), State News
(including casino coverage), Business, Panorama (two sections covering consumer news, food, health, travel, and gardening), Comics, TV, and Family
Weekly. The daily news hole also is impressive. Averaging 25 pages, it is the
third largest in the state.

The editors are proud of the size of the news staff and of the quality of the
reporters. To do the work once done by "copy boys," the paper employs
college-educated "editorial assistants," waiting for their chance to become
full-fledged reporters. "Ten years ago we would have hired them as reporters,"
said Jobson, who figures he has hired all but 10 of the current news staffers.
"There were periods when I had to dredge people out of the streets. I got stuck

with a lot of bad apples. Now so many people want the jobs . . . in the last six or eight years the intellectual level has gone up. We have about 25 reporters and editors who came through the editorial clerk program." Jobson also is proud that 43 percent of the news staff is female, and that many women hold middle-management positions, including Jody Calendar, the Red Bank bureau chief, and Paulette Browne, who is in charge of Asbury Park coverage.

The *Press* emphasizes training and motivation. William Marimow, a Pulitzer Prize-winning reporter for the Philadelphia *Inquirer*, was brought in to explain to the staff how he turns routine assignments into engrossing work. Gary Deckelnick, the paper's state editor, has met with group after group— the sports staff, the night desk, the bureaus—to bring them up to date on libel law, privacy rulings, and other aspects of newspaper law and ethics. And the *Press* has begun a writing coach system. Reporters are assigned to one of four coaches, Christine Garsson, a regional section page editor; Ray Ollwerther, the assistant to the editor; Lawrence Benjamin, the night suburban editor; or

Long-time *Asbury Park Press* editors Thomas Jobson and Si Liberman (standing) consult on a story.

bureau chief Calendar. A coach reviews a reporter's raw copy for two weeks, and then they discuss the work extensively—the flaws, the problems encountered in writing, and what might have worked if the writer had had more time.

"I'm really proud of the staff," Jobson said. "We do things to motivate them and send them to everything." Six staffers are sent to the Washington Journalism Center each year (for seminars on such coverage issues as the economy, health care, energy, and the environment), and the business editor regularly attends conferences at the Wharton School in Philadelphia. When three reporters asked for time off to attend the national convention of the Society of Professional Journalists in 1981, the newspaper sent them with pay.

Second Takes, an in-house publication (like the Bergen *Record*'s *A Second Look*), comments on coverage, finds fault (without naming names), and hands out bouquets (using names). One issue of *Second Takes*, for example, commented on the increasing quality of *Focus*, the paper's soft-news people profile, and included tips on how to take portrait shots. Another characteristic comment read:

> We do not use trade names unless essential. In this usage the brand name is not essential: "Two sailors, bound for Florida and other points south aboard a homemade boat, aren't eating gourmet meals, but they're eating—bread, peanut butter and Budweiser." The headline correctly said "beer." Another point: How do you eat beer?

The *Press* has no ombudsperson, but carries a list of editors as an invitation to comment. "We correct errors ungrudgingly," Jobson said. Ethical issues frequently are discussed at the weekly editors' meetings. After one session, the *Press* set a policy against taking pictures of grieving families at funerals. "We have a pretty strict code of ethics," Jobson explained. "When we get gifts of any sort through the year we put them in a closet. Then we have a raffle at the end of the year, on Christmas morning, and auction them off." The proceeds are given to an environmental group. "But," he added, "we don't pay our way into the stadium yet."

For all its growth, the *Press* remains a distinctly local newspaper. The 85 municipalities of Monmouth and Ocean counties are divided into six areas, and are covered in detail by bureaus located in Asbury Park, Red Bank, Toms River, Freehold, Brick Township, and Manahawkin. Thus the *Press* is a truly suburban newspaper, with even its home base, Asbury Park, the responsibility of a bureau chief rather than a city editor.

The *Press* looks for a local angle to every story. The attempts of Sakharov's daughter to join her husband-by-proxy in the United States and thus get out of the Soviet Union engendered a "local reaction" story in the Sunday *Press*. The story worked because the reporter interviewed a couple with local connections who had experienced a similar situation and were able to provide incisive views about what was happening. When a West Coast blood bank decided not to accept blood from homosexual donors because of the possible danger of spreading Acquired Immune Deficiency Syndrome (AIDS), a *Press* reporter was sent out to survey the local blood banks. And the opening of the Vietnam Memorial in Washington led to a local story about an elderly man who was unable financially to make the trip to view his son's name on the memorial list. This article resulted in an effusion of community support, and a follow-up story by the *Press*.

"What's of interest to our readers is local," Jobson said. "Nothing, for instance, is more local than TV. If there's a 'To Be Announced' in our listings, I want the blank filled in before press time, and we try to get it. What's happening with the Common Market affects the price of Toyotas and video games, and how much we're spending this year for Christmas presents."

While the *Press* sees itself as a local newspaper, it does attempt to avoid provincialism. The newspaper makes extensive use of wire service and syndicated copy, and maintains bureaus in Trenton and Atlantic City. (The Trenton bureau is staffed by Adrian Heffern, a columnist and associate editor, statehouse reporters Bob DeSando and Karen DeMasters, and an editorial assistant.) Four full-time staffers write and edit business news, and the paper's business coverage has expanded from 14 columns to as many as 24 columns every day except Monday. Ten "general assignment reporters" concentrate on various specialized news topics, including energy, the environment, crime, welfare, and health care. The newspaper has a weekly science column and plans a science beat. And sections such as Sports are so large—55-60 columns daily and 17 staffers—that everything gets covered from the New York and Philadelphia pro teams to local shore sports like sailing.

In addition, every two months each local bureau reporter is relieved from covering municipal meetings to work on more in-depth material. This rotation system produces many of the paper's soft-news articles, including "A Closer Look," a continuing feature that updates old news stories, and "Reflections," a series of taped interviews with former newsmakers. "But our beat reporters are the heart of the paper," Jobson admits. "If we had to cut we'd drop the general assignment people first." And about sports, Jobson says, "We cover sailing like there's no tomorrow. This is a sailing area." The emphasis clearly is local, local, local.

Some local bureau reporters feel limited by the concept that the beat is all-important. "Management says that it's a lateral move when you go from a beat to Sunday staff or general assignment," one reporter said. "But it's perceived as a promotion. The *Press* is a big paper that still has a small-paper mentality. Most of the people running the *Press* have grown up at it—they've been here since they started out as beat reporters. The paper has grown almost

OCEAN COUNTY EDITION

THE ASBURY PARK PRESS

SATURDAY

SINCE 1879

Store Price 25 cents

September 15, 1984

Great Adventure indicted in fire deaths

Amusement park, 2 officials to face manslaughter charges

By PAUL D'AMBROSIO
and RICHARD C. HALVERSON
Press Staff Writers

TOMS RIVER — Six Flags Corp. and its Great Adventure amusement park in Jackson Township, along with two high-ranking corporate officials, have been indicted by a special Ocean County grand jury on manslaughter charges in the deaths of eight teen-agers in the Haunted Castle fire at the park May 11.

The corporation and park were indicted for aggravated manslaughter, Ocean County Prosecutor Edward J. Turnbach announced at a press conference yesterday. The only crime more serious than aggravated manslaughter, he said, is murder.

David Paltzik, vice president and general manager of Great Adventure, and Larry Cochran, a Six Flags vice president and general manager of the park when the Haunted Castle was built in 1978, were indicted for manslaughter, a second-degree or lesser crime than aggravated manslaughter.

If convicted, the corporation faces a maximum fine of $100,000. The two corporate officers, if convicted, face prison sentences of up to 10 years and maximum fines of $100,000 each.

Turnbach said the grand jury is still at work. Although Turnbach said he expects no more indictments, the grand jury could hand up presentments, or findings of things done or not done by public agencies, as well as findings of building or fire code violations, and recommendations for improvements in how those agencies function.

At a press conference following Turnbach's, Bruce Neal, director of public relations for Six Flags, denounced the indictments as "inappropriate, unfortunate and unprecedented" and said the corporation would vigorously defend itself and its two executives.

The next step in the proceedings is

scheduled Sept. 28, when pleas will be entered in Superior Court here.

Turnbach said the grand jury based its charges on findings the corporation and the two men "recklessly endangered the lives of human beings."

Turnbach refused to give details of the evidence upon which the indictments were based or to say whether the grand jury determined if the Haunted Castle, a maze of 17 tractor-trailers linked with a common facade, violated the state building code.

George Mahana, East Orange, designed and built the Haunted Castle under a $495,000 contract with the park.

"In our view, no one should have been criminally charged."

— Bruce Neal,
Six Flags
spokesman

William M. Connolly, head of the Division of Housing and Development in the state Department of Community Affairs, refused to describe his officials' testimony before the grand jury.

Previously, the division disclosed its investigators found 12 code violations in the ruins of the castle. The most serious was the failure to install fire sprinklers designed to put out a fire automatically and the use of flammable plywood in the corridors that made up the structure.

The fire spread so rapidly that the eight victims, all teen-agers from New York and New Jersey, died from smoke inhalation before they could escape.

"There wouldn't have been a manslaughter charge if the grand jury hadn't found negligence," Connolly said.

In previous statements, Great Adventure had said it took out no building permit to erect the castle because it was only a temporary structure made of tractor-trailers that could be readily towed away.

As a result, no one from the Jackson building department inspected it during construction or issued a Certificate of Occupancy attesting that the building complied with all building and fire safety codes.

But Connolly said it was "definitely a permanent structure that required a permit. If it had been inspected and a CO issued, there would have been no code violations."

"The responsibility for obtaining a building permit rests with the owner," Connolly said. "The responsibility for detecting building done without permit rests with the building inspector."

Armand Battista was the building inspector for Jackson Township until his retirement to Florida in 1983. Battista has said he never saw the Haunted Castle during inspection visits to the park.

Other Jackson Township agencies, however, noticed the building. When it opened in 1979, the township assessor placed at least the permanent facade of the structure on the tax rolls and the Board of Health forced Great Adventure to close the structure for two weeks and install air conditioning.

Connolly said he is scheduled to testify before the ongoing grand jury proceedings Thursday.

The state Fire and Safety Commission, which conducted its own investigation in July, is scheduled to release its findings within the next 10 days, according to state Sen. John Caufield, D-Essex, commission chairman. The

Ocean County Prosecutor Edward J. Turnbach (above left) and state police Maj. Louis Toranto yesterday discuss Great Adventure fire indictments, which Bruce Neal (right), a Six Flags spokesman, later called "inappropriate." The fire site (below) has been turned into a mini-park at the Jackson Township amusement park.

See FIRE page A2

Doctor rebuked for misconduct

By JOYCE NICKOLAUS
Press Freehold Bureau

FREEHOLD TOWNSHIP — The assistant chief of staff at Freehold Area Hospital has been reprimanded by the state Board of Medical Examiners for failing to obtain written, informed consent from a patient before performing a mastectomy.

Dr. Ignacio Cruz, a Freehold Township surgeon who joined the hospital when it opened in 1971, was found guilty of professional misconduct by the board at a meeting Wednesday in Trenton.

The patient involved in the incident and who brought the case to the attention of the medical board was Dr. Eddy Zeidenberg, a Freehold Township pediatrician affiliated with Freehold Area Hospital.

The board voted to issue a reprimand, which becomes a part of the doctor's permanent record on file with the state board, and to make him pay the state's court costs of $769.

Cruz can appeal the decision to state Superior Court, appellate division, said Charles Janousek, board executive secretary.

Cruz's lawyer, John R. Orlovsky,

Toms River, said he is "considering an appeal."

In its decision, the board modified the recommendation of a state administrative law judge in Newark, who listened to six days of testimony during a hearing in the spring.

Judge Sybil R. Moses ruled that Cruz was guilty of "gross malpractice" and his license to practice medicine should be suspended for 18 months, the three months actively and 15 months on probation, according to the 29-page court decision.

The medical board could affirm, modify or reject the judge's decision.

A mastectomy is the removal of the breast.

Cruz performed a biopsy on lumps found in Dr. Zeidenberg's left breast and armpit on Jan. 16 to discover if the nodes were malignant, according to the judge's findings.

Dr. Zeidenberg, who practices in Freehold Township and lives in Marlboro Township, had signed a consent form for the biopsy.

Cruz had assured Dr. Zeidenberg and her husband, Ralph, that the

See DOCTOR page A2

GOING HOME — Residents of Long Beach, N.C., head for home under downed utility poles yesterday after Hurricane Diana passed through the town causing heavy damage. Story, page A2

Auto union strikes GM in Linden

The Associated Press

ABOUT 60,000 United Auto Workers members, including about 4,800 employees at the Linden assembly plant, struck General Motors at midnight yesterday over local issues following authorization from their national bargaining unit.

Meanwhile, bargaining continued in Detroit on the national contract, which expired at midnight.

The UAW struck 12 other General Motors Corp. plants in eight states last night, but said it would keep most of its workers on the job and continue bargaining on a national contract.

In a statement, UAW President Owen Bieber said the union was "still making progress in some areas. However, we will continue the national negotiations and work without a new national agreement."

The strike is the first coast-to-coast walkout against the world's largest manufacturer in 14 years.

The UAW represents 350,000 workers at more than 130 GM plants

See STRIKE page A2

Jury convicts ex-inspector of taking bribe

Press Toms River Bureau

TOMS RIVER — Joseph J. Griso, a former state transportation inspector, could face a maximum of 40 years in prison after being found guilty yesterday of two counts of bribery and two counts of theft by extortion.

A jury of six men and six women deliberated less than three hours before

two contractors to approve curbing and asphalt work at the Laurel Square Shopping Center, Brick Township, in 1980, and having one of the contractors do concrete work at his home at no cost in 1981.

Earlier this year, Griso was tried on charges that he solicited a bribe in return for approving work on a Stafford Township sewer project, but a

The contractors, Edward J. Steitz, owner of Le-Ed Construction, and Dan McLaughlin, president of Avis Paving Co., each testified that Griso took the $200 bribe after threatening to find their work unacceptable and order them to do the job again.

Steitz testified that in August 1981 he did between $400 and $500 of curbing and driveway work at Griso's

worked for the department for six years in Freehold Township.

Griso's earlier trial ended Jan. 25 in a mistrial after the jury deadlocked.

In that instance, Griso had been charged with taking an $800 bribe from a construction firm in Stafford Township on May 14, 1982, in return

INSIDE

In the swing

Three government reports indicating the economy is slowing may prompt lower interest rates. Business/A15

Factions

Iran is beset with several bitterly antagonistic factions.

In the swing

in spite of itself. The attitude is still small-town." Nevertheless, the reporter added, morale is not a major problem at the *Press*. It is a pleasant, affable workplace where management is generally sympathetic.

Like most evening newspapers, the *Press* actually is published in the morning, but the paper's first press run is particularly early—6 a.m. "It doesn't hurt us," Jobson said. "We miss some acts of God but we'd miss some whatever our deadline." Fortunately for the *Press*, its chief competitor in Monmouth County, the *Daily Register* of Shrewsbury, has an equally early deadline. The *Press* publishes four editions: First Monmouth, which goes mostly to newspaper stands; Ocean; Southern Ocean, which was added to counter the *Atlantic City Press*, moving its way north up Route 9; and the last edition, called Monmouth Final, which goes to press at 9 a.m. The newspaper's printing plant is in Neptune, connected to the editorial and business offices in Asbury Park by laser technology. The 10-unit press was expanded to 14 units at the end of 1982, allowing the paper to print its Monmouth and Ocean editions at the same time, but not improving the early morning deadline. In 1984, the paper began construction at the Neptune site of a new administration building designed to house the editorial and business staffs.

There is competition from every direction. The *Daily Register* has grown from 18,000 readers in 1959 to 30,000 today, fighting the *Press* for every subscription. And the New York newspapers, the *Star-Ledger*, and the Woodbridge *News Tribune* also circulate in Monmouth County. The 23,000-circulation *Ocean County Times-Observer* covers Ocean County, the *Atlantic City Press* has a bureau in Stafford Township, and Philadelphia newspapers are available. But the *Asbury Park Press* is clearly the advertising and circulation winner in Monmouth and Ocean counties. And its circulation continues to grow while that of the *Daily Register* and the *Times-Observer* appears stagnant. The company also owns a radio station, a free shopper, a direct-mail operation, a travel agency, and a printing facility. It produces cable television shows and has applied for low-power television licenses.

The local coverage of the *Press* has been highly rated for many years. In the 1974 survey of reporters and editors conducted by the Center for Analysis of Public Issues, the *Press* was ranked second in local coverage (behind the *Record* of Hackensack). But the journalists surveyed at that time did not rank the *Press* among the state's leaders in any other category.

The 1974 *Asbury Park Press* was in the midst of tremendous growth. Its circulation was 86,715 (sixth highest in the state), twice the size of its readership ten years earlier. The study of 1974 New Jersey newspapers conducted by the Center for Analysis of Public Issues found the *Press* to be a 69-page newspaper with 43 pages of ads and 26 pages of news. Thus it was physically the second largest paper in the state. It was third in advertising, and first in news, with a larger news hole than even the *Star-Ledger*. The *Press* ranked first in the quantity of local news, second in national news, third in state news, and 17th in foreign coverage. By all quantitative measures, the 1974 *Asbury Park Press* was already a very good and complete newspaper, although at that time reporters and editors across the state thought of it only in terms of its local coverage.

The content analysis of 1977 New Jersey newspapers conducted for this project supports the conclusion that the *Press* is one of the four best newspapers in the state. By 1977, the newspaper's circulation had hit 96,000, and was the fourth highest in the state. Its advertising had apparently dropped a bit to 37 pages (fourth best), and its news hole was 25 pages (third after the Camden *Courier-Post* and the *Star-Ledger*). The *Press* ranked third in the total number of news and feature stories, tied for first in the amount of local news, tied for fourth in national news, tied for fifth in state news, and tied for ninth in international news coverage. It tied for second in the production of locally originated stories, and ranked fifth in the use of wire service and syndicated material. In addition, it ranked third in the number of longer stories carried daily, and tied for sixth in the use of photographs.

Jobson believes the *Record* and the *Press* are the state's two best newspapers. Editors and reporters interviewed for this project generally agreed that the *Record* was the best newspaper in New Jersey, but few mentioned the *Asbury Park Press* until they were prompted to do so. When asked specifically about the *Press*, journalists throughout the state responded positively, often praising its local coverage as they did back in 1974, and ranking it as one of the top five or six papers in New Jersey.

Perhaps the *Press* is thought of as too provincial to be ranked any higher. Clearly its circulation is rising faster than its reputation. The *Press* has grown and prospered (beating back its rivals) as a distinctly local product. Jobson says, "If we were to become an international newspaper and give up what we're doing, we'd create a void that somebody would fill."

The *Press* is the right paper in the right place at the right time. It is a very good newspaper, getting better every year, and deserves to be considered one of the four best newspapers in the state.

The Awakening of the *Courier-Post*

The *Courier-Post*, one of the 10 largest dailies in the Gannett chain, is among the most highly regarded newspapers in New Jersey. Its weekday circulation was the third largest in the state until 1983, when it slipped to fourth. Its Sunday edition, which began publication in 1979, also ranks fourth in readership. Many news people rate the *Courier-Post* among the state's three or four best newspapers, often comparing it, as did *Post* Executive Editor William Chanin, with the *Asbury Park Press*. Like the *Press*, the *Courier-Post*'s 100-member news staff covers the world from its backyard, ingeniously finding a local approach to nearly every story.

The *Courier-Post* was the first New Jersey daily to flee the inner city, leaving Camden in 1955 for nearby Cherry Hill. It traces its lineage back to two 19th century dailies, the *Courier*, which began in 1882, and the *Post*, which dates back to 1875. The newspapers were combined in 1949 by the Stretch family. In 1959, the Gannett chain bought the *Courier-Post*, but management remained in the hands of William Stretch as publisher. Under Stretch, circulation increased from 89,803 in 1963 to a static 123,000 in the mid-1970s, while the paper was commonly thought of as just another sleepy daily.

The awakening of the *Courier-Post* began in the latter half of 1975 when Gannett brought in Sal DeVivo from Niagara Falls to become editor. In February 1976, Bob Dubill was hired away from the Associated Press, where he had been New Jersey bureau chief, to become assistant managing editor. Within a short time DeVivo was publisher, Dubill was executive editor, and Stretch was president, a position with few decision-making powers. A number of highly talented reporters, many of them proven performers, came aboard as well, and by 1977 the *Courier-Post* was a different newspaper.

The *Courier-Post* was already a good newspaper in 1974 when the Center for Analysis of Public Issues conducted its study of New Jersey dailies. It ranked fourth in advertising with 43 pages, and its 22-page news hole was the fifth largest in the state. The *Post* carried more foreign news than any other paper, and ranked fourth in the amount of national news, 10th in local coverage, and 11th in state reporting.

Reporters and editors surveyed in the same year chose the Bergen *Record* as the best all-around newspaper in the state by an overwhelming margin over the second-place *Star-Ledger*, but four of those polled picked the *Courier-Post*, which became the third-place finisher. Nevertheless, the *Post* was not ranked among the leaders in any specific category.

Gannett star editor Bob Dubill, the man who turned the *Courier-Post* around.

The 1977 *Courier-Post*, the product of DeVivo and Dubill, was a vastly improved newspaper as shown by the content analysis conducted by David B. Sachsman for this report. While its 43 pages of advertising now ranked third best, its news hole had been greatly expanded to 29 pages, the largest in the state. International news coverage was much the same, with a first-place tie with the *Star-Ledger*. And national news was also unchanged, with a fourth-place tie. But in the amount of local coverage, the *Post* now tied for first with the *Asbury Park Press*, and in state coverage, it ranked second behind only the *Ledger*. In the number of locally originated stories, it tied for second with the *Press* behind the *Ledger*, and it used 10 more photographs daily than any other paper. In the total number of news and feature stories, it ranked second behind the *Ledger*, but in the number of longer stories, a quantitative measure related to in-depth reporting, it ranked first, just edging out the Newark-based paper.

The new *Courier-Post* was a distinctly local newspaper, with solid state coverage and a flair for investigative reporting. Anthony Mauro came from the AP to direct court coverage. Dubill emphasized "special projects" and created an investigative team to cover them. Ralph Soda, managing editor at the *Saratogan*, another Gannett paper, was brought in to head "special projects" as a senior investigative reporter.

The staff at the *Courier-Post* soon began to see the extent of Dubill's commitment to enterprise reporting. A probe of the area's municipal courts was conducted not only by the special projects reporters, but by eight to 10 newsroom regulars, who attended court sessions incognito. Other major special projects covered Teamsters, adoptees, a group of ministers who had been playing fast and loose with federal funds, and exclusive private clubs that systematically excluded Jews, blacks, and women.

"The fact that we had a couple of people designated as special projects reporters was basically to provide a continuity and let people know we were there," said Dubill, now executive editor of the Gannett News Service and national editor of *USA Today*. "When you have a special projects team, you sometimes get tips over the transom."

The *Courier-Post* got more than tips. It began receiving reporting awards from the New Jersey Press Association, the Philadelphia Press Association, the Society of Professional Journalists (Sigma Delta Chi), and a number of national groups including the American Bar Association. The newspaper was developing a reputation, and stories in the *New York Times* and the *Los Angeles Times* about the Gannett chain, with its more than 80 daily papers, would single out the *Courier-Post* as the Gannett paper making the most waves.

Planning for the Sunday edition began during the DeVivo-Dubill era. "Some of the kinds of journalism that we were doing, it's best to put them in the Sunday paper," Dubill said. "That's when people have time to read it. I think people read the Sunday paper more completely."

The *Post*'s ombudsman column also came out of the DeVivo-Dubill era. It was designed to give the public insight into how editorial decisions are made, and to develop the paper's credibility, explained Dubill.

One of the first-rate reporters acquired by Gannett was John McGowan, who, like Dubill and Mauro, came from the AP. McGowan covered the statehouse for the *Courier-Post* and Gannett's other New Jersey newspaper, the *Courier-News*. McGowan answered to Dubill, and he said Dubill instructed him, on sending him to Trenton, to look for important statewide stories.

The presence of top-notch reporters on a New Jersey daily is nothing unusual. What made the *Courier-Post* particularly attractive was the presence of top-notch editors. In addition to Dubill, Peter Halden, the night editor, was noteworthy. Halden had a talent for bringing young reporters along, teaching them the rudiments of good reporting and writing, and furnishing strong leadership. Like Dubill and Mauro, Halden is a lawyer. He later left the newspaper to practice law in Camden County.

The *Courier-Post* was at its best during the 1976-79 DeVivo-Dubill period. It had come to be regarded as one of Gannett's standout newspapers, a prestige paper. And for all its holdings—its dailies and weeklies, television and radio stations, and subsidiaries—prestige had eluded Gannett; its newspapers generally lacked distinction. The company rewarded Dubill by moving him to

USA Today

The Gannett Company, in a quest for a national presence, launched *USA Today*, a gaudy, process-colored, satellite-beamed national daily newspaper, in 1982. Slick and attractive, it featured comparatively short stories, and was criticized as shallow journalism. The company soon brought in Bob Dubill as national editor to strengthen the paper's newsgathering efforts.

USA Today became Gannett's top priority, and the resulting shift in finances and personnel from many of its local and regional newspapers to the new national paper put a strain on the smaller dailies, including the *Courier-Post* and the *Courier-News*.

As of the first quarter of 1984, Gannett's corporate earnings were still being affected by the start-up losses of *USA Today*, according to *Editor & Publisher*'s May 19, 1984 report. Nevertheless, quarter earnings were up 8 percent to $34.8 million on revenues of $425.2 million. *USA Today*'s circulation was around 1.3 million, and the chain's total daily circulation was more than 4.7 million.

the Gannett News Service, and a number of the *Post*'s journalistic stars
followed. Mauro became a media and court reporter for the news service, and
Soda an investigative reporter. McGowan moved to the New York office,
where he would become bureau chief.

The news service now is regarded as a first-rate newsgathering organization,
a prestige operation. It has won 15 major awards in the last few years,
including a 1980 Pulitzer Prize for public service. Some of Soda's work on
Abscam, which has earned high praise, actually began when the special
projects team was looking into the affairs of Camden Mayor Angelo Erri-
chetti, who was subsequently convicted of charges stemming from Abscam.

McGowan said of Dubill's years at the *Courier-Post*: "He made quite a
difference. I think the *Courier-Post* suffered a bit by his loss, but he moved on
to a more important position. It [the paper] is coming back, I suppose, but he's
a hard guy to lose. He breathes spirit into whatever he touches."

Meanwhile, the *Courier-Post* has continued to win prizes. The paper won
14 awards, from first place to honorable mention, in Philadelphia and New
Jersey Press Association competition in 1983. "It is one of the better papers in
the state," McGowan said. "I think it does a fine job of covering its area, and it
is well staffed." Top staffers today include Lillian Micko, who covers the
statehouse; Dave Marziale, one of the state's best political reporters; and
Judith Petsonk, who has won a number of awards for enterprise writing.

The transition from DeVivo and Dubill to the current administration of
Publisher Robert T. Collins and Executive Editor William Chanin was not an
altogether comfortable one. In between, N.S. "Buddy" Hayden, who had been
a Gannett publisher in Oregon, spent a number of months as publisher of the
Post before moving on to the Philadelphia *Bulletin*, and Jerry Bellune, a
respected journalist who had helped the Bergen *Record* start a Sunday paper,
served briefly as executive editor. Bellune's tenure was brief because he and
Collins, who took over in 1980, did not see eye to eye.

"He [Collins] wanted to cut everything to the bone," said Bellune, who is
now a newspaper consultant. "He didn't want to spend any money. He and I
had a series of disagreements. I thought we could work them out in time. He
finally got to the point where he didn't think we could. He told me to pack my
bags and leave. So I did."

Whether any of this internal squabbling affected the daily operation of the
newsroom is hard to say. But at least one reporter, who asked not to be
identified, feels there is a big difference between the management of the
Courier-Post a few years ago and management today. "To be fair to Bill
Chanin, he is certainly a competent guy, but his hands are really tied," the
reporter said. "There's very little he can do. Jerry Bellune, his predecessor,
tried to fight these drastic cutbacks and got fired. Got canned overnight. One

day he was our executive editor, the next day he was gone. It's hard to judge a man when he has no resources to work with."

To be fair to Publisher Collins, the *Courier-Post* still has plenty of resources. Its newsroom staff of around 100, while having the added burden of putting out a Sunday as well as a daily newspaper, is hardly a skeleton crew. By Gannett standards—and by New Jersey standards—the *Courier-Post* continues to be a solid operation.

The local emphasis, begun under DeVivo and Dubill, is now the paper's key feature. Collins stresses local reporting to the utmost. For example, the front page of the *Post*'s March 2, 1982 edition contained five local stories. The only wire story to make the page was an Associated Press tie-in to a locally produced story about the mounting problems of getting aid for college.

The front page of the following day, March 3, demonstrated the *Post*'s independent news judgment. The lead stories were two related pieces concerning Arco's decision to drop credit card sales at service stations. The main article was written by James A. Walsh, a *Post* business writer. The side story, by staffer Karen Curran, dealt with local reactions of service station operators, mostly negative, to Arco's decision. The *Courier-Post* probably was the only paper in the nation to lead with the Arco story. The paper did so partly because Arco is the largest gasoline retailer in the South Jersey-Philadelphia area, but the main reason, said Executive Editor Chanin, was that the editors liked the comprehensive, solid feel of the copy.

Also on the front page that day was an article by staff writer Judith Winne about research on early detection of prostate cancer, played as a local story because the work was done by a New Jersey researcher.

Most of the newsroom staff at today's *Courier-Post* work on general assignment, with beats deemphasized, especially geographic beats. Staff reporters cover some major meetings, but many meeting stories are assigned to stringers and placed in a separate section of the newspaper. The *Post* has a two-person Gloucester County bureau, a two-person Burlington County bureau, and a three-member Camden bureau. In addition to the Gannett statehouse operation, it maintains a reporter of its own in Trenton. It also has two business reporters, two police reporters, a political writer, an environmental reporter, and a staffer who covers education on a part-time basis.

"We have a very strong local sports section, the strongest of any paper I've ever worked for," Chanin said. The staff covers Philadelphia professional teams, making road trips selectively.

The *Courier-Post* has enterprise reporters but has dismantled the special projects team assembled by the previous editors. "I think of that as an elitist system," said Chanin. "I think all reporters should be investigative reporters." When the paper found out about a toxic waste landfill near Atlantic City that

▬ INSIDE TODAY ▬

Section A—State-Nation-World
Section B—Local-Living-TV
Section C—Sports-Money
Section D—People-Classified

Astrology	4B
Classified	3D
Comics	11C
Crossword	11C
Dear Abby	4B
Editorials	10A

Experts	4B
Letters	10A
Movies	5B
Obituaries	2D
Television	6B
Weather	2A

Rose out

1C Phillies Pete Rose is missing spring training while he nurses a sore back.

A&P closings

6C A&P plans to close three South Jersey stores and 26 others in the area.

Here's looking at

Bogart and Bacall

Page 3B

WEATHER
Today: **Cloudy**
Tonight: **Snow**
Tomorrow: **Sleet/rain**
Details: Page 2A

COURIER-POST

A GANNETT NEWSPAPER SERVING SOUTH JERSEY   TUESDAY, MARCH 2, 1982   25 CENTS

Waste ban not lifted in state

By LEE SEGLEM
Of the Courier-Post

New Jersey will continue to prohibit the disposal of containers of liquid chemical wastes in landfills despite a decision by the U.S. Environmental Protection Agency (EPA) to lift a federal ban on such activity, state officials said yesterday.

"We will continue to enforce New Jersey's standards, which prohibit the dumping of anything considered as toxic," said a spokeswoman for Robert E. Hughey, commissioner of the state Department of Environmental Protection (DEP).

The spokeswoman, Loretta Brennan, indicated that state officials were concerned about the potential for a legal conflict between the federal and state positions on the issue. Neither Hughey nor other ranking DEP officials would comment further until they received more details concerning EPA's move.

Meanwhile, the federal agency's decision, which was issued late last week but not publicized until yesterday, sparked protest from environmental and industrial groups alike.

Jackie Warren, a senior staff attorney for the Natural Resources Defense Council in New York City, said EPA's lifting of the nationwide dumping ban represents "a quantum leap backward" into circumstances that allowed hazardous wastes to poison the Love Canal area of Niagara Falls, N.Y., and to threaten the drinking water of Atlantic City as a result of an old chemical dump near there called Price's Pit.

"I don't think we should be putting liquid wastes underground at all because you can't control where it

Please see N.J., Page 7A

Hijacking averted   *Associated Press*
John Celestin restrains would-be hijacker Gillermo Lazaro Major-Diaz on a Chicago-to-Miami flight last night in this photo by passenger Daniel Pinto. Major-Diaz threatened to ignite a bottle of liquid unless the plane landed in Cuba. The pilot flew over the ocean, then returned to Miami, where Major-Diaz was arrested.

Stolen art found

By LINDA JANKOWSKI
Of the Courier-Post

CAMDEN — City police have recovered an oil painting believed to be a 16th Century Italian artwork worth more than $25,000 that was stolen from a car in North Camden last month and later sold on the street for $15.

Police said they placed the value of the painting, "Madonna and Child with St. John the Baptist," at between $25,000 and $30,000 based on information supplied by Meredith Newton, who, along with her husband Anthony, owns the painting and had reported it stolen.

However, Mrs. Newton could not be reached for comment yesterday and her husband said he was uncertain of the value of the painting. Police said the couple had not had the painting appraised.

Police had distributed flyers within the department on the missing painting and the Newtons had offered a $100 reward for the safe return of the artwork.

The Newtons had just paid $1,000 to have the painting restored, police said.

Please see STOLEN, Page 2A

Grand jury to get Auto Train probe

By BOB COLLINS
Of the Courier-Post

Auto Train is the story of the little train that could, but didn't.

For 10 years the train ferried passengers and their cars between Lorton, Va., 20 miles south of Washington, and Sanford, Fla., less than a half-hour's drive from DisneyWorld.

Families could board the red, white and lavender trains in Virginia, enjoy a motion picture or live entertainment in the club car, go to sleep in the Pullman cars and wake up the next day under the sunny skies of Florida.

The concept caught the fancy of stock analysts and many investors who scurried to buy the 1.6 million shares offered on the American Stock Exchange.

WHEN THE company went public in the middle of 1971, its $10-a-share stock skyrocketed to more than $65 a share before the first train even left Auto Train's specially built terminal in Lorton, Va., on. Dec. 6, 1971.

Profits soared following the maiden run, spiraling upward through 1974, slipping slightly in 1975 and rising to a peak of $1.7 million in 1976.

Company officials talked about placing a terminal near Newark, N.J., in the heart of the heavily populated Northeast.

But before that happened, Auto Train began to lose steam.

Finally, on Sept. 8, 1980, its officials filed for protection of the court under the provisions of Chapter 11 of the federal Bankruptcy Act.

TODAY, AUTO TRAIN Corp. exists only on paper. Murray Drabkin, a Washington attorney appointed by the bankruptcy court to settle creditors' claims, continues weeding through the maze of records in an effort to close outstanding accounts.

Federal officials, including the FBI and Securities and Exchange Commission, continue to probe the company's collapse.

The information will be examined this week by a federal grand jury in Washington

Please see GRAND, Page 6A

Lobbying at home urged

Associated Press

WASHINGTON — College student activists urging Congress to oppose President Reagan's deep cuts in programs that help pay for their schooling are being advised that their real work awaits them after they return home.

At a rally yesterday on the Capitol steps, in a packed congressional meeting room and in private sessions with lawmakers, the students were repeatedly told that to protect their aid programs they must win over the members of Congress who voted for Reagan's initial round of budget cuts last year.

Please see STUDENTS, Page 12A

Help for students   *Courier-Post photo by Ron Karafin*
Paul Petrowski, assistant financial aid director at Temple University, directs students to some of the forms for grants and loans still available.

Funds dwindle for students

By JULIE BUSBY
Of the Courier-Post

PHILADELPHIA — Bright dreams of college are being clouded over by dark nightmares of where to get financial aid.

And next semester, the nightmares will get worse.

Under proposed federal reductions totaling more than $3 billion, the major sources for student loans will be cut 9 percent for the 1982-83 academic year and by 67 percent for the following year.

"There's money out there. The bad news, though, is that it's dwindling more and more each year. The reality of it is that people are going to get hit harder and harder," Paul Petrowski, assistant director of financial aid at Temple University,

1983 federal budget

● President vows he will not change his course: **Page 3A**
● Congress will not be asked to speed up gas decontrol: **Page 3A**

told a group of a dozen students assembled for a workshop on receiving aid.

The average cost for a private school is $6,885 this year, up 13 percent from the 1980-81 term, while the typical cost for a public school is $3,873 annually, up 14 percent from last year.

For students expecting to attend Temple and other places of higher academic learning for the first time,

Please see FUNDS, Page 12A

Assembly OKs bill that could stem local tax hikes

By LILLIAN MICKO
Courier-Post Bureau

TRENTON — Scores of municipalities state's so-called gross receipts tax on utilities.

In total, the towns would realize an estimated $650 million in additional revenue

In the Legislature
● Prison hiring bill passed: **Page 1B**
● Sex club bill approved: **Page 3D**

posted for a Senate vote next week, towns would anticipate 100 percent of their expected utility tax proceeds in the budgets they are in the process of adopting

the additional money in their surpluses — working capitals — this year, making it easier for them to meet expenses during the year.

was affecting the water supply, Chanin noted, the environmental reporter and another reporter did the investigative work, which resulted in a 1981 first place award for interpretive reporting from the New Jersey Press Association.

Chanin looks for a staff-written "people" story every day to lead off the paper's People section. A sampling of 1982 stories includes pieces about a 13-year-old Cherry Hill boy appearing in television commercials, a Deptford woman who fought isolation and discrimination because of her deafness and now teaches sign language at Gloucester County College, and an 87-year-old Haddon Township minister whose ancestors came to the area as newly freed slaves.

Collins is one Gannett publisher who, contrary to the usual complaint, comes from the area. He started as a copy boy at the *Post* in 1960, and worked as a reporter and manager on several Gannett newspapers before returning to South Jersey. Collins insists on quality reproduction not only for news photographs but for advertisements. "If we see anything not up to our standards," he said, "we remake it for the later run." Although the *Courier-Post* publishes two editions daily, they are not zoned. Rather, they are in effect simply an early and a late edition. The early edition runs by 8:30 a.m. to get to newsstands by the lunch hour, and the second edition goes to press about noon.

The daily edition of the *Courier-Post* was losing readers in 1981, a showing that Collins attributed to poor service. Consequently he gave much of his attention to improving distribution. Circulation has continued to drop in the city of Camden, but the paper is doing especially well, he said, in Burlington County. The *Post* is becoming more aggressive along the shore, from Brigantine to Cape May, although it has no shore bureau.

The death of the Philadelphia *Bulletin* in January 1982 set the *Courier-Post* into action. "When the *Bulletin* closed we approached the carriers immediately and asked them if they'd like to deliver the *Courier-Post*," Collins said. "By Monday we had 376 former *Bulletin* carriers delivering our paper."

New vending racks went out on street corners and in shopping centers, and free samples began being delivered to nonsubscribers in an expensive attempt to find new readers.

On the news side, the Gannett News Service lent McGowan to the *Post* for several weeks to write Philadelphia stories. "The idea was not to sell in Philadelphia but to sell to people on the Jersey side who are interested in Philadelphia news," explained McGowan. It did not last. When McGowan returned to New York, the *Post* discontinued its regular coverage of Philadelphia.

The *Courier-Post*'s circulation had been 115,745 daily and 100,571 Sundays in September 1981. By March 1982, it was 134,000 daily and 125,000 on Sundays. But these gains soon began to dissipate, and by September 1982, daily circulation was 123,496 and Sunday sales were 111,397. The *Post*'s circulation continued to fall in 1983, down to 117,927 daily and 107,488 on Sundays. While the *Post* should be able to hold on to its basic readership—no mean feat for an evening newspaper in the 1980s—it is unlikely to see major long-term growth.

The Sunday edition now appears to be one of the *Courier-Post*'s chief strong points. The Sunday *Courier-Post* of August 22, 1982, for example, ran 88 pages plus inserts. It carried a 38-page news hole, 50 pages of ads, Comics, Family Week, Parade, Pennywhistle Press, a television guide, and four advertising inserts—an impressive package for what was then a 3-year-old product.

Today's *Courier-Post* may not be as exciting as it was under DeVivo and Dubill, but it has retained the legacy of quality reporting and solid local coverage, and it remains one of the very best newspapers in New Jersey.

3

Staying Alive in Northern New Jersey

Northern New Jersey is the territory of the Newark *Star-Ledger* and the Bergen *Record*, newspapers rich in circulation and advertising dollars. To the west lies suburban and rural Morris County, where the *Daily Record* thrives and the *Daily Advance* struggles to survive. To the northwest lies rural Sussex, home of the isolated *New Jersey Herald*.

Sandwiched between the *Star-Ledger* and the *Record* are the newspapers of Passaic County, the once-mighty Passaic-Clifton *Herald-News* and Joe L. Allbritton's Paterson *News*. To the east are the Hudson County papers, the *Jersey Journal* and Allbritton's Hudson *Dispatch*, while to the south is the Elizabeth *Daily Journal* in Union County.

The newspapers of northwestern New Jersey are in competition, a competition only the *Daily Advance* is losing. The newspapers of northeastern New Jersey are not just competing with each other—they are virtually falling over each other. Faced with the lack of population growth in the area, the only way to gain a subscriber is to take a reader away from another newspaper. Furthermore, the black and Hispanic populations now inhabiting the core cities tend not to buy general dailies in the same numbers as did their predecessors. The *Star-Ledger* and the *Record* are tough competitors, holding their own, but the other newspapers in the area are in trouble. Their efforts are not so much a struggle to gain circulation as to keep from losing readers.

Are there too many newspapers in northeastern New Jersey? Can they all survive? Or will one or two more go the way of the Bayonne *Times* and the Paterson *Call*, both of which folded during the last generation?

Morris County's *Daily Record*

The *Daily Record* of Morristown and Parsippany became a morning newspaper in October 1981. "We decided about three months before to do it," said Norman B. Tomlinson Jr., the publisher and editor. "Our primary reason was the general trend toward morning newspapers—instead of fighting the TV viewing habit at night—plus the fact that our biggest competitor is the *Star-Ledger* and we might as well meet them on their own turf, so to speak. We did not do a survey. I've never been hot on surveys. We'd rather use the money on promotion. We had a feeling that it would work—everybody seemed enthusiastic."

When rural Morris County began becoming suburban in the 1950s, the *Daily Record*'s chief competitor was the *Newark News*, which for many years outsold the *Record* in Morris. Reporters from those days recall that the period after lunch was known as the "heartburn hour," when Tomlinson, then editor serving under his father the publisher, would open the *Newark News* searching for a local story that was not in his own paper. The *News* maintained a large bureau in Morristown, and the *Daily Record* was beaten often.

In those days the circulation of the *Daily Record* hovered around 18,000 and the night news editor doubled as sports editor. By 1963 circulation was still only 23,000. But with the decline of the *Newark News* and the further residential development of the county, including enormous growth in the Parsippany area and western Morris, the *Daily Record* grew. By 1973, the year after the *News* folded, circulation had reached 44,000. The chief competitor then became the *Star-Ledger*, which opened a major bureau in the county and attempted to take the place of the *News*.

Other rivals have less clout. The Dover *Advance* has been losing circulation steadily, falling below 13,500 before it converted to morning publication in 1983. The 17,748-circulation *New Jersey Herald* of Newton holds the line in southern Sussex County, and the *Courier-News* of Bridgewater reaches up to the Somerset Hills (Bernardsville) area. The *Daily Record* has never sold well in the northern end of Morris County, which is more allied in its retail interest to Paterson and southern Passaic County, but the newspaper has carved for itself an enviable niche in the heart of Morris.

The *Record*'s daily circulation reached 57,703 in 1980. The paper was healthy, but had stopped growing. Daily circulation was 56,686 in 1981 when the decision was made to switch to mornings. By the end of 1983, daily readership was up to 60,245. The Sunday newspaper, inaugurated in 1973 (also without a survey), grew phenomenally in the 1970s. Its circulation leveled off in 1980 at 65,631. At the end of 1983 the figure was up slightly to 67,294.

The *Record* dropped its Saturday evening edition in 1970. (At that time the notion of switching to a Saturday morning paper had not yet emerged.) Upon converting to morning publication, the *Record* reestablished the Saturday edition as a tabloid. Its circulation reached 53,970 within a matter of months.

Nineteen-seventy also was the year the *Record* moved to Parsippany, the backbone of its circulation and the junction of routes 10, 46, 80, 202, and 287. The paper continued using its old building on the town square in Morristown for administration, accounting, circulation, and outside advertising sales.

The *Record* has a full-time news staff of 66, with about 75 stringers and part-timers. "Our thrust is local," Tomlinson said. "The metropolitan papers can beat us on world and national news, so we beat them on local news." Most of the assignments are geographical by municipality, but the paper has some subject beats, which are called "horizontal." It has three business writers— "you have to in this area," said Tomlinson. The sports staff numbers seven full-time people. They cover New York teams at home but not away.

The *Record*'s strength in local and state reporting is illustrated by its high rankings in the study of 1977 newspapers, where it was seventh in local coverage and tied for fifth in state news. The paper tied for eighth for its use of photographs, and tied for 11th for its use of locally originated stories. It tied for 12th for the size of its news hole, ranked 13th for its use of longer stories, tied for 13th for international news, and tied for 14th for national news.

Five days a week the *Record* publishes a single all-purpose edition, but on Wednesdays (the big supermarket advertising day) and Sundays it zones some pages for both news and advertising. Much of the news on these pages is low-priority material—"honor rolls and things that we wouldn't otherwise run," explained Tomlinson. The paper's deadline is 11:30 p.m., and the press run begins about an hour later.

The *Daily Record*'s trademark is a color picture on the front page every day. "We felt it was a circulation builder," Tomlinson said. "We started with the Sunday paper and gradually kept enlarging until we were into process color seven days a week."

The newspaper is family-owned, and Tomlinson's wife and daughter work as top administrators. Selling the paper has never been considered seriously,

Morris May Have Four Congressmen — See Page 17

FINAL ★ Edition

Daily Record
The Paper That Cares

Number One In Northwest New Jersey

WEDNESDAY, DECEMBER 16, 1981 | VOL. 82 NO. 159 | 25 CENTS

Winter Renews Onslaught

Staff Photo by STUART DAVIS

Karin Ardin, 11, catches frozen raindrops while Laura White, 9, protects candy canes Scout Troop 626 were passing out in Dover.

Judge Warns Morris Road Crews: Go To Work Or Lose Your Jobs

By RICHARD E. HARPSTER And JAMES KULLANDER Staff Writers

Morris County employees who participate in wildcat strikes will be fired if they ignore court orders to return to work, Superior Court Judge Reginald Stanton said yesterday.

The comments came on the heels of a wildcat walkout by some 100 county road workers who left work Monday about 1 p.m., just as the snowfall began. They all said they were sick.

Stanton issued a back-to-work order Monday at 6 p.m., and all but one or two workers reported to work by 8 p.m.

The snowfall, the first of the season, created massive traffic jams and accidents in the Morris County area.

The walkout — called over frustration with the slow pace of contract negotiations with the county — accomplished what was intended, said Allen Hantman, attorney for Civil Service Council 6, the union representing the workers.

"Now people are aware that all is not hunky-dory in the land of Wynken, Blynken and Nod," Hantman said of the Morris County negotiations. "If the road department had gone on strike in July, how many residents would care one way or another?"

Freeholder Alfonse Scerbo, public works chairman, favored firing those who walked out but said it is not possible. He wanted to know how the freeholders could reprimand those involved.

The superior court judge's authority to fire workers defying a back-to-work order has never been challenged in appellate court, Hantman said. He said he does not believe the court has that power, although he said he recommended the orders be obeyed.

"Does someone want to risk his job to find out?" Hantman asked. "I'm not making that request."

Edward Horan, county labor relations director, told the freeholders yesterday he was told the road department personnel voted unanimously to accept the county's new contract offer.

The county reportedly has offered 9 percent salary raises for 1981 and 1982, upgraded hospitalization and disability plans and a more-generous sick leave proposal.

The walkout took place for the same reason as last summer's strike by workers at Morris View, the county nursing home, Hantman said. He said the workers' feeling that the freeholders don't care about their contract was reinforced when two freeholders told radio reporters they had not been aware there was a problem.

Morris County municipal road crews yesterday were still tabulating how much sand and salt they used on county roads when they stepped in for the county road workers who walked off the job as the snowfall started Monday.

Freeholder Alfonse Scerbo promised the county would resupply the towns with any materials used to clear the 300 miles of county roads. Yesterday, however, those plans had not been settled, Scerbo said.

Some towns reported they had trouble recording how much was used on county roads alone. Some town officials said they don't know if they will bill the county for the average two-to-three extra hours their road workers put in.

Motorists Face Icy Peril

Roads throughout northwest New Jersey may be icy today, because the rain that started yesterday afternoon turned to sleet last night before changing to snow. Sleet melts slowly and it's like throwing ice cubes on the road, said Frank Lombardo of Ion Weather Inc. at Morristown Airport.

Accumulations of up to 6 inches were expected in parts of northwest New Jersey.

Two lives were lost in this area since Monday's storm.

Cheryle Eichner, 26, of Durban Avenue, Hopatcong, died in a two-car collision yesterday afternoon at Route 15 and Berkshire Valley Road in Jefferson Township. Diane Hahn, of Pennsylvania, died on Monday after a head-on collision on Route 206 in Roxbury.

Michael Covert, 3, Metro Trail, Hopatcong, was involved in the Jefferson accident and remained in critical condition yesterday with a fractured skull, said a Dover General Hospital spokesman.

A woman in the Roxbury accident, Kristine Holmes, 21, of Montoursville, Pa., was in guarded condition yesterday, the spokesman said. A third victim in that collision, Karen Mowry, 20, of Piscataway, was in satisfactory condition.

Police reported few accidents last night.

Pole Workers Continue To Defy Crackdown

By The Associated Press

Polish troops drove sit-in strikers from some of Poland's biggest plants, but the martial-law regime was unable to get them working again yesterday as workers across the country continued to defy the crackdown on the independent labor movement.

Reliable reports from Warsaw said troops and riot police in armored cars invaded the Huta steel mill in Warsaw and the giant Ursus tractor factory outside the capital Monday night and evicted thousands of workers occupying the plants.

About two dozen striker leaders at the steel mill and about 60 at the tractor plant were reported arrested.

The reports said the two plants were idle yesterday, with riot police guarding the gates.

Reports reaching Warsaw from Gdansk said the sit-in there at the giant Lenin Shipyards, the birthplace of the Solidarity labor federation, also had been ended, but this could not be confirmed.

Arrivals from Gdansk said "many places" in the Baltic industrial center were on strike.

Solidarity activists in Warsaw who escaped the police roundup when martial law was proclaimed early Sunday reported union chief Lech Walesa had sent word that the workers should use only non-violent protests and should strike only in factories where such a protest would be effective.

But Solidarity's Warsaw chapter circulated a leaflet calling again for a general strike. "The group which staged a coup began a war with society," it said.

The union sources said Walesa, who is being held by the government somewhere outside Warsaw, gave his message to Roman Catholic Archbishop Bronislaw Dabrowski, who visited him.

Walesa reportedly told the archbishop: "Don't allow the moral spirit of the nation to be crushed."

The sources said the government wanted to arrange a meeting of Walesa and Premier Wojciech Jaruzelski with Archbishop Jozef Glemp, Poland's Roman Catholic primate. But they said Glemp insisted the meeting be held at his palace and that advisers be present, and the government vetoed this.

In Stockholm, Olof G. Tandberg, secretary of the Swedish Academy of Sciences, said he had indirect reports from Polish colleagues that shots were fired in Warsaw and Poland's southestern mining region, apparently by soldiers.

U.S. Reacts, See Page 9

Pope Condemns:

- Contraception
- Divorce
- Abortion
- Polygamy
- Trial Marriage
- Pornography
- Prostitution
- Machismo

— See Page 12

Israel Prepares For Syrian Retaliation

MAJDAL SHAMS, Golan Heights (AP) — Israeli army convoys headed north and Jewish settlers cleaned out bomb shelters yesterday in a show of readiness for possible Syrian retaliation over annexation of the Golan Heights.

Defense Minister Ariel Sharon toured military bases on the Golan. His office announced that "all necessary steps" were being taken to deal with any flareup over Monday's abrupt legal takeover of territory captured from Syria in the 1967 Middle East war.

Sharon cabled Egyptian President Hosni Mubarak and assured him Israel planned no military action on the Syrian front or in Southern Lebanon, Israeli TV reported.

Golan Druse Arabs declared a three-day protest strike starting today, and religious leaders threatened to blacklist any members of the sect who did not participate.

The military chief of staff, Lt. Gen. Raphael Eytan, broke off a visit to Cairo and flew home as trucks carrying armor and supplies headed in the direction of the heights.

There was no sign that Syria was preparing to use force to counter the annexation of the 458-square-mile plateau, despite talk of war in the government-controlled Syrian press and some official statements.

Acting without any warning, Prime Minister Menachem Begin's government rammed a law through Parliament at almost record speed Monday night and extended Israeli law to the Golan after almost 15 years of military occupation.

Shimon Peres, the opposition Labor Party chief who was out of the country when Parliament acted, said he was "really shocked and sad" at the way the bill was so quickly passed.

The move provoked worldwide censure, including statements from Cairo and Washington that Israel was violating tenets of the U.S.-sponsored 1979 Camp David accords between Egypt and the Jewish state.

The Israelis took the diplomatic offensive. Foreign Minister Yitzhak Shamir said the law was adopted "to show to Golan residents, Arabs and Jews alike, that the heights are an inseparable part of the state of Israel."

Reacting to U.S. criticism, Shamir was quoted by Armed Forces Radio as saying "American and Israeli interests are not identical. We have to guarantee our own national interests, even if they cause conflict in our relations with the U.S."

The Israelis insisted they annexed the heights out of despair at Syria's refusal to make peace.

Arabs On Edge, See Page 8

FYI

Weather

Today — Cold, Chance of Snow
Tonight — Windy, Cold
Tomorrow — Snow Likely

— See Page 2

Today

Today is Wednesday, Dec. 16, the 350th day of 1981. There are 15 days left in the year.

On this date in 1773, American colonists, dressed as Indians, staged the Boston Tea Party, dumping 342 chests of tea off a British ship.

Short-term parking fees at New- Reduced-rate long-term parking charges will remain unchanged. The new fee structure will help offset the increasing costs of operating and maintaining public parking, according to the Port Authority.

President Ronald Reagan will hold the sixth news conference of his 11-month-old presidency at 2 p.m. tomorrow.

Reagan's last news conference was Nov. 10.

A second public meeting on the selection of a new landfill in Morris County will be held at 7:30 p.m. to- in the jury assembly room as it was last Thursday.

I'D BETTER START LOOKING FOR MY CHRISTMAS LIST. ONLY 9 SHOPPING DAYS LEFT!

Quote Of The Day

"But this time the tree talked back to him and he really got excited."

— Kathy Kasper, teacher of the mentally retarded, relating the effect a talking tree had on one of her students. See story, Page 11.

Ann Landers 33
Business 14-15, 51
Classified 54-56
Comics 38
Crossword Puzzle 38
Editorial 4
Lottery 2
Obituaries 2

Today's Brite

BROOKLANDVILLE, Md. (AP) — The folks at St. Paul's School for Girls have just the Christmas gift for the person who has everything. . A yurt.

They are offering the yurt, a portable Mongolian shepherd's hut, for free.

"We're saying free Mongolian yurt to a good home," said Carol Maus, director of development and alumni affairs at the school in this Baltimore suburb. She said it can easily be moved and would make a

although offers have come regularly through the years. "We're approached four or five times a year," noted Tomlinson.

On family ownership, Tomlinson said, "It really depends on the nature of the family. If they're interested in the community and in staying abreast, they can do as well as anyone else. We've been able to stay in the forefront of modern technology and we're probably as advanced as anyone."

On chain ownership, he added, "I'm not impressed by claims that the chains give complete editorial independence to their newspapers."

The *Daily Advance* Struggles to Survive

The Drukker family, the owner of the Passaic-Clifton *Herald-News*, in 1962 purchased the *Dover Advance*, a newspaper then publishing twice a week. The Drukkers converted it first to a three-times-a-week newspaper and then, in 1965, to a Monday-through-Friday evening publication. In 1978 the *Daily Advance* began offering a Sunday edition as well.

In the 1960s the *Advance* did well. The heightened activity of the Picatinny Arsenal during the Vietnam War was a major factor in the boom times, explained Publisher Austin Drukker. With the close of the war and the 1974 recession, the fortunes of the *Advance* took a downward turn—a turn that became acute when the new Rockaway Mall decided to ignore the *Advance* and give the bulk of its advertising to the *Daily Record* in Morristown and the *New Jersey Herald* in Newton.

The *Advance*, even before the advent of the Drukkers, had referred to western Morris County and the Lake Hopatcong region as "the Lakeland area," attempting to differentiate what it viewed as its own territory from that of the *Daily Record*. The Rockaway Mall was within these boundaries, and yet it treated the *Daily Record* as *the* Morris County daily newspaper. The *Advance* was left with downtown Dover as its main source of advertising—a business district that was none too stable to begin with, and which began deteriorating when faced with competition from the nearby mall.

During this period, Austin Drukker, who had been directing the operations of the *Advance*, had been called back to manage the *Herald-News* because of the death of his father, Richard Drukker. With his attention elsewhere, Austin Drukker said, the *Advance* slipped. Meanwhile, the *Daily Record* was growing. Advertisers and readers would find at the *Daily Record* a Sunday edition, newer presses with sharper reproduction, state-of-the-art front page color, and, as of 1981, a morning newspaper.

The circulation of the *Daily Advance* in 1974 had been 22,098. By the end of

1981, the newspaper's readership had fallen to 14,224 on weekdays and 13,332 on Sundays. The territory of the *Advance*, from Boonton and Denville in the east to Hackettstown in the west, was a competitive battleground, with the *Daily Record* advancing, the *New Jersey Herald* holding its ground, and the *Star-Ledger* making inroads.

The Drukkers' other daily newspaper, the *Herald-News*, also lost readers in the late 1970s, but in Passaic the circulation base remained large enough to justify continued publication. In Dover, the Drukkers were fighting the tide, and in February 1982, the *Advance* was converted to a tabloid format.

The conversion was done by the newspaper's editors, with some artistic direction from Passaic. The type faces used in the full-sized *Advance* were retained. "We wanted to keep some elements that the readers would recognize," explained Managing Editor H.C. Jackson Jr. "We didn't want to scare people off with a total change, and the type faces that we had been using seemed eminently adaptable to tabloid."

Jackson, who came over in 1981 from the *Herald-News* (where he had been assistant news editor) said the management held meetings with the staff to discuss changes in story length, and that the conversion "has forced reporters to write tighter than before." He ventured, however, that the conversion has not changed the news hole much, if at all.

Some features such as weddings, engagements, and club news have been taken out of the daily paper and moved to the Sunday edition in order to provide more room for local news. "I about doubled the amount of space that I give to local news," Jackson said, "increased by half again the amount of space I can give to world and national, and give about the same space to state news that we previously gave."

Considerable time has been devoted to insuring that world, national, state, and local news have their own designated parts of the paper. Jackson said this had been done in the pre-tabloid *Advance* only in part: "So once you got beyond the first few pages of the old paper, you really didn't know what you would come upon in the next page, until you got to the sports section."

The old *Advance* was not a good newspaper. The study of 1977 New Jersey newspapers conducted by David Sachsman ranked the paper third from the bottom in the overall standings. The *Advance*'s news hole tied for 24th place, and the paper was near the bottom in every category, except "use of photographs," where it ranked 11th. The *New Jersey Herald* did not score much better, but the *Daily Record* and the *Star-Ledger* did, and it is not surprising that the old *Advance* lost readers to its competition.

The new *Advance* also has a new press time, many hours earlier than the old 8 a.m. start. "When we analyzed it," Jackson said, "with an 8 a.m. press start we were still giving people virtually the same news we are now giving them. Obviously there are some late-breaking things that will go on after 1 a.m. that

the daily
Advance

25 cents   Vol. 81 No. 186   **Tuesday, October 16, 1984**

Advance Staff Photo by Marc Bellagamba

Sen. Bill Bradley buys three dozen donuts 5 a.m. Monday at the Viking Bakery in Denville to kick off his 21-county, 600-mile day of campaigning. Bradley ended his marathon in Little Falls in Passaic County. **See story, page 3.**

Mt. Olive council disputes tactics

By JEAN ZIPSER
Advance Staff Writer

MT. OLIVE — Residents attending Monday night's council workshop meeting to discover what tactics the council will use to fight the state's siting of the county landfill at Camp Pulaski saw a rift among council members concerning those very tactics.

Although the council had appropriated $150,000 Sept. 25, some council members seemed reluctant Monday to spend that money on anything but expert testimony and legal fees.

Council President Larry Brown appointed a committee to organize the township effort against the Camp Pulaski siting, but when he called for a vote on spending any money to advertise a public rally on Oct. 22, the council split 3-3.

At a workshop meeting a tie vote means the measure is effectively tabled, according to Mayor Charles Johnson, who

said he could have broken the tie if it had been a public meeting.

Five residents, including John and Mary McNamara, Robert Parker, Anne Marie Steward, Cathy Hedden, Environmental Commission member Wendy Erhard and council members Barbara Swasey, John Rucki and Earl Spino had asked the council for an appropriation of $3,000 for advertising the rally against the Camp Pulaski siting.

Camp Pulaski, a 350-acre site owned by the county, became the number one landfill site when two Rockaway sites were eliminated from the DEP lists recently.

When the council divided on the advertising issue, Parker said funds could and would be raised privately.

Council Vice President Richard Kamin, Councilman Steve Bruder, and Brown, all of whom voted against the funding, said that they could not "in good conscience" agree to spend taxpayers money on advertising when that money might be needed for legal and consulting fees in the future.

Brown said he did not see why the advertising issue was so critical. But, according to Swasey, the siting of a landfill at Camp Pulaski is imminent. She drew to the council's attention that Oct. 26 is the date that Superior Court Judge Arnold Stein has set for a determination to be made concerning the placing of a county landfill.

Brown, Kamin and Bruder said they were counting on the township environmental consultants to refute Camp Pulaski's top listing on the county's landfill list.

"We've handled landfills in the past with a nuts and bolts approach from our experts and consultants," Kamin said.

Residents present at the meeting, however, did not agree with Kamin, Bruder or Brown. John McNamara of Lozier Road said the situation was a political one.

"We have reams of technical data. Months ago, we thought the issue was dead, due to the amount of professional information. Now, the DEP has changed all the questions we thought we'd answered with scientific information. We can't rely on a subtle, business-like approach," McNamara said.

Jury deliberates on Castellano's fate

By BILL GANNON
Advance Staff Writer

"I am not embarrassed to stand here and plead for Stephen Castellano's life ... he is not an evil man," said the convicted murderer's attorney, Stephen S. Weinstein, to a Morris County jury Monday.

"There is only one question left for you to decide, and that is

who will decide when he dies — you or God," Weinstein concluded.

"It is an awesome responsibility, but it is one you can handle," Morris County Assistant Prosecutor Allan J. Iskra told the jury moments later.

"This man," said Iskra, pointing to a head-bowed Castellano, "he made a choice then; he

decided 'Mr. Bernknopf - you are to die,' and he sentenced him to death."

Three women jurors quietly dabbed their eyes as attorneys in the sentencing phase of the case made their final statements to the panel in a Morristown courtroom around noon.

Today, the seven-man, five-woman jury that convicted him

of murder is expected to decide if Castellano should be sentenced to life imprisonment, without chance of parole for 30 years, or to death by lethal injection.

The burly 31-year-old man from Kearny was convicted Oct. 4 for the ball-peen hammer murder of his longtime friend

See ATTORNEYS, page 3

Rockaway corporate center plan presented

By P.L. WYCKOFF
Advance Staff Writer

ROCKAWAY TWP. — Developers for the proposed Rockaway 80 Corporate Center presented the Planning Board Monday night with an overview of the $100 million office park.

"This will become the most notable viewing point across northern New Jersey," Morton Salkind, agent for the developer, Weiler-Arnow Investment Co., told the board.

Salkind said as many as 4,000 people are expected to be employed at the offices, which will be rented to "Fortune 500" type corporate clients. He said the complex's tax payments should reduce taxes for township homeowners by 25 to 30 percent.

Architect Frank Richlan explained the 72-acre site, located between Route 80 and Mt. Pleasant Avenue, and the Rockaway Mall and Route 15, would have a "park-like atmosphere" and that as much as possible of the natural vegatation would be saved.

Richlan said four eight-story buildings would be built, each with about 260,000 square feet of office space. There would be two access roads into Mt. Pleasant Avenue, and cars would park in a double-deck lot stretching in front of the building, he said.

Because of the grading and landscaping, only one deck of parking would be visible from the buildings, he added.

"The most notable thing... is

the amount of green space," Richlan said. He also said two retention ponds would be built, both to handle drainage and to increase the beauty of the site.

The buildings will have a blue, metallic glass facade on their eastern sides, and a concrete facade on their western sides, Richlan noted.

Engineer Ted Cassera told the board the complex would tie into township sewer and water lines, which, by the time construction is completed, are expected to be able to handle the increased demand.

Anthony Leichter, a vice president of the developer, said his company had chose. Rockaway from a number of sites because of the transportation capabili-

ties of Route 80, the excellent workforce in Morris County and the increasing development of such complexes in the western part of the county.

Weiler-Arnow owns and operates a number of buildings nationwide which are used for corporate offices and headquarters, Leichter said, but this would be the company's first project in New Jersey.

Shire National sold the property to Weiler Arnow in late spring, Salkind said.

Planning Board Chairman William Kersey told the developers the board was interested and would study the project's documentation closely. A public hearing will be scheduled for the project, he said.

we won't get, but . . . the number of times that happens is so slight that we're still providing essentially the same service."

The newsroom deadline of 11:45 p.m. has caused occasional problems for reporters covering night meetings. When the deadline arrives, reporters at late meetings call in what they have. "We haven't cut down anything on the night meetings because as a local paper that's very important," said the managing editor, adding that the deadline can be pushed back somewhat for an important story.

The *Advance* in 1982 was still regarded as an afternoon daily because it was still being home-delivered in the afternoon, but it now reached the newsstands by 6 a.m. along with its morning competitors. The paper had taken its first steps toward morning publication.

The *Advance* has a newsroom staff of 22, including seven reporters, three sports people, four night copy desk editors, and two photographers. There are no specialized areas except sports and lifestyle, and the paper publishes no weekly feature sections other than a Wednesday food section.

The *Herald-News* and the *Advance* combine their efforts in some limited ways. The papers trade big stories of interest to both, and Ed Mullin, the *Herald-News'* political writer, sometimes supplies the Dover paper with a story out of Trenton. The *Advance* prints the *Herald-News'* TV book and does other occasional jobs. The Drukker family also owns four weekly newspapers in Warren and Morris counties that are printed at the *Advance*, but have their own composing rooms, news staffs, and management.

The *Daily Advance* struggled for survival throughout 1982, changing its format, reorganizing its news pages, and moving up its press time to compete on the newsstands with morning newspapers. But by the end of the year, there was virtually no change in its Sunday readership (13,406), and its weekday circulation had dropped to 13,629.

In summer 1983, the newspaper gradually began morning delivery on a zone-by-zone basis. The paper's daily circulation was continuing to decline (to 13,082), while holding its own on Sundays (13,316). If it is to survive as a daily, the *Advance* will do so as a morning newspaper.

The *New Jersey Herald* in Rural Sussex

A weekly newspaper until 1962, the *New Jersey Herald* began to publish on Sundays in June of that year, and expanded from twice weekly to daily publication in 1970. The *Herald* was growing along with Sussex County, the last frontier in northern New Jersey for residents seeking a rural way of life.

But while the *Herald* benefited in the 1970s from an increase in retail advertising (including the Rockaway Mall in Morris County), circulation has not kept up with population growth. Readership in 1983 was 17,748 Monday-to-Friday and 25,352 on Sundays, not very different from the 1974 figures of 15,008 weekdays and 20,622 on Sundays.

The *Herald* editorial staff numbers about 20, plus an equal number of stringers and part-timers. The newspaper has no specialists except for four full-time sports people and one lifestyle staffer. It publishes little in the way of special weekly features, although on Sundays it produces a tabloid leisure section that includes locally written leisure-time articles as well as the standard TV listings. *Herald* reporters are assigned to local news—almost exclusively within Sussex County—and local coverage is the only thing the *Herald* does well.

The study of 1977 New Jersey newspapers conducted for this project found the *Herald* tied for 13th in the number of local news stories, a good score considering the paper's small circulation and 12-page news hole (which tied for 22nd place). The *Herald* tied for 20th for the total number of news and feature stories, tied for 19th in state coverage, tied for 20th in international news, and tied for 21st in national coverage. While it tied for 17th for its use of photographs, it ranked 22nd in the number of longer stories, and tied for 22nd for locally originated stories.

The *Herald*'s emphasis on local news—a real advantage over its competition—has not led to a significant increase in circulation because of a number of special problems. Many residents of the county are relative newcomers who have not yet become interested in local affairs, and many work outside the county and are more interested in news of the area in which they work than the area in which they live. "Until they have children or become involved," said James Collins, *Herald* vice president and general manager, "then they have to come to our paper to find out what happened."

Most of the *Herald*'s news staff works at night, covering meetings, and almost all the local news is written at night. In the morning, a small staff wraps up any loose ends in local news and selects wire stories in time for an 8 a.m. deadline for the newsstand edition and a 10:15 a.m. deadline for the normal press run. The Sunday paper goes to press at 11 p.m. on Saturday.

Until the last few years "you might say that if news didn't happen at a meeting, as far as the *New Jersey Herald* was concerned, it didn't happen," Collins said. "We're changing that philosophy. We're still covering meetings, but we're not just automatically sending reporters to cover a meeting unless it warrants covering. And we're trying to change our local news to issues that affect all of Sussex County" as well as trying "to use more people coverage."

The evening newspaper's chief competitor, according to Collins, is the *Star-Ledger*. The Morris *Daily Record* made a major drive into Sussex a few

The New Jersey Herald

Copyright / 1984 The New Jersey Herald, Inc.

Sussex County's Daily Newspaper

NEWTON, N.J.   Established 1829   WEDNESDAY, OCTOBER 10, 1984   HOME EDITION   25¢

Good afternoon!

PARTLY SUNNY

Details, Page A2

CONTRACT REJECTED. The Hampton Township Committee again rejected a garbage service contract with Hamm's, saying the cost of picking up trash is too high. Page A4.

MORE WATER. Another source of potable water has been found in Franklin, a discovery that will help to dry tears once shed over the borough's drinking supply. Page A4.

NO RATE HIKE. A request for a 9.9 percent rate increase that would have affected 80 percent of New Jersey drivers has been rejected by acting Insurance Commissioner Kenneth Merin. Page A3.

CASINO REVENUES. A slowdown in revenues at Atlantic City gaming halls is causing concern among casino executives and could stall plans for industry expansion there. Page A3.

COPYCAT BURNING. A Milwaukee man set his wife on fire after watching a TV movie about an abused wife who killed her husband by setting fire to his bed. Page A8.

BROKEN PROMISES. Democrats say Ronald Reagan will not keep his promise about keeping his hands off Social Security benefits if he wins a second term. Page A8.

DUARTE GREETING. President Jose Napoleon Duarte was cheered as he returned home to El Salvador, where leftist rebels have agreed to his offer for peace talks. Page A7.

ANN LANDERS A10
BRIDGE B8

Backlog pinches health agency

By MARGARET McGARRITY
Staff Writer

FRANKFORD — Sussex County Health Department employees are now working a 40-hour week, expanded from 35, to cope with backlogged inspections, complaints from municipalities and the department's efficiency and the recent loss of five county inspectors.

According to county Health Director Frank Wilpert, who took office last month, the changes were needed largely because of "an exodus of personnel," many of whom left because of low wages.

WILPERT SAID another inspector just resigned, again for higher pay elsewhere, and that the 40-hour week, by bringing proportionately higher wages, may help make the job more attractive.

He said most of the employees are happy with the new hours because of the higher wage — about $2,000 higher for sanitary inspectors — although four workers have said they cannot make the change.

Wilpert said he will discuss today whether those four will be permitted to remain on a 35-hour schedule. The new schedule took effect last week.

On a 40-hour schedule, the department's six sanitary inspectors will make between $15,635 and $19,248, while two senior sanitary inspectors will earn between $23,963 and $27,534. The department also has one 40-hour inspector trainee and a third

senior inspector who will remain on the 35-hour schedule.

Eight other laboratory and office workers will also move to 40 hours.

WILPERT SAID the department is behind on inspections, a problem cited by Wantage officials as one reason they had considered setting up their own Health Department, possibly in conjunction with Vernon and Frankford.

At Tuesday's freeholder meeting, Wantage Township Committeeman

Richard Dunn, who is a construction contractor, said officials and builders in that township were "very dissatisfied with the services from the county."

He said the department is "definitely understaffed" and gives "very, very poor service," including inspections that are delayed a day or two and poor coordination of inspections in the same area.

See HEALTH, Page A2

CONTRACT DISPUTE — John Totin Jr., Newton school superintendent, looks on with concern Tuesday night, as the Board of Education nullified a long-term
(Anna Murphy photo)
contract for the official which the board termed illegal because it would bind future boards to the pact.

Board voids 4-year pact with Totin

By TRUDIE WALZ
Staff Writer

NEWTON — The town School Board on Tuesday failed to ratify the second year of School Superintendent John Totin Jr.'s contract and declared its four-year contract with Totin illegal because it would bind future boards.

School Board President Greta Kemether said the board "has found it can only ratify the first year of the contract. It refuses to ratify the remaining three years."

When asked about the implications of the board's action, Mrs. Kemether said the board is unable to bind subsequent boards to a contract with a tenured employee.

"The contract is not legal," she said at Tuesday's meeting.

ACCORDING to the contract, Totin, whose salary during the 1984-85 school year is $62,700, would receive a 6 percent salary increase during the 1985-86 school year, a 5 percent salary increase during the 1986-87 school year and a 4 percent increase during the 1987-88 school year.

Totin, whose contract with the School Board took effect July 1, has served since July 1977 as superintendent. His contract expires June 31, 1988.

Mrs. Kemether said the board "would go with a contract for each year."

"Mr. Totin is an employee of our school district. At this point, he has a one-year commitment. But he is a tenured employee," she added.

FOLLOWING the meeting, board Attorney Robert M. Tosti said, "In our opinion, the board does not have an option of ratifying the contract beyond the second year."

In a letter to the School Board,

Tosti said unless Totin's contract is "ratified by the subsequent Board of Education, the contract dated April 3, 1984, has no viability beyond the 1984-85 school year.

"Our research reveals the salary provisions of the long-term contract are invalid for all years after the first year of the contract."

Tosti recommended "the board consider the contract anew" to decide whether to ratify the contract in its second year or "to limit ratification to the first year of the contract only."

TOSTI SAID because Totin is a school superintendent, "only once in his career can he be given a long-term contract," which went into effect when Totin was first hired as superintendent.

The terms of Totin's subsequent contracts differ from teachers' contracts "because of the nature of his position," Tosti said.

Tosti's letter was a reply to an inquiry about the legality of the contract, which Mrs. Kemether said she initiated.

When Mrs. Kemether was asked how the question of the contract's legal aspects arose, she said, "Because we had quite a few (members) of the public question the need for a four-year contract." Totin, she added, gave his resignation "in four years" when the contract was signed.

MRS. KEMETHER said the board acted little more than three months after the contract went into effect "because we prefer to do it at this time."

Totin, who was named secretary-business manager of the board in 1959 and assistant superintendent for business affairs in 1965, did not speak on his behalf during the meeting. Afterward, however, he said, "It actually works out to my interest."

Reagan's debate showing prompts age controversy

WASHINGTON (AP) — Democrats are saying President Reagan's performance in the presidential debate may be a sign of advancing age, but Republicans are shrugging it off as an "off night" compounded by poor staff work.

Politicians in both parties are watching whether Reagan's age will become an issue in the closing weeks of the presidential campaign.

Rep. John McCain, R-Ariz., said Tuesday that the strength of the age issue may depend on how Reagan does on Oct. 21, when he and Walter F. Mondale will debate a second time, this one devoted to defense and foreign policy.

EVEN JAMES Lake, spokesman for the Reagan campaign committee, conceded the president had an "off night" on Sunday, but he denied it was a sign of age.

"Why he had an off night, I can't define for you," said Lake. "I can tell you it had nothing to do with his chronological age."

Asked if Reagan's age might become an issue, Lake said, "Absolutely not."

At 73, Reagan is the oldest man ever to serve as president. If reelected he would be two weeks short of 78 at the end of his second term.

NEITHER MONDALE nor his staff were raising the age issue, but other Democrats were becoming less hesitant.

"He looked old, acted old," said Rep. Tony Coelho of California, who flew with Mondale on Monday from Louisville, Ky., site of the debate, to New York City.

Rep. Claude Pepper of Florida, at 84 the oldest member of Congress, said, "There were lapses in the thinking apparently and the alertness of the president during the debate that might well be attributed to his increasing years."

The president's age also was being discussed in the media.

The lead story in Tuesday's Wall Street Journal was headlined: "New Question in Race: Is Oldest President Now Showing His Age."

DAVID BRODER, political columnist

See AGE, Page A2

Registration drives swell state voter totals

TRENTON (AP) — Voter registration drives that had volunteers signing up residents at shopping malls and on unemployment lines may have swelled New Jersey's registration rolls to a record of nearly 4 million voters.

"We're definitely going to be setting a new record," said James

according to Kathleen Smith, administrative clerk of the county Board of Elections.

"They have been coming out of the crevasses, the rocks, the fields and streams," she said of residents who registered Tuesday, the deadline for voter registration before the Nov. 6 election.

The municipal clerks were swamped yesterday, there were so

Current county registration totals were not available, but Ms. Smith said there were about $3,000 registered voters as of last month. A breakdown by party affiliation was not available.

Statewide, Nosuchinski said there were 3,709,173 registered New Jersey voters for the June 5 primary, the latest figures available.

presidential election.

Christine St. John, director of the election division, said New Jersey residents were registering to vote at a rate 22 percent above the same period in 1980.

MS. ST. John said that as of August, 69 percent of New Jersey's voting age population was registered, compared to 64 percent

dents who had not registered for the June 5 primary.

Rep. James Courter, chairman of the New Jersey Reagan-Bush campaign, said the campaign has registered about 50,000 people for the November election.

As he rolled a wheelbarrow filled with forms to the Division of Elections here Tuesday, Courter said he

years back but pulled out again because of lack of success. As for the Dover *Daily Advance*, Collins believes its days as a daily newspaper are numbered, but feels that the Drukker family, which also owns a number of successful weeklies in the area, might continue the *Advance* as a weekly or twice-weekly publication. Even the *Star-Ledger*, he said, has been less aggressive in Sussex than it has been in Morris County. "Even with us, with our circulation, it's a very costly county in which to distribute a paper," said Collins, because of its rural nature. "The *Star-Ledger* or anyone else runs into the same problems but the magnitude is greater because they might have only one newspaper per mile."

The *Herald-News*: "You Might Even Ask Why We Exist"

The Passaic-Clifton *Herald-News* suffered an enormous loss in circulation in the late 1970s. By 1983, its readership was down to 64,682 daily and 58,597 on Sundays, in contrast to its 1974 daily circulation of 88,332 and its 1977 figures of 80,964 daily and 73,557 Sundays. Changes in the market, in the industrial base, and in the racial, ethnic, and socioeconomic makeup of Passaic had turned the tide against the once-mighty *Herald-News*.

The *Herald* was founded by Dow Drukker in 1918 and merged with the Passaic *News* in 1932. Austin Drukker is the third generation of the family to run the newspaper, which is deliberately poised on the Passaic-Clifton border and thus claims to be the hometown paper for both cities.

The management made changes when the downturn began. A more horizontal makeup was inaugurated. Concerned that the paper might have too conservative an image, the decision was made to abandon the American flag that had been the hallmark of the front page. A Sunday newspaper was begun in the mid-1970s, and was given away to subscribers for the first year. More recently the newspaper has relied on contests, while continuing to offer special discounts on subscriptions. Surveys showed that those readers who liked the *Herald-News* appreciated its local coverage, while those who disliked it wanted a more metropolitan approach.

The 1977 *Herald-News* tied for ninth for the size of its news hole (19 pages) in the study of New Jersey newspapers conducted by David Sachsman, while its 18 pages of advertising only tied for 14th. The paper was fifth in the number of locally originated stories, tied for 10th in local and state coverage, and was 12th in the number of longer stories. It tied for 14th in national coverage, tied for 19th for its use of photographs, and tied for 20th in international news. As the readership surveys confirm, the *Herald-News* is a good local and state paper, weak in national and international coverage.

"We are not the largest newspaper in any county," Drukker noted. "Passaic does not have a major department store and has never had one. We haven't had a shopping center opening in our area since 1967. You might call it a mature market. One reason why we're a survivor is Clifton, a good middle-class city. But we have no reason to be in Wayne, or Morris, or Bergen, or Essex County. You might even ask why we exist."

There is no natural base for the evening paper, Drukker suggested. It is not even the county-seat daily. Thirty percent of its sales are in Bergen County, a holdover from the days when Passaic was an industrial center in textiles, but these Bergen readers are growing older and are not being replenished. About 6,000 copies are sold daily in the Pompton area of Morris, and about the same in western Essex. The paper historically has tended to sell to the west and east rather than to the north and south—a phenomenon that shows the importance of highways in the culture, for until the coming of the Garden State Parkway, the area had no major north-south road.

In recent years, the *Herald-News* has eliminated some of its outlying circulation in areas where the number of copies sold did not justify the cost of distribution. It deliberately divested itself of a small number of subscribers and newsstand sales in Parsippany, Moonachie, Little Ferry, Ridgewood, and the Oranges.

The *Herald-News* publishes five editions daily. The first press run begins at 7:30 a.m., and the final begins at 11:45 a.m. The Saturday edition, a morning paper, has a single press run at 1 a.m., while the Sunday paper goes to press at midnight. Video display terminals have been in use in the newsroom for several years.

The newspaper staff has been unionized. In August 1980, 51 of the 79 newsroom employees voted to be represented by the International Printing and Graphic Communications Union. Two days after the election, the paper discontinued publication of the weekly column written by Mitchell Stoddard, a reporter who had actively supported the union. In 1982, an administrative law judge ordered the newspaper to restore Stoddard's column, and in 1983 the National Labor Relations Board upheld the judge's decision.

Despite the newspaper's difficulties, Drukker plans to hold on. "Allbritton [the owner of the nearby Paterson *News*] has come at me both ways," Drukker said, "offering to buy and offering to sell, with the argument that there's no room for both of us in Passaic County.

"One of the most exciting things about being a publisher in northern New Jersey is its highly competitive nature," he added. "We still have a lot of individually owned newspapers. When an individual owns his own paper, he

Mondale, Reagan back on the road	**A - 3**
Local recycling control questioned	**A - 6**
Giants and Jets come up winners	**B - 1**

The Herald-News

Serving the public for 113 years

COUNTY EDITION
MONDAY
October 15
1984

Vol. 113 No. 284

26 Pages in Two Sections   Price 25¢

Clifton detectives examine the body of the shooting victim outside the Howard Johnson restaurant-motel Sunday morning.

Herald-News Photo by Edmund R. Pompono

Cops seek motive in Clifton slaying

By Norm Mates
Of the Herald-News

CLIFTON — Local and Passaic County detectives are hunting the killer or killers of a 52-year-old Caldwell resident, who died in a gangland-stlye execution outside a Route 3 restaurant-motel Sunday morning.

Pronounced dead at the scene was a man tentatively identified as Cosmo Dominick Aiello, 52, of Caldwell, who was believed by police to have been struck by most of the nine bullets fired at him in the parking lot of the Howard Johnson Motel on Route 3, near Passaic Avenue.

Neither Caldwell nor Clifton police would confirm reports that the victim was known to have been associated with organized crime figures.

Police said the victim was apparently walking to his car with one or more people with whom he had had breakfast when the shooting occurred.

According to Detective Capt. Robert Kelly, the department received a report of the shooting at 11:26 a.m.

The first policemen to arrive at the scene found the man, believed to be Aiello, lying face down in the parking lot, Kelly said. The body had multiple gunshot wounds, but exactly how

many will be determined by an autopsy by the county medical examiner this morning, he added.

Nine expended shells were found in the parking lot near the body. They are believed to have been fired from a .22 caliber automatic handgun, Kelly said.

The proximity of the shells to the body indicated that the shooting was from close range, police said.

The small caliber automatic is reputed to be an imported weapon used by professionals because of the greater number of shots immediately available without reloading, but police would not confirm this.

Kelly said that members of the Aiello family were sought most of Sunday and would be brought to the county morgue this morning to confirm identification.

According to police, robbery was not a motive in the slaying.

No one else was injured in the shooting, despite the number of bullets fired, and there was no indication that Aiello had an opportunity to defend himself, since a weapon was not found.

On Aug. 3, 1983, and out-of-the-area resident was found shot to death in a room at the same mo-

tel, but it was later declared a suicide.

In another murder, it was also established by subsequent investigation that Albert "Tiny" Manzo, a well-known Passaic County restaurateur and political figure who is believed to have had links to organized crime, met with an unidentified person at the Ramada Inn, on the eastbound side of Route 3, a short distance from where Sunday's murder took place.

Manzo, who weighed more than

Restaurant employees react to scene Page A-4

300 pounds, was not seen again until his body was discovered in the trunk of his Lincoln Continental in a supermarket parking lot off Route 22 in Hillside on Aug. 22, 1983. The crime has never been solved.

On Dec. 27, 1983, the body of a former elementary school teacher, a Cuban immigrant then living in Portland, Me., was dumped from a passing car on Route 3 near the ramp of Route 21, also just a short distance from Sunday's murder scene.

There is no indication that any of these murders were connected to that of Aiello, but they all occurred in the same area of Clifton.

It's strictly the pits for 'Big Apple West' as Passaic bankers reject bonding plan

By Pat Politano
Of the Herald-News

PASSAIC — A lack of financing may sour the "Big Apple West" project.

Alex Parker, a partner in Market Street Associates, said he has been turned down by every bank in Passaic for financial assistance.

In December, 1983, Market Street Associates, a partnership of Parker of Oradell, and Rudolph Stewart of Tuxedo Park, N.Y., bought the former Uniroyal plant on Market Street and dubbed it the "Big Apple West."

In April, the partners received approval for a $12 million state Economic Development Authority bond for renovation of the 10-building site, but all city banks have declined to purchase the bond, Parker said.

Local banking officials were unwilling to confirm or deny ap-

plications for financing from the developers.

C. Richard Paduch, city community development director, said he was not told by Parker of any difficulty in receiving funding.

"He hasn't come to us and said he's had any difficulty with the city banks," Paduch said.

Under the state authority's bond program, developers can get tax-exempt loans, thus reducing their interest rates to 70 or 80 percent of the prime rate. The developer, however, must secure a bank to purchase the bond.

"It's been very difficult. Passaic banks are not too happy with Passaic," Parker said. "You would think they would be the first to lend us the money. All of the banks have turned us down. I guess we'll have to go elsewhere (for the loan)."

Parker said the developers have used their own money to begin refurbishing of the 600,000 square feet of building space at the site.

"As far as I know there hasn't been any movement on the bond since April," said Rose Smith, a spokeswoman for the economic authority.

Smith said it is not unusual for developers to begin construction with "interim financing." She said if work has begun on a project it is sometimes easier to get banks to purchase the authority's bond, using the beginning work as collateral.

Parker said earlier this year that he would develop a Songwriters' Museum of New Jersey, a riverboat restaurant, a commercial radio station, a Hollywood movie company and turn-of-the-century storefronts at the former rubber mill.

In almost a year since he bought the building, the only new business to move to the site has been a warehousing firm owned by Stewart.

Parker said 300,000 square feet, half of the available space in the buildings, has been rented. He said leases have been signed by six different firms, but refused to name the companies.

A person familiar with the issue, who asked not to be named, said Parker rejected renting one of the buildings at $5 per square foot for a proposed permanent indoor flea market. The $5 per square foot rent is considerably higher than the rental at most industrial buildings in Passaic.

The person said Parker also has twice refused to sell the property for $1 million, a 33 percent profit over the $750,000 paid last December.

Shortage of underground water prompts fears

By The Associated Press

New Jersey has "overtapped" its underground water supplies and state officials warn that there could be severe shortages if no controls are put in place.

John W. Gaston Jr., director of the state Department of Environmental Protection's Division of Water Resources, said about half of New Jersey's 7.36 million resi-

But he said there is too much strain on those delicately balanced and limited resources.

"It is a simple law of nature. You only have so much," said Gaston. "The ground water table is declining steadily, and in some cases, precipitously."

Gaston said experts are worried about several critical "target" areas in the state: the

treme southern Ocean County, including Atlantic City; eastern Middlesex County; and the area from northern and eastern Monmouth County to northern Ocean County.

"In Monmouth County, you probably have the severest problem. Many of the coastal communities rely on groundwater from very deep aquifers," he said.

homes and businesses — large amounts of water are being drawn from aquifers, but there is no time to replenish the supplies.

An underground water supplies become dangerously low, they become exposed to possible intrusion by pollutants and salt water.

And as the water table in the aquifers gets lower, it creates a vacuum that draws salt water

A **jubilant** pitcher Willie Hernandez is grabbed by catcher Lance Parrish after the Detroit Tigers beat the San Diego Padres 8-4 to win the World Series Sunday before their

AP Wirephoto

gives it much more attention. I'm thinking particularly of Borg [Bergen *Record*], Tomlinson [Morris *Daily Record*], and Newhouse, who is always at the *Star-Ledger*. They're all highly intelligent, capable, motivated, and I think they force the rest of us to show a lot of initiative and scramble. They're attuned to change."

His list did not include Joe L. Allbritton.

Allbritton's Thin Sisters: The Paterson *News* and the Hudson *Dispatch*

The Paterson *News* and the Hudson *Dispatch*, only 16 miles apart, are both the property of Joe L. Allbritton, a newspaper chain owner who buys troubled papers and tries to make them profitable by means of "survival journalism"—that is, by stripping expenses to the bone. Whether these sister newspapers, with their thin budgets, can stay alive in a competitive marketplace remains to be seen.

The Paterson *News* covers all of Passaic County, a little of South Bergen (the working-class part of the county), and a section of northern Morris County (the Pompton area that has always been more oriented toward Paterson than Morristown). The *Dispatch* of Union City covers most of Hudson County, and the communities on the eastern edge of Bergen County up to Ridgefield and Fort Lee. Both newspapers are located in no-growth areas and are completely surrounded by competitors. The Bergen *Record* covers all of Bergen County and parts of Passaic and Hudson, the *Star-Ledger* is ever present, the Passaic *Herald-News* covers the same ground as the Paterson newspaper, and the *Jersey Journal* is head-to-head with the *Dispatch*.

In the 1960s when the 35,000-circulation morning Paterson *Call* was still alive, the evening *News* had about 60,000 readers. At that time the Hudson *Dispatch* was in its heyday, with more than 67,000 readers. The death of the *Call* benefited the *News*, which by 1974 was publishing a 28,698-circulation morning edition and a 42,390 evening edition. Meanwhile, the morning *Dispatch* had slipped to roughly 50,000. When Allbritton was considering buying the newspapers, he probably used their 1976 figures. By then the Paterson *News* had dropped to a combined circulation of 64,543, and the *Dispatch* had fallen to 45,930 readers. The circulations of the two newspapers continued their decline in the early Allbritton years, approaching bottom around 1980 (by which time the *News* was a morning paper) and then slipping more gradually. By 1983, the Paterson *News* had a circulation of 48,114, while the Hudson *Dispatch* was selling 36,388 copies.

The Paterson newspaper purchased by Allbritton editorially was a very solid product. The Haines family's legacy can be seen in the content analysis of 1977 New Jersey newspapers, where the Paterson *News* was ninth overall. Its 21-page news hole ranked sixth, while its 21 pages of advertising were good for an 11th place tie. It tied for sixth in the number of locally originated stories, ranked ninth in the number of longer stories, tied for ninth in international news, tied for 10th in local coverage, was 12th in the national news and in the use of photographs, and tied for 16th in state coverage.

The 1977 Hudson *Dispatch* was not in the same class. The 28-page newspaper carried 15 pages of news, tying for 19th place in that category. While it ranked seventh in the number of longer stories and tied for 10th in state news, it ranked 13th in national coverage, tied for 13th in international news, tied for 22nd in the number of locally originated stories, ranked 23rd in the use of photographs, and tied for 23rd in local coverage.

The Paterson *News* of the 1970s had an editorial contingent of 70 people. Under "survival journalism," the number of journalists steadily declined. In 1982 the newspaper was at survival level—40 news staffers—the same number it would have two years later. A number of newsroom positions were also eliminated at the Hudson *Dispatch*, where rock bottom was judged to be a total of 44 journalists.

Reporters' salaries were stabilized at a level that can only be called *below* survival. In 1982 the *News* and *Dispatch* paid beginning reporters $180 per week and experienced writers about $20 more. Reporters were hired fresh out of college, and tended to move on to better-paying newspapers as soon as they gained experience. "Reporters can't live on such a salary," said Linda Cunningham, who was executive editor of the two newspapers at the time. "We're resigned to losing our good people, but I'd like to keep them three years instead of one. One year doesn't pay off; they're just learning when they leave. I've been after Allbritton for more money. Still, they get their clips while they're here—I suppose that's exploitation, but we do it."

Cunningham, who served as executive editor of Allbritton's *Trenton Times* as well as the *News* and *Dispatch* until her efforts were concentrated in Trenton, was not successful in raising salaries. "Beginning reporters are paid $180 a week, and reporters with experience $200," said *Dispatch* Managing Editor Mike Fistel in 1984. "The paper is seen as a training ground. For most people it is a first or second job."

Allbritton modernized the production facilities at the Paterson *News* soon after taking over. He also centralized some of the functions of the two newspapers. The *Dispatch*'s nightside copy editors were moved to Paterson, where the *News*' composing room became a shared facility. The two papers pool courthouse coverage in Bergen, Hudson, and Passaic counties (leaving the Morris County courts uncovered except for major events involving the Pompton area). The sports editor in Paterson oversees both newspapers, and the papers use the same state and national editorials.

The *News* publishes two editions, one for Paterson and the other for the rest of its area. Despite the paper's efforts of reshooting and replating pages and replacing news items, Cunningham said, suburban readers complain that the paper concentrates on Paterson and Paterson residents say it is filled with suburban news.

The *Dispatch* on Tuesdays publishes a Spanish-language tabloid section called "Ahora," which it circulates only in the Hudson County portion of its area. Because the influx of Cubans has made Union City a bilingual community, the paper seeks Spanish-speaking reporters, but with its low pay scale it has trouble holding them.

Local coverage is emphasized at both newspapers, although staff size makes achievement difficult. "There is a mandatory production quota of two stories a day," said reporter James Greiff, who left the *Dispatch* in 1983 and went to the New Brunswick *Home News*. "Quality slides while production goes up."

Greiff commented that at the age of 28 "I think I was the oldest reporter there." He added, "The political environment of Hudson and Bergen counties is an excellent training ground, but at the *Dispatch* you learn on your own. With little direction, it is sink or swim." He said the pressure was constant, the hours grueling, and the pay dismal.

Under "survival journalism," the heavy writing load and the lack of specialized news reporters act against the production of investigative or in-depth stories. But while this management technique can make a good newspaper mediocre, it can actually clean up some of the problems of an already mediocre newspaper.

The Paterson *News* was less of a newspaper in 1984 than it was in the 1970s, but the same cannot be said of the Hudson *Dispatch*. The 1977 content analysis found the *Dispatch* (with a 15-page news hole) to be a comparatively weak newspaper, and the 1974 study conducted by the Center for Analysis of Public Issues showed the paper (which then had a 12.8-page news hole) to be no better than mediocre. "The common nickname for the *Dispatch* in the old days used to be the 'Hudson Disgrace,' " said Greiff.

The reputation of the *Dispatch* among journalists for many years was tied to the reputation of the Hudson County Democratic political machine. In his September 1977 *New Jersey Monthly* magazine article "All the News That Money Can Buy," Robert Sam Anson told story after story about *Dispatch* staffers who received Christmas envelopes, held no-show jobs, or received money for writing press releases, all supplied by the politicians and other news sources they were covering. Reporters told each other these stories for years,

Joanne Woodward in Weekend Woman today

Weehawken, Leonia play to 3-3 tie
— Page 13

Fatal rally

Rep. wants probe of Belfast melee
— Page 3

Cubs, Sutcliffe stifle Mets
— Page 9

hudson
the dispatch

'First thing in the morning'

VOL. 111 NO. 222   2★ 3★   24 PAGES   **Saturday, September 15, 1984** $1.15 Weekly Home Delivery. Call 863-2000   25 Cents

Photo by Bruce Johnson

CARMINE A. BALZANO, a former North Bergen detective, listens, while his wife, flanked by their two sons, expresses shock as he receives a four-year sentence for arson yesterday in Hudson County Superior Court in Jersey City.

Balzano gets 4 years

By FRANCES ANN BURNS
Staff Writer

Convicted arsonist Carmine A. Balzano was sentenced to four years in prison yesterday. But an appellate court allowed him to remain free on bail pending appeal.

"This court is acutely aware that you have been a police officer in North Bergen for 18 years," Judge Maurice Walsh in Hudson County Superior Court in Jersey City said as he imposed sentence. "It is hoped that your incarceration will act as a deterrent, not only for you, but for others."

Balzano's wife, Mary Ann, sobbed as the judge spoke, but Balzano sat with his head lowered. As soon as the sentencing was over, he rose and hugged his wife.

Walsh refused to stay the sentence or allow bail pending appeal, but his decision was overruled yesterday afternoon by a three-judge panel of the Appellate Division of state Superior Court, sitting in Springfield. Balzano, who has been free on a $25,000 personal recognizance bond since his indictment, was ordered to put up bail of $50,000 by 2 p.m. Monday.

Paul DePascale, an assistant Hudson County prosecutor, said he expects the appeals process to take about a year.

Before the sentencing, Walsh also denied motions from Balzano's attorney, Michael J. Beatrice of Hackensack, to set aside the verdict and to dismiss the charges against Balzano.

Balzano was convicted July 30 of setting a fire last year that destroyed The Barn flea market on Tonnele Avenue in North Bergen in order to collect $300,000 insurance.

See BALZANO, Back Page

Great Adventure indicted in fire

By CAROLYN BELARDO
United Press International

TOMS RIVER—The Six Flags Great Adventure amusement park, its parent corporation and the park's current and former managers were charged with manslaughter yesterday in the deaths of eight teenagers killed by a fire in the park's Haunted Castle.

A special Ocean County grand jury investigating the May 11 fire found that insufficient safety measures and carelessness at the Jackson Township park led to the tragedy, Ocean County Prosecutor Edward Turnbach said in announcing the indictments.

The indictments, handed up Thursday but impounded until yesterday, charge the Six Flags Corp.

and Great Adventure Inc. with aggravated manslaughter in "recklessly causing the death" of the eight youths "under circumstances manifesting extreme indifference to human life."

Also charged were Larry Cochran, the former general manager of the park, and David Paltzik, current general manager. The two were charged with manslaughter for "reckless conduct" in causing the deaths.

Cochran was general manager of the park from October 1977 to September 1982 and is the executive vice president of Six Flags Corp. Paltzik became general manager at Great Adventure when Cochran was promoted.

If convicted, the corporations

could be fined up to $100,000, and Cochran and Paltzik could face a maximum sentences of 10 years in prison and $100,000 in fines.

Six Flags Corp. called the indictments "unfounded and unfair" in a statement released from its Chicago headquarters.

"The grand jury's action is an inappropriate, unfortunate and, we believe, an unprecedented reaction," the statement said.

"There is no question that last May's fire was a terrible tragedy," the statement said.

The fire broke out in the Haunted Castle May 11,trapping and killing five teenagers from Brooklyn and three from New Jersey. All of them were with school groups.

Poll: Reagan ahead in Hudson

By BILL GYVES
Staff Writer

President Ronald Reagan would carry Hudson County easily if the November election were held today, defeating challenger Walter F. Mondale by a 2-1 margin in a Democratic bastion of an otherwise large-

ly Republican state, according to a poll released yesterday.

The poll indicates, however, that nearly one of every three registered voters in Hudson County remains uncertain of which candidate they favor — leaving local leaders of both major political parties less than two months to swing those

voters into their respective camps.

The poll, conducted by Raritan Associates for the New Jersey Republican State Committee, surveyed 500 voters on their opinions concerning national, state and local issues. It is the first sophisticated

See POLL, Back Page

UAW to stay on job without contract

By MICHELINE MAYNARD
United Press International

DETROIT—The United Auto Workers announced last night it will continue to work without a contract with General Motors Corp. and will continue negotiations, but 13 local unions have been given permission to strike.

The announcement came from the union 20 minutes before the contract expired at midnight.

The 13 union locals cover about 70,000 auto workers. Members at a number of those locals were working the night shift at GM assembly plants, including the one in Linden, and members were expected to stop working immediately.

The 2 other plants are in Warren, Orion, Flint and two Pontiac, Mich. locations; Doraville, Ga.; Arlington, Tex.; Wilmington, Del.; Van Nuys, Calif.; Shreveport, La.; and Bowling Green, Ky.; and

Wentzville, Mo.

UAW President Owen Bieber said the 13 locals had been given permission to walk out based on local issues — a strategy that technically avoids a national walkout while giving the union some clout against the No. 1 automaker.

"Despite our repeated warnings that time was running dangerously short, the corporation delayed and stalled on key issues — most importantly on job security — and we have been unable to arrive at a satisfactory agreement," Bieber and UAW Vice President Donald Ephlin, head of the union's GM Dept., said in a statement.

Talks were expected to continue into the night, and the union said it is prepared to bargain "as long as necessary."

A union spokesman would not elaborate further on the decision. There was no comment from GM.

UPI Telephoto

POPE JOHN PAUL II kisses Janet Rushion during a visit to the Izaak Walton Killam Hospital in Halifax, Nova Scotia, yesterday, during the sixth day of his visit to Canada.

$202M in mortgages offered by state

United Press International

TRENTON—State officials said yesterday $202 million in low interest mortgages will be made available to moderate-income New Jersey residents next week on a first come, first serve basis.

The program, offered by the New Jersey Housing Mortgage Finance Agency, is slated to use the proceeds of tax-exempt bonds to provide fixed rate, 30-year mortgages at 10.65 percent interest to about 4,000 eligible first-time buyers.

Hundreds of people were expected to camp out at banks this weekend in order to be first in line when the mortgage applications become available Monday morning, said Julia Chabala, a spokeswoman for the agency.

Income eligibility limits and first-time homeowner requirements have been waived by the agency for many homes purchased in the designated

urban areas. First-time homeowners in other areas of the state cannot have an annual household income of more than than $37,500, except in in Bergen, Essex, Morris, Somerset and Union counties, where the maximum income is $42,500.

The program also offers people purchasing homes in 41 targeted urban areas to qualify for reduced-rate mortgages bearing an initial rate of 8.65 percent, which would increase during a five-year period to 10.65 percent.

Applicants must present proof of their income and a check for 1 percent of the mortgage amount in order to reserve the funds.

In order to apply for the loan, the applicants also must have a signed purchase contract for a specific property that is dated after Aug. 27.

More details about the program are available from the agency by calling 609-890-1300.

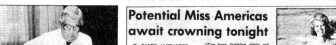

Potential Miss Americas await crowning tonight

By RANDY ALEXANDER
Special to The Dispatch

ATLANTIC CITY — The tension is mounting as the Miss

"I've been thinking about not winning any of the preliminaries," said the 25-year-old, 5-foot 9-inch blonde from West New York. "I'm trying to think of all

Miss NJ loves WNY and state

By RANDY ALEXANDER
Special to The Dispatch

and some of the ones repeated by Anson concerned events as recent as the early 1970s.

Under Allbritton, the *Dispatch* is a clean house, and even the nickname apparently has faded. Allbritton editors hire fresh, young reporters with good college backgrounds and push them to churn out as much copy as possible. These young people are out to make reputations for themselves and move on to better-paying newspapers. They have no long-term connections with the local politicians. They are unlikely to jeopardize their futures by taking Christmas envelopes, or even to contemplate such actions. "Reporters at the *Dispatch* are now young and straight from top to bottom," declared Greiff with assurance.

While survival journalism clearly affected the quality of the Paterson *News*, today's Hudson *Dispatch*, on balance, is at least as good a newspaper as it was before Allbritton took over. *Dispatch* reporters may be younger and less experienced, but the reputation of the newspaper has improved. Although few would argue that today's *Dispatch* is a first-rate newspaper, the jokes are gone and the paper survives.

Newspapers are expensive, labor-intensive propositions. When revenues are high, they can afford to carry some fat, especially in the form of excessive numbers of well-paid writers and editors. These extra journalists often deliver the goods, providing the specialized and in-depth coverage that is the hall-mark of a newspaper of the first quality. But when revenues are declining, newspapers are in jeopardy, and costs can kill them. The Paterson *News* and Hudson *Dispatch* were troubled newspapers when Allbritton purchased them. The *News*, in particular, had large numbers of back-shop workers, including 100 composing room employess. The financial cuts instituted by Allbritton at the *News* eventually led to a strike by the International Typographical Union, which hurt sales but did not halt publication.

Allbritton stripped the *News* and *Dispatch* to the bone, and the result is survival. "Some consider it a miracle that we're still here," Cunningham said in 1982. "In this particular market the competition is high. This is wall-to-wall newspapers. Every few miles there's another daily." Cunningham predicted that some of the newspapers in the area would not make it through the decade, but that the Allbritton papers would be among the survivors.

In the case of the Paterson *News*, idealists might argue in favor of a middle ground, somewhere between 70 news staffers and 40. But it is certainly possible that survival journalism was necessitated by financial reality. Regard-ing the Hudson *Dispatch*, the losses due to survival journalism appear bal-anced by the gains, a surprisingly positive end result. It really does not matter how good a newspaper *was* if it no longer *is*, and Allbritton's success will be measured by the continued existence of daily newspapers in Paterson and Union City.

Jersey City's *Journal*

If the *Star-Ledger* is the flagship of Newhouse Newspapers, the 31-newspaper chain created by Samuel I. Newhouse, the *Jersey Journal* is the tramp steamer of the fleet. Separated only by Newark Bay, the two newspapers are in direct competition. And yet the *Jersey Journal* survives—on street sales.

The *Journal's* reliance on newsstand sales for a large percentage of its circulation is unusual in New Jersey, where most newspapers depend on home-delivered subscriptions. But Jersey City and Bayonne are a world apart from suburban New Jersey, and in the core cities newspapers are still sold on the streets.

The *Journal* publishes its newsstand edition first to attract morning as well as afternoon sales. The newsstand edition carries a different flag than the others, and its deadline for copy is 5:30 a.m., very early for an afternoon newspaper. The second edition, designed for Bayonne, goes both to stands and homes there. The third edition is for home delivery in Jersey City and surroundings; and the fourth edition, with a 9 a.m. deadline, is for home delivery in North Hudson.

"When I first came over here [from another Newhouse paper], I was very uncomfortable that almost half my readers made up their minds every day whether they were going to buy the paper," said August Lockwood, who was editor of the *Journal* until he retired in the summer of 1983. "But I grew used to it . . . and I put more emphasis on a bit of the sensational."

Journal coverage coincides with the boundaries of Hudson County. Its expansionist aims lie to the north where it is outsold by the Hudson *Dispatch*. "Why, I don't know," Lockwood said. "We have more local news for North Hudson than they have. I've put my ruler on their paper and ours and measured it, and we have a hell of a lot more north news in our north edition and in our regular edition than the Hudson *Dispatch* does. And the same was true of the old Bayonne *Times* when I first came over here."

In the 1960s when the 15,000-circulation Bayonne *Times* was still alive, the *Jersey Journal* was a 92,000-circulation newspaper. In 1974 with the *Journal* serving both Jersey City and Bayonne, its readership was down to a still healthy 84,220. By 1977 its circulation had slipped to 73,151, and by 1982 the paper's circulation was down to 61,470. Although there was a slight increase in 1983 to 63,618, the *Journal*, with no Sunday edition to bring in advertising, was a newspaper in trouble.

While the *Journal* has become the predominant daily in Bayonne, it has substantial competition, especially in advertising, from two successful week-lies. "People still don't like the idea that the Bayonne *Times* died and sold its list to us," said Lockwood. "Bayonne looks with suspicion on Jersey City, and

the north communities look with suspicion on Jersey City, and we publish in
Jersey City. They see us as 'that Jersey City newspaper.' "

The editorial staff totals 54 people, which Lockwood called "thin." Most
are general assignment reporters who double by developing contacts and
specialty beats. One reporter, for example, keeps up with the Hackensack
Meadowlands Development Commission, an important agency to people in
the area. The *Journal* maintains small bureaus in Bayonne, Hoboken, and
West New York and stations a statehouse reporter in Trenton. As a member of
the Newhouse chain, it has a Washington, D.C. news resource, but usually
prefers to develop its own Washington stories, using the Newhouse facilities
only for research help. Otherwise, since a Newhouse-developed story would
be sent out over the wire, it might be published first by the *Star-Ledger*. "They
talk about the Newhouse group," Lockwood said when he was still editor of
the *Journal*, "but each one of us stands on his own feet. And I'm sitting in the
shadow of a big guy, so I have to be fast on my feet."

The paper covers important night meetings in person, and otherwise
depends on phone contacts. Under Lockwood, the paper looked for qualified
Hispanic reporters, especially to cover the northern part of the county, but did
not publish any news in Spanish. "We have not gone that route," Lockwood
said, "because very frankly we'd get a backlash from our non-Spanish-
speaking people."

The *Journal*'s break page features business on Mondays, food on Wednesdays, and entertainment on Fridays. On Thursdays the paper opens the break
page to its readers, who are invited to send in their own prose and
photographs.

The study of 1977 New Jersey newspapers found the *Jersey Journal* to be
right in the middle of the pack. Its 18-page news hole ranked 11th, while its 18
pages of advertising tied for 14th place. It was eighth in national news and in
the number of locally originated stories, 12th in local coverage, and tied for
13th in international news. The *Journal* tied for 15th for its use of photographs, ranked 19th in the number of longer stories, and tied for 19th in state
coverage.

The reputation of the *Jersey Journal* among journalists for many years was
linked to the reputation of the Hudson County Democratic political machine.
In his September 1977 *New Jersey Monthly* magazine article "All the News
That Money Can Buy," Robert Sam Anson called the *Journal* "the editorial
lackey of the Hudson County Democratic machine." And some reporters
familiar with *Journal* coverage of county politics through the 1960s say the
Journal not only ignored political corruption, but that a number of reporters
were part of it, taking part-time public relations jobs arranged by politically
related sources.

The *Journal* that 26-year-old Steven Newhouse took over as editor in

JERSEY
CITY
WEST HUDSON

THE JERSEY JOURNAL

and Jersey Observer

25 CENTS
Home Delivery
$1.10 weekly

Tonight: Clear, low in 60s.
Tomorrow: Sunny, high near 80.

FRIDAY, SEPTEMBER 21, 1984

118th Year — No. 122

A war is being fought in the Hackensack River

By John Kampfe

There is a war being fought each day that does not involve armies, guns or bombs.

The battleground is the Hackensack River, which cuts a 22-mile path through Hudson and Bergen counties. The fight is being carried out by Mother Nature against her sometime arch-enemy, man, and it appears that she now has the upper hand.

Mother Nature, with a nudge from Hackensack Meadowlands Development Commission environmentalists, is attempting literally to breathe life into a waterway that essentially died in the name of progress.

"You have here a river that has seen a rather marvelous return in the abundance of species and diversity of species," said Chester P. Mattson, the HMDC's former director of environmental programs and planning.

But, Mattson and Donald Smith, the HMDC's chief staff naturalist, agree that nature, rather than the restoration of the river to what it once was, has created something new.

"Yes, it's a rebirth, but not a rebirth of what it (the river) was 50, 60 or 70 years ago," Smith said. "This is a different ecosystem than what had been here."

While it is impossible for the environmentalists to determine what kind of system had been in place decades ago, they can say what caused its downfall.

It began in 1914. The Panama Canal construction and the many who died after being bitten by malaria-laden mosquitoes were fresh on everyone's minds.

See A WAR — Page 17.

The Byrne Meadowlands Arena is framed by vegetation growing along the banks of the Hackensack River.

Dems rolling out red carpets for visit by Ferraro

By Robert Larkins
and Patricia Scott

The visit that the Democratic Party's vice presidential nominee, Geraldine Ferraro, will be paying to Hudson tomorrow is already cheering Democratic officials.

Ms. Ferraro is scheduled to arrive at the Bayonne Democratic Club's annual picnic at about 2 p.m., after a stop in North Bergen, and stay for about half an hour. The picnic will be at Hudson-County Park in Bayonne.

"We're delighted," said Hudson County Executive Edward Clark of Bayonne, who is president of the club. "I understand the weatherman is going to cooperate and I'm looking forward to meeting her.

"I'm very happy," said Assemblyman Joseph Doria of

Bayonne. "It's important she comes to Hudson County. It's important for people to see the candidates, to get to know them."

At the formal announcement of the nominee's visit yesterday, Bayonne Mayor Dennis Collins predicted the Walter Mondale-Ferraro ticket would win in Bayonne by a "respectable" margin and would also win Hudson County.

Asked the reason for the visit to the city, Collins remarked:

"I like to think good politicians, like good hunters, go hunting where the ducks are, where the voters are."

The mayor characterized Bayonne as a "blue-collar" city that is concerned about what Collins sees as a tendency during the current federal administra-

See DEMS — Page 9.

Geraldine Ferraro
She'll campaign in Hudson

But, will party chairman support the candidate?

Bayonne Mayor Dennis Collins' said yesterday that he would talk with Jersey City Mayor Gerald McCann about McCann's attitude toward the presidential race — if McCann shows up at a campaign breakfast of Hudson Democratic leaders scheduled for this morning.

McCann hasn't said who he will endorse for president. He may endorse no one. He has been quoted as saying it's important to be with a winner.

"I've read some comments by Mayor McCann," Collins said yesterday at a press conference announcing the visit of Democratic vice presidential nominee Geraldine Ferraro to Hudson. "I regard his comments as regretable in view of the fact he's elected Democratic chairman of this county."

Asked about the importance of picking a winner, Collins said that seemed to him like "Monday morning quarterbacking."

"I have to tell you," he said, "that my attitude about this is you're either with me or against me, not piecemeal."

McCann has said he would support the rest of the Democratic ticket.

Today's meeting at Casino-in-the-Park was called by Rep. Frank Guarini, who heads the Mondale campaign in New Jersey. Invited to the meeting were Hudson's top Democratic officeholders, including the Democratic mayors, and other Hudson Democratic leaders.

McCann was invited. Guarini's office said yesterday that it was informed that McCann

See BUT — Page 9.

Dennis Collins
Questions for McCann

4 city agencies 'raid' boarding house

By Steve Dnistrian

Officials from four Jersey City government agencies raided and closed a four-story boarding house on Bergen Avenue yesterday, claiming 33 fire, health and building violations that made the structure uninhabitable.

Two Jersey City men on the premises were arrested on charges stemming from outstanding warrants. William Stevenson, 34, was arrested on an assault charge, and George Cavdra, 19, was wanted for contempt of court, police said.

Members of the Jersey City Police Department and nar-

cotics squad, the board of health, fire prevention unit and department of property conservation raided the house at 669 Bergen Avenue near Fairmount Avenue just before 2 p.m.

Police were unable to determine exactly how many people occupied the wood-framed structure since the landlord failed to keep a tenant register, according to Capt. John McAuley.

Police said that all but one of the house's 15 apartments appeared to be lived in.

Frank Pechillo, a city spokesman, said the owner of the boarding home is listed as S. Eshagpour of Queens, N.Y. Pechillo said the city will serve

the owner with a notice of the violations.

Fire officials found a propane container, open paint containers and stacked sofas and mattresses in the building's bottom floor. They also said that floor's smoke detector failed to set off other smoke detectors throughout the building when tested, which violates safety standards.

"If this place ever went up in flames," said public safety director Richard Harrison at the scene, "those people on the top floor would be dead."

Fire officials also allegedly found inadequate fire doors and escapes, along with faulty wir-

ing.

A department of health representative said half of the third floor was uninhabited because it was "unbelievably infested" by roaches and insects.

Joseph Galasso of property conservation said the building was cited for 133 violations in April.

Police said that neighborhood complaints about drugs allegedly being sold from the building and numerous other complaints led to the raid.

However, no arrests were made on those allegations.

Tenants of the building were relocated through the Red Cross in Jersey City.

Felix Gabrush, city director of property conservation, leads "raid" on boarding house at 669 Bergen Ave., Jersey City.

Court upholds Friedlands' disbarment

By Margaret Schmidt

NEWARK — The chief judge of the U.S. District Court

not be reached for comment.

Shaughnessy had argued that David Friedland's cooperation

May that he couldn't point to any case in which an attorney disbarred by the state was allowed to practice in federal court.

charges, according to court papers, included tax violations and attempting to influence a grand jury witness.

summer 1983 seemed to be a very different newspaper than the one that had been the subject of all the stories. Although the newspaper still had no formal "conflict of interest" guidelines, the issue had not reared its head for many years. But within two months, Newhouse was told by a veteran reporter that he had been asked to testify at a bribery trial involving waterfront development projects. As reported by Montieth M. Illingworth in the March/April 1984 issue of *Columbia Journalism Review*, the reporter told Newhouse that he had accepted a $1,000 advance for public relations work involving a development project, but that he had not been covering the issue at the time. A number of weeks later when Newhouse learned that the reporter had in fact written about the waterfront projects, he fired him. The punchline to the story is that many *Journal* reporters objected to the firing, and the Hudson County Newspaper Guild, by a narrow margin, voted in favor of filing a grievance. The old ways apparently die hard in Hudson County.

The *Jersey Journal*'s basic dilemma is much more difficult to solve than its ethical problems. While the *Star-Ledger* has been able to keep its readers when they moved to the suburbs, high distribution costs and competition from the *Ledger* and others have prevented the *Journal* from following former readers who moved out of Jersey City. For many years the *Journal*'s short-range strategy has been to go to the newsstands, trying to grab the public's attention with big headlines and scary stories. This has kept the *Journal* alive but declining, and it is doubtful whether any long-term strategy can be devised to change the newspaper's fortunes.

The *Daily Journal* of Elizabeth

When the *Newark News* closed its doors in 1972, one of the newspapers that appeared to be a likely beneficiary was the Elizabeth *Journal* (now the *Daily Journal*). Founded in 1779 and owned for many years by the Crane family, the *Journal* had been purchased in the 1960s by the Ingersoll group, which owned the *Trentonian*. The *Journal*'s coverage area was just south of Newark, and expansion seemed a real possibility.

Ingersoll actually attempted to expand into Newark itself, placing former *Newark News* reporter Jeff Stoll in City Hall and hiring a contingent of Newark reporters. More importantly, the *Journal* moved west to cover all of Union County, and south into Woodbridge and Edison. Unfortunately for the *Journal*, the expansion was temporary and unsuccessful. Although the paper was covering Newark, Irvington, Maplewood, Plainfield, and Woodbridge, it failed to make significant circulation gains in these areas.

"When we would talk to officials, we would have to explain what the paper was," said Joseph Bakes, a former *Journal* reporter. "And they were not able to see the next day what we had written. In Maplewood I was okay because I had worked on a weekly there and people knew me. In other towns people just didn't know what the *Journal* was."

The expansion attempt did not last long. "When they originally decided to go into Plainfield they sent five or six reporters," explained Christine Davies, another former *Journal* staffer. "But within a year they were down to one in the day and one at night."

The mid-1970s were difficult years for a number of New Jersey afternoon newspapers, which were faced with a general business recession and the struggle to hold on to circulation. The *Journal*'s bureaus began to close, coverage became more sporadic, and finally most of the towns marked for expansion were abandoned. Then a few reporters who had left the newspaper were not replaced. Eventually, Ingersoll dismissed 13 reporters and editors on the same day.

The *Journal* was sold in 1975. "The paper looked as if it was being house-cleaned for sale," said Davies, who left the *Journal* in 1978 and later became business editor of the *Courier-News*. "Of course you see that in hindsight. It was passed off at the time that the paper was tightening its belt. So whether it was a condition of sale or whether those people were just smart enough to clean up their books so it looked better, it's basically irrelevant."

The buyer of the *Journal* was Hagadone Newspapers of Coeur d'Alene, Idaho, and the results were devastating. Within a short time, a number of the *Journal*'s top people were gone, including Editor Joe Jennings, who was highly regarded within the profession. The newsroom attrition continued; people who left were not replaced. In February 1976 seven reporters, two editors, and a photographer were laid off, from the bottom, according to the paper's contract with the Newspaper Guild. When reporter Bakes began on the *Journal* in 1974, the paper had about 60 people in the newsroom. In April 1979 when he left, the newspaper's news staff had shrunk to around 25.

The lack of human resources affected the content of the newspaper. "We'd hear it on the streets all the time," Davies said. "'The paper's going downhill,' people would say, and, 'How come you don't cover my town anymore?' On any paper you'll hear general griping from the public, but this was different. People knew. Not only weren't they getting the coverage, but there were fewer editions, fewer pages, and the news lineage was going down in proportion to advertising."

The Center for Analysis of Public Issues' study of 1974 New Jersey newspapers had found the Elizabeth *Journal* to be a solid newspaper, averaging 19.9 pages of advertising and 16.6 pages of news. The paper had ranked fourth in state coverage, 10th in national news, 13th in foreign news, and 18th in the amount of local coverage.

The content analysis of 1977 New Jersey newspapers conducted by David Sachsman showed the decline of the *Journal*. In 1977, the paper was down to 18 pages of ads and 15 pages of news. It tied for 13th in state coverage, tied for 20th in the number of local stories, tied for 21st in national news, and carried the least amount of foreign news of any newspaper in the state. The *Journal* tied for 14th place for the number of longer stories, tied for 18th for locally originated stories, and tied for 21st for its use of photographs.

The circulation of the evening newspaper had declined as well, from 62,257 in 1974 to 52,090 in 1977. But the content of the 1977 *Journal* was not comparable to the other 50,000-circulation newspapers in the state. Instead, it ranked with the 11,833-circulation Bridgeton *News* and the 15,857-circulation *New Jersey Herald*.

While the content of the *Journal* was shrinking, Hagadone was improving the newspaper's technology. The chain wanted a new building and was seriously considering leaving Elizabeth. This was discovered when the local weekly paper in Cranford published news of the *Journal*'s application for a variance to construct a new plant there. The notice brought out a large crowd of residents, who opposed the variance at the zoning board meeting because the plant was to be located in a flood plain. Hagadone quietly dropped the proposal and instead built a new plant next door to the old one in downtown Elizabeth. The facilities were modernized, and the paper was converted to offset printing. Employees called the new building, a squat, unwindowed fortress, "The Bunker."

During the move to the new building, a general housecleaning was ordered. Many of the materials in the newspaper's nearly 200-year-old "morgue" were simply dumped, although management claimed that the items of historical importance were retained, or thrown out by accident. "They had no feeling of history or of the past," said Jean-Rae Turner, who was a *Journal* reporter in 1977 and now is a freelancer. "They weren't even interested in a morgue."

"This is what happens as the papers move from family ownership to chain ownership," Bakes said. "They have no feeling or regard for the area, and no time for history or sentimentality. The company is oriented solely to the bottom line."

As the news staff shrank, the pressure on the remaining journalists increased. "What we felt was very shorthanded," said Davies, by this point an editor in charge of the business and women's pages. "You'd have a good story in your hands and you'd look around the room and there was nobody to do it. If you could somehow squeeze the time to do it, you'd go ahead and do it

Local
Linden airport operator repays debt to city....................... Page 9

Sports
Dwight Gooden: National League strikeout leader............. Page 15

LOCAL
Edition

25 CENTS

The Daily Journal

MUCH WARMER: Weather details on Page 2

VOL 206 ISSUE 157

Serving Union County Since 1779

★★ TUESDAY, JULY 3, 1984

County

IF YOU'RE interested in borrowing a personal computer, something to do your household accounts on, or play games on or just fool around with to get the hang of a computer, the Linden Free Library may have what you're looking for. — Page 9

A MORATORIUM on apartment development in downtown Scotch Plains was proposed by a group of citizens and merchants at the planning board meeting Monday night during a hearing on a developer's plans to build a 37-unit apartment complex on Park Avenue. — Page 9

A RAHWAY councilman will testify before a state Assembly committee to support legislation which requires the state to halt investments of pension funds and annuities in companies or banks dealing with the Republic of South Africa because of the country's apartheid policy. — Page 11

AS FEDERAL funding for new senior citizen housing dwindles to two-thirds its former level, Rahway is continuing an effort to complete two approved 40-unit apartment residences for its elderly population. — Page 11

Nation / World

WALTER MONDALE insists pressure from women's groups will not sway his choice for a running mate but he also says Rep. Geraldine Ferraro is "clearly in contention" to complete the Democratic ticket. — Page 3

THREE SHARK fishermen whose boat capsized in shark-infested waters off the Florida coast said a pair of buoyant plastic coolers saved their lives. — Page 3

A BLACK CONSERVATIVE picked by President Reagan to head the U.S. Commission on Civil Rights says actions Reagan has taken this election year are "doing mayhem to the Constitution." — Page 7

ENVIRONMENTALISTS say President Reagan "should be ashamed of himself" for bringing former EPA chief Anne Burford back into his administration to head a national environmental advisory panel. — Page 7

ALEUTS who live in an Alaskan village clubbed nearly 800 seals to death on the first day of the annual kill — a controversial 200-year-old harvest that has triggered debate over aboriginal rights versus animal protection issues. — Page 24

Sports

DR. PAUL WARD'S involvement with the U.S. Olympic Committee ended Monday, a day after he was quoted as saying that he had given some Olympic athletes information about beating drug tests for anabolic steroids, banned by the International Olympic Committee. — Page 15

JIMMY ARIAS, seeded fifth, No. 11 Kevin Curran, No. 12 Johan Kriek and No. 15 Vitas Gerulaitis were upset victims at Wimbledon Monday as the men got down to their final eight. Kriek lost to Paul Annacone, the first qualifier to reach the quarterfinals since John McEnroe in 1977. — Page 15

MANY OF THE GENERALS, despite losing their first-round playoff game to Philadelphia, are happy with the team's 14-4 record in the first year of Donald Trump's ownership, and predict better things for next season. — Page 17

THE HEAVYWEIGHT championship boxing battle between unbeaten Larry Holmes and Gerrie Coetzee, canceled once, may be on again. — Page 18

Inside

Four towns declare trash emergencies

By VALERIE REITMAN
Journal Business Writer

Mayors of at least four Union County municipalities declared a state of emergency Monday as a garbage collection strike began to have an impact on nine counties in north and central New Jersey.

The situation created by the strike by sanitation workers and sympathizing landfill operators — which effectively closed at least two landfills in Middlesex County — was somewhat alleviated Monday when the union agreed to allow emergency truckloads of hospital and nursing home waste into the sites.

No quick end to the strike was in sight today as further negotiating sessions had not been set by a

state mediator asked to deal with the impasse.

Meanwhile, Gov. Thomas Kean formed a solid waste emergency task force of five cabinet officials Monday to deal with the Teamsters sanitation workers strike which moved into its third day today. Elizabeth Mayor Thomas Dunn, among others, had appealed to Kean to intercede in the matter to open the landfills for emergency municipal dumping.

Dunn, along with Union Mayor Michael Bono, Clark Mayor Bernard Yarusavage and Cranford Mayor Gene Marino, ordered residents in their municipalities to separate perishable and decomposable items from other waste such as boxes, cardboard and glass. Officials in other municipalities were urging their residents to do the same.

Several municipal administrators said they were confused about the situation and had received no guidance from the state.

Some local businesses said they had no idea what they would do if the strike continues.

Papetti's Hygrade Egg in Elizabeth, which cracks some 3.6 million eggs daily in the manufacture of its liquid egg product and generates 35 tons of eggshells daily, said it was desperate for a solution.

"We've got to do something by tomorrow," said co-president Arthur Papetti. The firm has three trucks already filled with eggshells but nowhere to dump them.

In announcing formation of his task force,

Continued on Page 4

How to handle your garbage

By VALERIE REITMAN
Journal Business Writer

The Union County Division of Environmental Engineering is recommending recycling to reduce the volume of solid waste which must be stored for the duration of the strike.

Recycling opportunities already exist in many municipalities for newspaper, glass, aluminum and steel cans. To learn which materials can be recycled in a particular Union County municipality and the location and schedule, county residents can telephone their municipal office or the county division's Environmental Resource Center at 654-6489.

In all affected municipalities, officials are urging residents not to leave their garbage on the curbs and to separate perishable solid waste

and store it in double bags to minimize health problems. To reduce volume, plastic containers and cardboard boxes should be crushed. Other measures include using household ammonia mixed with water to control odors, storing plastic bags in cool places, using cloth instead of disposable diapers, rinsing all containers before putting in bags, and storing paper and dry waste in safe locations to avoid fire hazards.

The following municipalities have outlined or plan to outline contingency measures:

CLARK — The municipal public works yard and dumpster service is closed until further notice. Pickup of bulky items will also be suspended. The branch-clipping operation will continue by appointment.

Continued on Page 4

GARBAGE is piling up already along Broad Street in Elizabeth's main shopping district as the sanitation workers' strike enters its third day with no new talks scheduled yet.
—Daily Journal Photo by Jon Delano

Reagan's sending message to Soviet

By HELEN THOMAS
UPI White House Reporter

WASHINGTON (UPI) — President Reagan is still probing the Soviets on the prospect of a meeting in Vienna in September and has given a message to Soviet Ambassador Anatoli Dobrynin to carry to the Kremlin later this week.

Reagan turned the other cheek when Moscow rebuffed his proposal to expand talks this fall on banning anti-satellite weapons to include a discussion of medium-range and strategic nuclear missiles.

"We stand by what we proposed yesterday and we are in communication with them," Reagan said during a Rose Garden photo session Monday.

The Soviets first raised the possibility of a meeting on Friday with a proposal to discuss in Vienna this fall the banning of anti-satellite weapons. The Soviet move followed statements by Reagan that the "door is not closed" to such negotiations.

Within a matter of hours Friday, Reagan agreed to meet with the

JUDGE MILTON A. FELLER
He approves public vote

Judge OKs referendum on officials' pay hikes

By WAYNE PARRY
Journal Correspondent

ELIZABETH — A Superior Court judge Monday ordered a referendum in which voters will decide whether to grant retroactive pay raises to Mayor Thomas G. Dunn, the city council and other municipal officials.

Judge Milton A. Feller ordered the referendum after the Citizens League of Elizabeth had gathered sufficient petition signatures challenging the raises.

The attorney representing the city said Monday he was not sure if an appeal would be filed.

"I'm delighted," Citizens League president Leila Poch said Monday. "After such a long unnecessary length of time the citizens will be able to excercise their rights under the democratic process.

"I'm delighted we'll be on the ballot in November," Poch said.

"We've waited a long time for this decision and it's because we stuck to it that the citizens will be able to exercise their rights in government," Poch added.

"I'm pleased at the result, although somewhat disappointed at the means to the end that Judge Feller took," said Gary Gordon, attorney for the Citizens League. "I'm happy that the citizens of Elizabeth will get to vote on the issue in November."

However, voters will only be permitted to vote on the retroactive raises, which run from Jan. 1, 1983, to Dec. 31, 1983.

The increases of between 9 and 15 percent will be permitted from Jan. 1, 1984, to the present because

Continued on Page 7

Top court expands Miranda ruling to include arrests in traffic cases

By SPENCER SHERMAN

WASHINGTON (UPI) — The Supreme Court ordered policemen nationwide to begin telling suspects arrested for minor and serious crimes alike that they have the right

the court said.

The police statement advising people being arrested of their rights is known as the Miranda warning — named after a landmark 1966 decision that said suspects in police custody must be warned of their

hamper the efforts of police to investigate crimes."

Miranda warnings should apply to arrests for lesser offenses, Marshall said, because they were designed "to ensure that the police do not coerce or trick captive sus-

yourself, and if you couldn't, it just wouldn't get done." The *Journal* no longer had an editorial writer, so Editor Richard Hight churned out editorials in addition to his other duties. And what was happening in the newsroom was happening elsewhere. Top advertising officials, for example, were on the telephone selling space.

The Newspaper Guild at the *Journal* was strong, including drivers, maintenance people, and the business office as well as newsroom personnel. By 1979, in addition to the expected disagreement over salary scales, the issue was job classification and union membership. The reduction in staff had led to a situation in which exempt employees (people whose job titles as management exempted them from Guild membership) were doing more and more of the work. Furthermore, Guild members believed the *Journal* was attempting to give employees management titles to exempt them from union membership.

The Guild struck the *Journal* on April 14, 1979, and closed the paper for a single day, a Saturday. The *Journal* does not publish on Sundays, and by Monday the paper was on the streets again, making do with wire copy, management personnel, people brought in from other Hagadone newspapers, and hired guards as drivers.

When it became clear that the strike would be protracted, the Guild began publishing a "strike paper" called the *Community Paper*. The strikers received some support from public officials and readers in Elizabeth, and a number of businesses were reluctant to advertise in what was regarded as a "scab paper," the *Journal*. The strike continued through most of the year, essentially ending in late November 1979 when the Guild decided it could no longer afford to continue funding the *Community Paper*. In the final settlement, the *Journal* made a buyout payment to the strikers, few of whom returned to the paper.

The 1980 Elizabeth *Daily Journal*, with a circulation of 42,244, was a shell of its former self. Its small staff of inexperienced reporters had not yet developed the contacts necessary to provide adequate coverage of the area. But a new publisher, Paul T. Miller II, and a new editor, Richard Vezza, were to help the newspaper begin its climb back to respectability.

"The *Daily Journal* is a paper in transition," said Vezza, when first interviewed in 1982. "Everybody knows that Miller is a good publisher. We also know the strike hurt us and that we have to get over it."

Under Miller and Vezza, the *Daily Journal* gradually added reporters, until by 1984 the newsroom staff consisted of more than 30 full-time journalists and about 15 part-timers. Coverage also improved significantly, and in April 1984 the *Daily Journal* changed from two editions to three zoned editions, remaking as many as four pages of news for each different circulation area. The *Daily Journal* was once again a real newspaper.

The paper's first edition, with a 9:00 a.m. press run, is aimed at Elizabeth, Roselle, and Roselle Park. The second edition, published an hour later, goes to Rahway and Linden, while the third edition is for the rest of Union County. The *Daily Journal* considers itself *the* Union County newspaper, although it apparently has conceded Plainfield to the *Courier-News*.

Vezza is a good editor and his thoughts on the newspaper business are worth repeating. "There are no tricks," he said. "A newspaper has to have depth. There's also a lot of important little news that doesn't mean that much alone but does mean a lot in accumulation. So a paper has to do a lot of small things and act as a communicator. A paper has to stay on top of trends and issues and find them before they become so overwhelming that anyone can see them. A paper should also have fun, with itself and with some of the things that it covers. It should have an element of surprise to it every day. It should be interesting, informative, and entertaining."

The *Daily Journal* lost very few readers in 1981 and 1982, and at that time Vezza argued that the newspaper was financially sound. He said that published reports that the paper was in trouble were based on appearances rather than reality. In 1983, however, the *Daily Journal's* circulation dropped 6 percent, down to 39,303. While the newspaper is fighting these numbers, as demonstrated by the move to three editions, the eventual outcome remains in doubt.

4

Suburban Central New Jersey

The once rural townships of central New Jersey are now almost totally suburban. Middlesex County is virtually filled to the brim, with many of its residents commuting each day to New York. The vast open spaces of Somerset County, which once boasted more horses than people, now host corporate headquarters and suburban housing developments.

The cities and towns that were the hubs of the region—Perth Amboy, New Brunswick, Plainfield, and Somerville—are no longer key commercial centers. The highways, routes 9, 1, 18, 22, and 287, are now the essential avenues of business and commerce for the area. Perth Amboy has been replaced by the Woodbridge shopping center, Plainfield and sleepy Somerville by routes 22 and 287. Only New Brunswick is being revitalized (by Johnson & Johnson), although shoppers have long since left it for the malls on routes 18 and 1.

The newspapers of the area, the *News Tribune*, the *Home News*, and the *Courier-News*, are now entirely suburban as well. The *News Tribune* moved from Perth Amboy to Woodbridge, and the *Courier-News* abandoned Plainfield for Route 22 in Bridgewater. The *Home News* stayed in New Brunswick, although most of its readers live in the more than two dozen suburban communities it serves.

These afternoon newspapers compete with each other on the borders of their territories, and all three are up against the morning *Star-Ledger*, which would like to blanket the area. The papers offer solid local coverage, the *Ledger*'s weak point, and appear to be holding their own, although all seem faced with no-growth situations.

The *Home News*: On the Banks of the Raritan

The *Home News* is a century-old family-owned newspaper still loyal to the city that gave it birth. In 1957, as the paper was outgrowing its plant in downtown New Brunswick, the board of directors chose a new site that appeared to be in the suburbs, but actually lay within the city limits. By 1959 the paper had moved away from the arteriosclerotic downtown area, which was becoming choked with traffic because of the limited access routes and bridges across the Raritan River.

"None of us ever foresaw the traffic congestion that has come," said Publisher William Boyd, who finds his paper again surrounded by creeping development. "In spite of that, it was a very good decision to stay. Our past and our future are connected with the city of New Brunswick." The publisher noted that the newspaper's first choice had been to build along the Raritan River on a tract owned by Johnson & Johnson, the pharmaceutical giant based in the city. J & J decided not to sell the land, Boyd explained, because its master plan was incomplete and the tract had potential importance in the company's future plans. In fact, it was to become a key element in the construction of Johnson & Johnson's new world headquarters two decades later.

While New Brunswick stagnated in the 1960s and 1970s, the *Home News* remained healthy. Advertisements from area shopping centers and from the miles of stores on suburban Route 18 kept the newspaper in the black, and population growth in the surrounding communities resulted in a largely suburban readership. *Home News* circulation rose from roughly 46,000 daily and Sundays in 1963 to 58,840 daily and 67,481 Sundays in 1974, as the newspaper expanded its coverage area to include more than two dozen municipalities in addition to New Brunswick. The *Home News* stretched its circulation area to the boundaries already established by its rivals, the *Courier-News* in the west, the Woodbridge *News Tribune* in the north and east, and the Trenton dailies to the south. But the *Home News* found it difficult to capture territory controlled by others, and as its own suburbs filled, the newspaper became stuck in a no-growth situation. By the end of

1983, although Sunday circulation was up to 73,044, the daily readership of 56,406 actually was slightly less than it had been nine years earlier.

With about 85 percent of its circulation outside of New Brunswick, the *Home News* is clearly a suburban newspaper. But it sees the city as the hub of the region, and believes that the future of the city, the region, and the newspaper, itself, are inevitably linked. "There's no question in my mind that the fortunes of the *Home News* are tied to the economic health of the whole region and irrevocably tied with the fortunes of New Brunswick," explained Publisher Boyd.

Johnson & Johnson's decision to build its headquarters on the downtown site, the creation of New Brunswick Tomorrow (a massive plan to revitalize the city spearheaded by J&J), the construction of a downtown Hyatt Regency Hotel, and the completion of a new bridge across the Raritan River have given Boyd and others hope for the future of the city. "New Brunswick is on its way to becoming a showcase city," said Boyd. "New Brunswick Tomorrow people say calls are coming in from all over the country about it."

The *Home News* operating committee has continuously voted to support New Brunswick Tomorrow, contributing a total of $45,000 through the years.

Sticking with New Brunswick has influenced how city leaders feel about the *Home News*, and being a full taxpaying entity has lent its counsel considerable weight. "We saw later what happened to the *Courier-News* [when it moved from Plainfield to suburban Bridgewater]," said Boyd. "The *Courier* moved out and I think a price was paid. Maybe the tradeoff was worth it—better and easier distribution and so on. But we've heard people from Plainfield and South Plainfield talk against the *Courier* for leaving the city."

The *Home News* decision to stay with New Brunswick represents the kind of responsible optimism for which family-owned newspapers are traditionally noted. But it has also exacerbated the perennial *Home News* question: Is the newspaper too cozy with the city fathers and Johnson & Johnson?

The *Home News* has a long history of journalistic integrity and excellence. The late Hugh Boyd, publisher and chairman of the board for many years, and Robert Rhodes, the executive editor in the 1970s, built a newsroom filled with a remarkable array of exceptional journalists. The stories of the 1970s included pieces on high fees for municipal lawyers, the Old Bridge school board's trip to Las Vegas, questionable land sales, double billings for Monroe's sewer lines, and ties between New Brunswick's garbage contractors and organized crime. Although Hugh Boyd's style was that of high commitment to particular issues, it was also scrupulous and introspective. Much of his time was occupied with long debates and self-arguments about whether to support issues such as New Brunswick Tomorrow, and about how to draw the line between a positive attitude and uncritical support. Hugh Boyd sometimes allowed his personal beliefs to affect newsroom operation, as in the case of his opposition to casino gambling, but such occurrences were few and far between.

Home News coverage of New Brunswick in the 1970s generally was fair to all sides, and it remains reasonably well-balanced today. In fact, the newspaper has been criticized by city fathers and business interests for being negative. Ralph Williamson, the managing editor for news, says the paper has tried to stay away from puffery and drum-beating, and that New Brunswick Tomorrow and city officials have complained that the newspaper never says "anything nice" about New Brunswick's development projects.

William Boyd commented: "We've been criticized by the usual people who feel we're not as supportive as they'd like us to be."

Nevertheless, one veteran reporter complains that the newspaper under Watson Sims, the current editor, is less aggressive than it was under his predecessor, Rhodes. "Sims wants to appear positive," the reporter said. "The go-get-'em attitude isn't around anymore. The pendulum has swung the other way."

Reporter Rudi Larini says that officials from New Brunswick Tomorrow and its subsidiary, the New Brunswick Development Corporation (called DevCo), complained to the *Home News* about his coverage of development issues. Not long afterwards, Larini says, he was offered a job as the paper's second education writer. "Needless to say, I was dumfounded," Larini recalled. Although the editors never expressed dissatisfaction with his work, Larini said Sims told him later: "We think we need a new direction in our downtown coverage."

Larini also was offered a job as copy editor, but he went job-hunting instead, and jumped to the *Star-Ledger*.

Sims says that no changes were made as a result of outside pressure. "I don't say they liked everything he wrote," Sims explained, "but we don't respond to pressure. If we did, we'd be reassigning people every day."

The Larini incident was an isolated case. While it shows that the newspaper is under considerable outside pressure, the consistent fairness of news coverage through the years demonstrates the basic integrity of the operation.

New Brunswick also is the home of Rutgers, the state university of New Jersey. Interestingly, there was a time (up into the 1960s) when the *Home News*' coverage of Rutgers consisted primarily of sports stories. But by the early 1970s, with reporter Stuart Diamond assigned to the beat, Rutgers had become a major area of interest for the newspaper. A study of *Home News* coverage of the university conducted in the 1970s found that the paper was publishing an average of five Rutgers stories a day, and that the paper was using nearly half of the press releases supplied by Rutgers' news service. This level of coverage has continued to the present day. Because the *Home News* makes use of so many releases—and because press releases usually tell "good

Hugh Boyd Versus Casino Gambling

Under the leadership of Hugh Boyd, the *Home News* became the foremost opponent of casino gambling in New Jersey.

Boyd was determined to keep casinos out of the state. He believed casinos were an unsound solution to Atlantic City's problems, that they would create an unseemly atmosphere in the state, and that they would prove an additional inducement to bribery and to the infiltration of organized crime.

The publisher called on Hank Messick, an authority on the mob, to write a *Home News* series on organized crime ties to casinos. A reporter was sent to Las Vegas and returned to write a series on casinos in Nevada. Another series on the growth on legalized gambling across the nation appeared in 1976.

Hugh Boyd

Home News statehouse reporters regularly covered the legislative committees dealing with casinos, and often found the publisher, himself, attending the hearings on the subject. The only other reporter regularly on the scene represented the *Atlantic City Press*, the pro-casino newspaper. Curiously, the two papers share office space in the statehouse.

The *Home News* articles and editorials raised such dander that Boyd was attacked on the floor of the Assembly by pro-casino forces who suggested, wrongly, that he was in league with Las Vegas interests who wanted to confine casinos to Nevada.

Although Boyd did not work with any organized groups to campaign against casino gambling, his influence may have been evident in the solid vote of the Somerset and Middlesex legislators against putting the question on the ballot.

"He tried terribly hard to be fair," William Boyd said of his father. "He and I used to talk about it a lot because he was so personally involved in this issue. I felt I should talk to him about the possibility that we would not be objective. But he was scrupulously careful and fair in our approach. We certainly had our most experienced reporters working on it."

news" stories—the newspaper's coverage of Rutgers is generally positive, but no close relationship has developed between the paper and the university.

The *Home News* is a serious newspaper, with a full-time news staff of 74 plus a dozen or so professional part-timers. Many of its municipal reporters cover a single town. It has a four-person business staff. One reporter is on permanent assignment in Trenton, while a second helps out on legislative days and writes state stories from elsewhere. A reporter who covered environmental and energy issues has not been replaced, but in his stead there is a full-time science and medicine writer. An education writer covers Rutgers University, the state education department, and the New Brunswick schools. The paper covers the Middlesex and Somerset county offices and court houses, and has three police reporters. One reporter covers senior citizens on about a half-time basis, and there is an enterprise-investigative reporter, although he is expected to help on daily coverage from time to time. There is a large sports staff, and the paper produces much of its own entertainment writing.

It is an excellent staff, even though many of the star reporters of the 1970s have moved on, including Stuart Diamond (to *Newsday*, and now with the *New York Times*), investigative reporters Michael Norman and Ron Gollobin (to the *Trenton Times*, and now with the *New York Times* and the ABC Boston affiliate), reporter Robert Windrem (now a producer for NBC Nightly News), and reporters Michael Hoyt and Daniel Lazare (to the Bergen *Record*). Windrem explains, "What happens on a recurring basis at the *Home News* is that a good staff comes along because the paper is unionized and pays well."

The *Home News* has three editions. The first, for towns north of the Raritan River in Middlesex (in competition with the Woodbridge *News Tribune* to the east and the *Courier-News* to the west), is out by 10 a.m. The Somerset County edition follows, stretching as far as Bridgewater and Montgomery (in competition with the *Courier-News*, and the Trenton dailies to the south). Then comes the "South County" edition, which circulates as far south of the Raritan as South Brunswick and Plainsboro (in competition with the Trenton dailies), and as far east as Old Bridge, Sayreville, and South Amboy (against the *News Tribune* and even the *Asbury Park Press*). While the last edition is normally out by 11:30 a.m., it can be held until 1:30 p.m., as it was for the inauguration of President Reagan and the simultaneous release of the hostages in Iran.

The *Home News* wants to be a complete newspaper, unlike the *News Tribune*, which has reconciled itself to purely local coverage. But in order to be able to afford to expand its news coverage, the *Home News* needs to break out of its no-growth situation.

One attempt came in 1978 when the *Home News* moved into Woodbridge,

Fall foliage tours
On the go!

The Home News

Housing
starts drop
B6

Living in style
A17

SERVING CENTRAL NEW JERSEY SINCE 1879 ★ THURSDAY, SEPTEMBER 20, 1984 25¢

TALKING WITH THE POPE

Pope John Paul II accepts a "talking stick" in Vancouver, Canada, from John George, an elder of the Salish Nation. The stick bestows on the recipient the authority to speak at public occasions. The pope yesterday promoted a "new vision of humanity." Story on Page A4.

Dems: Extra cash should fund string of state programs

By TOM HESTER
Home News Trenton Bureau

The Democrats also want to use surplus funds to provide pay increases for teachers, especially those who excel in teaching mathematics and science, Karcher said. Money also would be used for displaced homemaker and infant health care programs.

TRENTON — The Legislature's Democratic leadership was proposing to Republican Gov. Thomas Kean today that the record state budget surplus be used to fund a string of programs, including the cleanup of hazardous-waste sites, construction of sewers and pay increases for teachers.

The Democrats also planned to propose giving a portion of the money back to taxpayers. Assembly Speaker Alan J. Karcher, D-Middlesex, said yesterday that he wants taxpayers to get a $75 credit on their state income tax return as reimbursement for the gross receipts utility taxes they pay.

Kean said yesterday, "Our priorities are not going to be that different," but he wants his proposal for a one-time increase of the homestead rebate from $39 to $86 to be the taxpayer giveback, rather than the tax credit proposed by Karcher.

The governor, Karcher and the rest of the Legislature Democratic and Republican leaderships were scheduled to meet at the Statehouse on what to do with the surplus, which is expected to be at least $417 million by June 30.

"I think we are in tune with the governor," Karcher said after the Democrats discussed their strategy at a luncheon meeting yesterday in Princeton. "I think our thinking is running parallel with the governor's."

"Good. That's just what I asked them to do," Kean said when told of the

impending Democratic proposals. "They will present some of their priorities and we will present some of our priorities. Once we see what the priorities are, we'll match them against the potential revenue."

Karcher said the Democrats want to create an infrastructure bank that would help fund the cleanup of hazardous-waste sites and the construction of sewer lines and solid-waste treatment plants. He said that after initial funding with surplus revenue, the bank could be financed by dedicating 1 percent of the current 6 per-

See SURPLUS, Page A20

Reagan stumps in Hammonton; talks patriotism

By ROBERT WADE
Associated Press

HAMMONTON — This small ethnic Republican stronghold unfurled a red, white and blue welcome as a campaigning President Reagan came to town to tell more than 10,000 flag-waving supporters they "are what America is all about."

The crowd chanted "Four more years!" as Reagan's 20-car motorcade reached the downtown business district yesterday, proclaimed "Ronald Reagan Day."

As Reagan left the farming community of 12,000 between Atlantic City and Philadelphia, state police received a report that a gunman had been seen along the motorcade route. But officers found only a man with a camera apparently trying to photograph the president.

Against a backdrop of bunting and streetlight poles each adorned with three American flags, Reagan told the crowd:

"I think there is a new feeling of patriotism in our land, a recognition that, by any standard, America is a decent and generous place, a force for good in the world — and we're a little tired of hearing people run her down.

"We've come through some rough times, but we've come through them together — all of us, from every race, religion and ethnic background," he said from a flag-flanked podium in front of a bank.

Reagan noted that his Democratic challenger, Walter F. Mondale, announced his package of tax increases and spending cuts in Philadelphia last week.

He said Mondale could have proposed his plan in Atlantic City, where there is legalized gambling, "but then, that would have been unfair."

"The people who go to Atlantic City gamble with their own money, not yours," Reagan said.

He attacked the deficit-reduction

SEA OF FACES — President Reagan addressing a crowd estimated at 10,000 people yesterday in downtown Hammonton, a South Jersey community.

trust fund Mondale has said he would establish for revenues from his $177 billion additional tax revenues over four years.

"I don't think you in South Jersey

believe your families were put on this earth just to help them (the Democrats) make government bigger. They want to enact a massive

See FLAGS, Page A20

P. Amboy boy dies in eight-story fall

By BARBARA S. GREENE
Home News staff

A 21-month-old boy fell to his death from an eighth-story window yesterday afternoon at the Gelber Apartments housing project on Huntington Street in Perth Amboy.

Police are treating the incident as an accident but continue to investigate how the child, Anthony Quiles, maneuvered himself from a crib to the window of a bedroom in the apartment.

His mother, Egrid Quiles, apparently had placed him in the crib to take a nap shortly before the incident occurred. She returned to the bedroom to check on Anthony about 2 p.m., police said, but did not see him. She then was drawn to the window by a commotion outside.

The baby was pronounced dead on the scene by a doctor at Perth Amboy General Hospital who was in communication with the hospital's Mobile Intensive Care Unit crew by a telemetric hookup. The Perth Amboy First Aid Squad also responded.

An autopsy was scheduled today by the Middlesex County Medical Examiner to determine the exact cause of death.

Police could not determine from the report whether the baby landed on the sidewalk surrounding the apartment building or on the dirt just beyond the pavement.

There are no guards on the window of the nine-story, low-income housing project.

Home News staff writer Jack Lutton contributed to this story.

Woodbridge to vote on appointed school board

By TED SERRILL
Home News staff

WOODBRIDGE — Township residents will decide Nov. 6 whether the Board of Education should be appointed by the mayor.

Woodbridge residents have voted down the school budget proposed by the elected Board of Education for 25 consecutive years. With an appointed board, the budget no longer would be submitted to voters. Final approval would come instead from a Board of School Estimate, which would be composed of the mayor, Township Council members and school board members. The mayor and elected council members would outnumber the school board members on the Board of School Estimate.

New Brunswick and Edison have the only appointed school boards in Middlesex County. There are 32 appointed boards among the approximately 600 school districts in the state.

The Township Council approved placing the question on the ballot by a 5-4 vote Tuesday.

Several previous attempts were made to place the question of an appointed board on the ballot. This time, the council decided to put the question before the electorate.

Six of the nine council members support Republican Mayor Philip M. Cerria.

The council vote was prompted by Tex Perry, a longtime citizen "watchdog," who asked that the matter of an appointed board finally be settled.

U.S. EMBASSY ANNEX ATTACKED

Explosive-packed car kills 10 in Beirut

By TERRY A. ANDERSON
Associated Press

BEIRUT, Lebanon — A car filled with explosives crashed into the U.S. Embassy annex in east Beirut today, severely damaging the six-story building and reportedly killing at least 10 people.

U.S. Ambassador Reginald Bar-

tholomew was among about 20 people reportedly wounded, according to the Christian-owned Voice of Lebanon radio. Its report said the casualties included people inside the annex compound and outside, but it did not give a breakdown of the victims' nationalities. There were reports Bartholomew was hospitalized in intensive care.

It said Bartholomew suffered "various wounds" in the explosion and was taken to hospital. Several diplomats on the scene were bloodstained with bandages and bloodstained clothes, refused to comment on the report.

The Voice of Lebanon said four floors on the west side of the annex sustained considerable damage from

the blast that went off shortly before midday.

In Washington, State Department Press Officer Sondra McCarty said: "Apparently a car did approach the embassy, went through the gate and blew up the embassy annex. There was some severe damage. There are injuries and deaths, but we have no figures now. As of right now, there are no known American deaths. Our

See BLAST, Page A20

Weather
Today: sunny, warm; low 80s.
Tonight: clear, around 50.

INSIDE TODAY

World
China to regain Hong Kong in 1997 .... A4
Pope urges 'new vision of humanity' A4

the largest municipality in Middlesex County and the home of the largest shopping center in the area. Because the *News Tribune* has no Sunday edition, the *Home News* tried to step in and fill the void, assigning one of its top reporters to write about Woodbridge for the Sunday paper. The effort has not been very successful, largely because of logistical problems. "It's hard to start a Sunday-only route for a carrier and then try to convert a Sunday reader to a seven-day reader," explained Boyd. As a result, the second step, a major move into Bridgewater, home base of the *Courier-News*, has never really been tried, and Princeton continues to be viewed as the province of the Trenton dailies.

The *Home News* emphasis on providing a complete newspaper suggests that it has come to see the *Star-Ledger* as its chief rival. Sims and Boyd confirm that the *Home News* is seriously considering conversion to a morning newspaper. (Its Saturday paper has already been converted.) Its Sunday edition, although healthy and outselling the daily product, is thinner than the *Star-Ledger* and more expensive. "It's really rare that a metropolitan paper sells for less than a suburban Sunday," Boyd noted. "I'm more concerned about the *Star-Ledger* as a competitor for price than about ad lineage."

In addition, a study done for the paper by Belden Associates of Dallas suggests that the *Home News* should not be too localized in its approach, and that it should increase its state coverage. While Boyd said that the paper would continue to look for the local angle in state news, the *Home News* clearly wants more regional reporting, and is placing less emphasis on the faithful recording of long and dull municipal meetings—even if this means getting beaten occasionally. Williamson explained that most of the suburban report-ers, who normally work nightside covering meetings, now put in part of their time in the afternoons doing interviews for stories beyond their regular nightly beats. This emphasis on regional reporting is exemplified by Laura Sanders' 1982 series on the impact of vacancy decontrol of rental housing in Middlesex County towns, and by Todd Bates' series in the same year on the Wheelabrator-Fry proposal for a garbage-to-energy plant in East Brunswick. To do the Wheelabrator-Fry piece, Bates went so far as to visit the company's facilities in Saugus, Mass.

"We have more substance," Williamson said. "A lot of newspapers went overboard a few years ago on stories about how to mend lawn chairs. People are baffled; they want help, information to make decisions. The print media play a very large part in that."

Despite the *Home News*' problems trying to break into Woodbridge, Williamson believes the *News Tribune* will have trouble surviving. "The central Jersey market will eventually shake down to two papers," he said. "It may take 10 years or 15 but the market's got to condense. It will be Gannett [the *Courier-News*] and us."

Although frustrated by the no-growth situation, no one at the *Home News* is worried about survival. They are betting on the New Brunswick turn-around, and the strength of the organization, now a mini-conglomerate owning five weekly newspapers, seven radio stations, two television stations, and one-third of *New Jersey Monthly* magazine. And they are betting on their own high quality as a newspaper.

The content analysis of 1977 newspapers conducted for this project supports the view that the *Home News* is an excellent newspaper. The study of 1974 New Jersey newspapers done by the Center for Analysis of Public Issues, on the other hand, painted a rather ordinary picture. It showed a 42-page newspaper with 26 pages of ads and 16 pages of news—ninth in advertising, but only tied for 12th in news. The 1974 *Home News* ranked eighth in the amount of national news, ninth in state news, 12th in local news, and 18th in foreign coverage. Journalists surveyed by the Center in 1974 ranked the paper fourth best in investigative reporting, then its strongest suit.

The Sachsman study found the *Home News* to be a superior newspaper—fifth best in the state. The 1977 *Home News*, with 23 pages of ads and 20 pages of news, ranked eighth in advertising and tied for seventh in news. It ranked seventh in the total number of news and feature stories, tied for fifth in state news and international coverage, and was sixth in the use of longer news stories. The paper tied for eighth in local coverage, tied for ninth for locally originated reporting, and ranked 10th for its use of photographs. Every score was in the top 10, and only four other newspapers (the Camden *Courier-Post*, the *Asbury Park Press*, the *Star-Ledger*, and the Bergen *Record*) ranked higher on average.

While the future of New Brunswick is still an open question, the self-confidence of the *Home News* clearly is well deserved.

"Where the Hell Is Bridgewater, New Jersey?"

In its location at least, the *Courier-News* is the quintessential suburban newspaper. Its plant lies in Bridgewater, a vast suburban tract whose only distinction is that it affords ready access to routes 22 and 287. These are vital roads for a newspaper with a circulation area covering all of Somerset and Hunterdon counties and parts of Union, Mercer, and Morris counties. While the readership is primarily suburban, the area includes many rural townships, and inner-city districts such as Plainfield.

The *Courier-News* was once the Plainfield newspaper, but it moved out to its new plant in 1972. The move made perfect sense in Rochester, N.Y., the home of the Gannett chain (which owns 85 daily newspapers including *USA Today*). Plainfield was on the eastern end of the newspaper's circulation area, which had been expanding steadily westward. And Plainfield, itself, was viewed as a city of declining circulation, decreased retail sales, and increased racial minorities. Many Plainfield residents resented the move, arguing that the *Courier-News* was a rootless paper run by an absentee ownership whose only consideration was the bottom line.

The anti-Gannett argument is clearly stated by Lore Fiedler, who retired from the *Courier-News* in 1980 after 18 years of service. She contends that the people in the newsroom are not personally committed to the local communities the newspaper covers. They are interested instead in advancing their own careers, in moving up through the fluid Gannett organization—a system that offers reporters rare opportunities for advancement as executives, managers, or national Gannett News Service writers.

"It's a paper full of internal machinations," Fiedler said, "of young people who want to move ahead. They come here not because the *Courier-News* is a good paper, but because it's a Gannett paper."

Gannett editors and publishers, the argument goes, are also people on the move, and the 1970s saw a number of leadership changes at the *Courier-News*. One newly appointed publisher, according to an apocryphal tale told by Fiedler, when assigned to the *Courier-News* asked, "Where the hell is Bridgewater, New Jersey?"

While there is some truth to the anti-Gannett argument, the move to Bridgewater was a wise business decision, making distribution of the newspaper faster and easier. And the news product of the *Courier-News* is much better than it was a generation ago, when the paper had a reputation for civic boosterism rather than professionalism. Furthermore, in recent years the leadership of the paper has been solidly grounded in the state. David Mazzarella, a Newark native who was once editor of the Rutgers *Targum*, was editor of the *Courier-News* from 1977 to 1979 and publisher of the paper from 1979 to mid-1983. Executive Editor Charles W. Nutt Jr., who was born in Dover, worked for the *Courier-News* for nine years, then moved on to the *New York Times* and the editorship of the Easton (Pa.) *Express*, returning to the Gannett fold in 1981.

The style and substance of today's *Courier-News* is the product of Mazzarella and Nutt, although Mazzarella has now moved up the Gannett ladder to become general manager of *USA Today* in the New York market area. The current publisher of the *Courier-News* is Thomas Curley, formerly publisher of the Norwich (Conn.) *Bulletin*.

The *Courier-News* has a full-time staff of 54, plus 20 part-timers. Normally this would be considered a reasonable newsroom for a 56,932-circulation

The Courier-News in the 1970s

The mid-1970s was a very good time for a number of New Jersey newspapers, but for others, like the *Courier-News*, it was a period of very little change, with no growth in circulation, no growth in advertising, and no improvement in its news pages.

The study conducted by the Center for Analysis of Public Issues showed the 1974 *Courier-News* to be one of the top 10 newspapers in the state. The 43-page newspaper had somewhat more than 26 pages of advertising and slightly less than 17 pages of news. With these numbers it tied for seventh in advertising and ranked 10th in the amount of news. It was fifth in local coverage, seventh in national news, 10th in foreign news, and 20th in state coverage.

The content analysis of New Jersey newspapers conducted by David Sachsman just three years later found the 1977 *Courier-News* to be very similar in size and makeup to its 1974 counterpart. But while the Bridgewater newspaper had stayed the same, other New Jersey newspapers had improved significantly, and in the rankings the *Courier-News* was no longer among the top 10.

The Gannett product was now a 37-page newspaper with 21 pages of ads and 16 pages of news. In 1977, the *Courier-News* still tied for 11th in advertising despite the apparent loss of five pages of ads, but its news hole only tied for 15th, even though it was virtually the same size as it had been three years earlier. It tied for fourth in the number of local stories, tied for ninth in international news, ranked 11th in national news, and tied for 19th in state coverage. Because only its local stories were locally written, it tied for 15th in the number of locally originated stories. It tied for 17th for its use of photographs, and tied for 20th for the number of longer stories. In 1977, the *Courier-News* was indeed a rather ordinary New Jersey newspaper.

---

newspaper with no Sunday edition, but the *Courier-News* covers 43 municipalities, four county governments, and four county courthouses, and thus *Courier-News* reporters are spread pretty thin. With so many municipal beats to cover, the newspaper has little room for specialized reporters. Nevertheless, it houses sports, lifestyle, and business writers, an entertainment writer, an education writer, a consumer reporter, and a medical-health writer (who also does environmental reporting), and it has a position for an investigative reporter.

The paper does not employ a political writer because, Mazzarella said, "We would have to sacrifice something else, and we can use our resources more fruitfully." Nutt said that most of the political figures in the area (a jumble of county lines and legislative districts) are not sufficiently well known to warrant extensive coverage. On the other hand, samplings have shown that people want medical and health news.

Courier-News marketing surveys consistently point to reader interest in local news, and thus the newspaper's assiduous coverage of individual municipalities. In 1980, the paper introduced the "Town Crier," a page or more of highly localized news, which is made over for each of the paper's three different circulation zones. And in 1981, it revamped its front page, adding a "News Break" section, which also is remade for each edition.

The *Courier-News* is not alone in this local emphasis. Municipal meeting coverage is a giant undertaking for many of the state's regional newspapers. Most of the meetings are at night, which creates a busy nightside. Reporters and editors coming in from other states often are astonished at the coverage of New Jersey's local municipalities, particularly if they come from areas where county operations are more important and local government is minimal.

In recent years, the *Courier-News* has been moving away from slavish coverage of every municipal meeting. "This is the way we use part-timers," Nutt said. "We don't physically show up for as many meetings as we did 10 years ago. We try to keep on top." Reporters are expected to know what is coming up, and to attend any meeting that promises to produce news. The paper is willing to live with an occasional slip-up, Nutt said.

The *Courier-News* uses aggressive editing to explain how local news items have meaning for other towns in the area, the editor said, and in-depth reports sometimes grow out of such local coverage. A story about colleges recruiting students by education writer Marilyn Marks originated with a number of local examples, and a story on counterfeit name-brand items by business writer Victoria Shannon followed from a local arrest.

The *Courier-News* also has increased its use of columnists and wire and international news, aiming to provide a complete news service rather than just a local newspaper. "One problem we've faced," Nutt said, "is that on one side there's the *Star-Ledger* news hole, which goes on forever with complete, if rather dry and uninteresting, coverage of state government. And on the other side we have weeklies like the Hunterdon *Democrat*, with a circulation of 20,000, and the Somerset *Messenger-Gazette*, with a circulation of 15,000. Does the *Courier-News* find a role that fits somewhere in between these two, or does it become a complete newspaper, the best of both? We want our readers to think they can get our paper and don't need another. We don't have to be a second paper."

Mazzarella said he is not sure which newspaper is the *Courier-News*' chief competitor. "In terms of instinct, one would have to say the *Star-Ledger*," he observed. "It's big, and therefore it's an easy target." In addition to the *Ledger* and the many weeklies in the area, the *Courier-News* competes with the

Rockin' Jersey

Prince, Elton John and ZZ Top lead the fall concert roster

— Story on Page C1

Expanded sports

Expos 7, Mets 0
Indians 11, Twins 10
Red Sox 5, Orioles 4
Cardinals 4, Cubs 1
Padres 4, Braves 2
High school football:
Somerville 0
Bridgewater East 0
—D Section

The Courier-News

A cool weekend: 60s today, Sunday In 40s both nights

Weather details, Page A-2

A Gannett Newspaper Serving Central Jersey   Bridgewater, Saturday, September 29, 1984   722-8800   25 Cents

---

Behind the burgers

Fast-food firms offer first jobs, flexibility

By LESLIE WERSTEIN
Courier-News Staff Writer

HILLSBOROUGH — It's 5:30 a.m., hours before even fast-food junkies start thinking about french fries, but the McDonald's restaurant on Route 206 already has its grill fired up.

Like a director making last-minute checks before the curtain goes up, assistant manager Debbie Van Norman runs over to check the coffee.

"You guys all ready to open?" she yells. "Yep, all ready," comes a reply from behind the grill. Tony DiMarchi, 18, cracks a few eggs and grabs bread from a toaster. At 6 a.m., Van Norman unlocks the doors.

Across the country, thousands of similar fast-food crews are braced for another day. Van Norman and DeMarchi are two soldiers in the army of 800,000 fast-food workers nationwide, a legion growing in numbers and diversity.

By 1995, the fast-food labor force is expected to grow by 37 percent, to 1.1 million, or about 1 percent of the labor force, according to Samuel Ehrenhalt, regional commissioner of the U.S. Bureau of Labor Statistics in New York.

But as an entry-level employer, the effect is broader than its statistics: It's a nationwide job training center. Each year, it hires and trains hundreds of thousands of people few others fill; many of them move on within single season.

The industry traditionally has offered a first job for teen-agers. But today, it increasingly provides

Sarah Walsh bags fries at the Hillsborough McDonald's on Route 206.

Courier-News Photo by Kathy Johnson

jobs for unskilled workers, mothers, senior citizens and others who need part-time work and flexible hours.

Behind the counters, first-time workers absorb good work habits, said Ted Gershon, operations director of Frank Quinn Inc., which owns and operates four McDonald's stores, including the one in Hillsborough.

And others take advantage of the flexible schedule. One example is 27-year-old Kathy Hussey, a single mother raising a son, who first found a spot at the East Windsor

McDonald's and now works at its store here.

"If I need a half day or to change my hours because my son is sick or something, I can get it because of the flexible hours," Hussey said. "You can't find that and good benefits at many other places."

Van Norman's job is her livelihood, but she recognizes that some of her co-workers are too young to know the meaning of dedication and responsibility.

"A lot of them take it as just some extra spending money," she

said. "They don't always care, and they'll just call out (sick). In my position, you'll always be here and work late because you know you have to keep the job."

Van Norman started behind the counter — in the industry jargon, a crew worker — and she aspires to be the youngest and only woman store manager in the Quinn chain.

But she doesn't want to move beyond that in the corporation because "I'd be pulling myself away

Continued on section's back page

Reagan, Gromyko trade views on arms

WASHINGTON (AP) — President Reagan, bent on improving U.S.-Soviet relations in the twilight of his first term, conducted nearly four hours of "very strong and useful" talks yesterday with Soviet Foreign Minister Andrei A. Gromyko, but no breakthroughs or agreements were announced.

After the meeting, Gromyko issued a statement saying the conversation with Reagan "does not, unfortunately, make it possible to draw a conclusion about practical

positive changes in the foreign-policy course of the U.S. administration."

When asked whether Reagan and Gromyko had agreed on anything during their talks, Secretary of State George P. Shultz told reporters: "They agreed to keep in touch."

"It was a very strong and useful interchange and Mr. Gromyko expressed his views very powerfully and aggressively, as he always does,

Continued on section's back page

Mystery sickness baffles officials

By LEE McDONALD
Courier-News Staff Writer

FRANKLIN (Somerset) — A mysterious illness is plaguing workers at the Federal Express center here, and so far, it has stumped an array of public and private investigators.

The problem began last month, when seven employees reported symptoms including weakness, dizziness, sore throats and shortness of breath. It hit its peak on Tuesday, when 60 employees went home sick with the same symptoms, company spokesman Armond Snyder said yesterday.

"We still have no idea what caused this," said Snyder, who flew in from company headquarters in Memphis,

Tenn., to help deal with the problem. "All we can say is that we are doing the best that we can, and we should find the cause very soon."

The investigation has expanded to include representatives from the township Board of Health and state health organizations, toxicologists from Rutgers University and officials from the Occupational Health and Safety Administration.

The Federal Express call center, on Belmont Street, employs 592 workers; 400 are on duty during peak business hours, Snyder said. It serves as the area's main pickup and delivery center and is the customer

Continued on section's back page

Special-interest contributions become hot campaign issue

By PAT ORDOVENSKY
Gannett News Service

WASHINGTON — Money, once called the mother's milk of politics, vividly is becoming an issue on its own in the 1984 campaign.

Charges are becoming louder and more frequent that special-interest political committees — commonly called PACs — are pouring so much money into congressional races that they're corrupting the democratic

process and buying a stranglehold on the U.S. Capitol.

"There's a growing awareness that the PAC system is a rotten system ... It's undermining the integrity of Congress," says Fred Wertheimer, president of Common Cause, the self-styled citizens lobby.

On the other side, people who run the PACs say they're exercising their members' right to take part in the political process by contributing

money to help their friends stay in office.

"I hope the public realizes that PAC money is contributions from thousands of individuals organized for a common purpose," says Austin Atkinson, PAC director for the National Association of Life Underwriters.

Wertheimer says the money is buying influence in Congress and tilting the legislative process in favor of the special interests. Atkinson says

PACs are just helping their friends "meet the enormous cost of campaigns."

"There's no question, the fact that we contribute increases our access (to Congress members) so our story can be told when legislation important to us arises," says Tom Baker, PAC director for the National Association of Home Builders. "It seems to us an obvious right that we should have."

"They say they're only buying ac-

cess," says Common Cause's Wertheimer, "but even if that's all they were getting it would be dead wrong. Buying access is no more acceptable in our democracy than buying influence or buying results."

In the presidential races, Ronald Reagan and Walter Mondale each face a spending ceiling of $40.4 million — all of it from the U.S. Treasury. Because they're taking public funds, they can't accept private donations from individuals or PACs.

The political parties, however, have found loopholes to raise private funds to help their presidential candidates with such activities as voter registration and turnout. The private money won't count toward the $40 million limit.

And groups such as the National Conservative Political Action Committee are spending millions on their own — instead of giving it to candidates

Continued on section's back page

Teen found innocent of slaying at dance

By MICHAEL J. KELLY
Courier-News Staff Writer

ELIZABETH — A 17-year-old Plainfield youth was found not guilty yesterday of killing a Fanwood teen-ager, seven months after the murder conviction of another teen-ager deemed as the defendant's ac-

However, the jury did conclude that Kelly was at the scene and did fire shots: It found him guilty of possessing a handgun for an unlawful purpose and possessing a handgun without a permit.

The accomplice in the shooting — Jerry "Rock" Lee, 18, of Plainfield

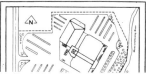

Developer plans mall overlooking river on Hunterdon border

By TOM NUTILE
Courier-News Staff Writer

An enclosed shopping mall that would overlook the Musconetcong River and feature gourmet food

Washington Borough and six miles from Clinton, the architect, Cyril Beveridge, said from his Clinton office.

The mall could be complete by the

Covering Plainfield: Access to Crime News

Although the *Courier-News* moved out of Plainfield in 1972, the city continues to be an important area of coverage for the newspaper. So important that in July 1980 the paper published a special 48-page, no-advertising tabloid supplement on the city and its life. "A lot of ink has been flowing for a lot of years about the big cities—Detroit and Philadelphia and many others—but less has been written about the smaller towns," Mazzarella said. "That's why we called it 'Plainfield, U.S.A.' "

When Mayor Everett Lattimore took office in 1982, Plainfield became a difficult city to cover. Lattimore decreed a new crime news policy: information would be withheld from the press until police officials reviewed and deleted whatever they regarded as unnecessary for the public to know.

The *Courier-News* took issue with the policy on its editorial pages, and made news stories out of several incidents in which information had been slow in coming. In one case in February 1982, the police provided the newspaper with meager details about an armed robbery, not mentioning that a 10-year-old boy had been shot during the holdup. It took the *Courier-News* almost three days to get the story after police in a neighboring community provided a tip.

Charles Allen, the Plainfield public safety director, admitted that one reason for the policy was concern about the city's image as a high-crime area. But he said that the policy was designed primarily to protect crime victims from further distress or even further harassment.

Nutt acknowledged that it was often painful for crime victims to read details in the paper, but maintained that reporting such details as the locations of crimes constituted a public service. The editor said that the problem of access to crime news ranges far beyond Plainfield, and is actually more prevalent in

Easton *Express* in western Hunterdon County, the *Trenton Times* in northern Mercer County, the *Home News* in border towns like Piscataway, the *News Tribune* in South Plainfield, and the Elizabeth *Daily Journal* in Westfield.

Mazzarella said the *Courier-News* is not particularly interested in expanding its coverage into additional areas. "We cover 43 towns and we're spread thin as it is," he said. "To cover a 44th and 45th we'd have to diminish our coverage elsewhere." Furthermore, he said, moving into another newspaper's territory rarely works. People buy the paper for a time as a novelty but eventually revert back to the more home-based paper.

Through the 1970s and into 1981, the circulation of the *Courier-News* held consistently around 59,000. The enormous population growth in the Bridgewater area had ended, and everyone was waiting for southern Somerset

rural areas, where a reporter's access to information often depends on the whim of the senior police official on duty at the time.

"We know from the police reports that we print each month that there are a lot of crimes that the police don't tell us about," Nutt said. "In some cases, that's simply because the departments are so small that the people aren't there. In other cases, maybe they've been so busy they don't want to be bothered. And sometimes maybe they have deliberately withheld it because they don't want their community to get a bad reputation."

In Plainfield, the access issue seemed to simmer down in late 1982 although the screening process continued. It flared up again in spring 1983 when the *Courier-News* received a tip that a well-dressed young man had been knocking on the doors of elderly people asking to use their phones, and then had been robbing them. The Plainfield police had reported this simply as a robbery on X block, keeping the public in the dark as to the robber's method of operation.

And then in June 1983 the police reported that a sexual assault had occurred, and gave the block number. Ten days later the prosecutor's office asked the police to release a composite sketch of the assailant to the *Courier-News*, and gave the details of the case to the paper. Again a public safety issue was involved since the assailant was still at large, and the woman in the case had simply been waiting at a traffic light while driving through the city at night when she was pulled from her car and sexually assaulted.

Clearly the public needs to know when and where to exercise a reasonable degree of caution, and such information is the by-product of crime news. When access to crime news is restricted, the details that are withheld often contain precisely that information the public needs to know. "Plainfield really woke us up," said Nutt. But the editor fears that some public officials may have learned the opposite lesson from the Plainfield situation, and that the trend toward restricting information may be on the increase.

County and Hunterdon County to take off. "Any afternoon paper that doesn't lose circulation is growing," Mazzarella quipped in 1982. But by the end of that year, the *Courier-News*' circulation had slipped to 56,932, and advertising (especially help-wanted advertising) was showing the effects of the nationwide recession. Mazzarella and Nutt had been building up the full-time staff from 54 in 1979 to 60 in 1981. But management responded to the economic conditions by cutting costs, reducing the size of the newsroom—by attrition—from 60 full-time staffers back down to 54. (Attrition comes naturally at the *Courier-News*, a nonunion shop that hires young people, works them hard, and expects them to move on, either inside or outside of Gannett.)

By 1983 circulation was down to 55,619. Nutt argues that the *Courier-News* was a top-10 newspaper in the 1970s with 54 news people, and that it can be a top-10 paper today with the same number of staffers. Others disagree, and in general the newspaper receives rather mixed reviews from professionals questioned. All agree, however, that today's *Courier-News* has integrity and credibility. Its leadership and staff represent newspaper professionalism.

The Very Local *News Tribune* of Woodbridge

A decision of some moment was made at the *News Tribune* in 1981: the newspaper stopped running college graduation lists.

"I hated to do it, but I agreed," said Editor Charles Paolino. "What killed us was the county colleges." The newspaper still runs a graduation item as a personal if it is sent in directly by the graduate or the family, he said, explaining, "For those to whom it's important, we'll use it." Otherwise, the college list has gone the way of the Dean's List, which also was dropped by the *News Tribune* for lack of space.

Nevertheless, the newspaper still runs high school graduation lists—and sends reporters to cover the ceremonies—because "it's a pivotal point in a family's history," Paolino said. And a photograph of the bride is still run in wedding stories, because, said the editor, "we think once in a lifetime people should open the paper and see somebody they know who hasn't been murdered or arrested."

That's how it goes at *The News Tribune*, known as *TNT*—a name and set of initials it chose for itself when it moved out of Perth Amboy more than a decade ago and dropped the name of the *Perth Amboy Evening News*. (To be known just as *The Evening News* sounded too much like the still breathing *Newark Evening News*.)

Paolino, who started at *TNT* as a reporter in 1965, and Managing Editor Lois DiTommaso, who has been there almost as long, labor continuously to produce a newspaper that remains very, very local—even though some staff members have chafed at what they considered excessive provincialism.

Local coverage, however, does not mean just municipal meetings. "We are tending to get away from the myopic idea that everybody lives in the municipal building," Paolino said. "We still give people municipal coverage, of course, sometimes in spite of themselves, because they should have it and know about it. But we try to supply their wants as well as their needs. In the amalgam, a municipal beat reporter should be painting a picture of the town, and that's more than just city hall reporting."

Some reporters balk. "The Cub Scouts are a bone of contention with us," the editor said. "The management considers the paper in a way a public utility, something we have to place at the disposal of people. We don't want to get into a lot of stuff about somebody whose sofa wasn't properly upholstered, but we want to help people with serious problems." For example Paolino pointed to coverage of Hand-In-Hand, a support group for the retarded and their families.

Geographical beats are central to the newspaper's operation. Out of a newsroom complement of 58 (not counting stringers), *TNT* fields 11 municipal beat reporters, most of whom cover more than one municipality. The paper also has two people in the Middlesex County complex in New Brunswick (one for county government and one for courts), a reporter in the Monmouth County complex in Freehold, and a statehouse reporter in Trenton.

The newspaper's local emphasis extends to the statehouse. The reporter in Trenton (currently Tom Damm) concentrates on regional legislators and their doings, augmented on legislative days with a second staffer. The emphasis on local legislators "has been easy," said Paolino, because people like Assembly Speaker Alan Karcher have played leading legislative roles.

Nine staffers are assigned to sports. ("I want at least one local story on the lead sports page each day," Di Tommaso said.) The paper has two lifestyle writers (the section is called "Tempo"), a full-time arts writer, and a senior citizens writer. In recent years *TNT* has stepped up its non-news leisure features. Its weekly tabloid insert, "This 'N' That," is the counterpart to the *Home News'* "Enjoy!" and the *Courier-News'* "Friday Plus" and "Weekend." And the Thursday Youth Page, which was inaugurated in 1981, was designed to provide feature material for teenagers. ("Hopefully it will cause people in their teens to read a newspaper," Di Tommaso said at the time. "We would like them to buy the paper someday.")

All in all, the newspaper has few specialized news reporters. This lack of specialists may be due in part to the fact that *TNT* does not publish a Sunday edition. Sunday publication is often a financial justification as well as an outlet for in-depth, specialized coverage. Without Sunday ads to pay the bills, and Sunday space to be filled with long stories, *TNT* may not be able to afford or have the room for a host of specialists.

TNT reporters are encouraged to write about subjects that interest them, said Paolino. Reporter David Schratwieser, before moving on to New Jersey Public Television, wrote a number of investigative stories about toxic waste disposal, even though he was not designated by the paper as an investigative specialist. "Investigative reporting is a matter of disposition," Paolino said. "In a way, most good reporting is investigative." *TNT* also lacks a political reporter. Election campaign coverage often is assigned to a number of reporters, usually in addition to their normal beats.

The 1960s and 1970s were growth years for the *Perth Amboy Evening News* and the Woodbridge *News Tribune*, with the rise of area shopping centers, and an increase in circulation from 39,894 in 1963 to 55,269 in 1974. But by 1977, readership was down to 51,845 and the situation was stagnant (1981 circulation was 51,561). Although the numbers improved in 1982 (to 53,362), they dropped back down to 51,597 in 1983. The population growth in *TNT*'s area is over, and the newspaper cannot be expected to do more than hold its own.

Paolino attributes some of this difficulty to the general problems of afternoon dailies. DiTommaso points to the competition. "We feel the competition very strongly," she said. "There's a head-on competition through much of our circulation area." *TNT* is surrounded by the *Asbury Park Press* and the *Daily Register* to the southeast, the Elizabeth *Journal* in the north, the *Courier-News* in the west, and the *Home News* in the south and west. And throughout its area it faces the New York papers and the *Star-Ledger*.

TNT is putting up a real fight. It covers South Plainfield (*Courier-News* territory), Highland Park (just across the river from the *Home News*), and Rahway (in Union County). All of them are covered—despite meager sales— because they are adjacent to high-circulation areas like Edison, Metuchen, and Woodbridge.

"The problem with coverage areas," Paolino mused, "is that newspapers tend to see themselves as the center of all there is." Some readers become annoyed that the newspaper refers to "the *TNT* area," especially in sports stories, just as some *Home News* readers for many years wondered what the "twin counties" of Middlesex and Somerset had in common, other than that they were both in that paper's coverage area.

TNT publishes three editions, replating various pages and moving up stories to be featured in particular circulation areas. The first edition, called Middlesex County, has a 7:30 a.m. deadline and the paper is off the floor by 9 a.m. The Monmouth County and South Middlesex editions go to press at 9:00 and 9:30 a.m. and are off the floor by 11 a.m. "The *Home News* occasionally beats us on a court story because of its later deadline," DiTommaso said. "The deadline has some significance, but I don't think that changing them would give us an advantage." She is not even sure that the *Home News* is *TNT*'s principal competitor: "We have a tendency to lose circulation to the *Star-Ledger* rather than the *Home News*, but in news content we are closer to the *Home News*."

DiTommaso regards the *News Tribune* as superior to both the *Home News* and the *Courier-News*. She said she thinks *TNT* is more thorough than the *Home News* and more local.

While the *News Tribune* does appear to be slightly more local than the *Home News*, this is not necessarily an asset. The New Brunswick newspaper is probably local enough to satisfy almost everyone, and it carries more total stories and more longer stories than its Woodbridge rival. For a suburban newspaper of its size, the *Home News* is very well balanced, and it deserves to be rated among the best papers in the state. Perhaps precisely because the *News Tribune* places such emphasis on local and state coverage—and because the editors want it that way—*TNT* is not a very well-rounded news product.

In the study of 1977 New Jersey newspapers conducted for this project, the *News Tribune* tied for 12th for the size of its news hole (17 pages), and tied for 15th for the total number of stories. It tied for fourth in number of local stories, tied for fifth in state coverage (with the *Home News* and the *Asbury Park Press*), and tied for ninth (again with the *Home News*) in locally originated stories. But it tied for 13th in foreign coverage and for the use of photographs, tied for 19th in national coverage, and tied for 23rd in the number of longer stories. When these numbers were put together *TNT* fell into the middle of the pack, well below the *Home News* but not far from its other rival, the *Courier-News*. The question of whether the Woodbridge or the Bridgewater newspaper is superior is too close to call.

Former *TNT* copy editor Eliott Sefrin, who worked for the paper for 10 years before leaving in 1981, sees the *News Tribune* as provincial and self-limiting, uninterested in much outside its area. But he also said, "You can read *TNT* and discover what's going on in your town." Sefrin added that *TNT* covers the story ultimately most important to its readers—the environment—with dedication.

"The *News Tribune* is a place where a lot of young reporters come and if they're good they move on," Sefrin said. "They learn the lessons that they have to learn, collect the clips, and move on. The management doesn't see that as all bad."

DiTommaso is proud of the *News Tribune*'s alumni. The paper has produced a score of leading journalists, including Serge Schmemann, who became a Moscow correspondent for the *New York Times*; Marcia Chambers, who became a *Times* legal writer; and Jonathan Kwitny, who went on to the *Wall Street Journal* and has written two books of solid investigative reporting.

Not bad for a very local newspaper in Woodbridge, N.J.

5

The Great Trenton Newspaper War
. . . and Peaceful Levittown

Daily newspapers are published in 1,541 cities in the United States. Two or more dailies are published in 148 of these cities. But most of the two-newspaper cities are one-publisher cities, with a single owner controlling both a morning and an afternoon paper.

While there is still a great deal of newspaper competition in America, between metropolitan and suburban papers and on the borders between newspaper territories, head-to-head competition in the same community is a vanishing phenomenon. There were only 35 two-publisher cities in 1978, compared to 51 in 1963, 109 in 1948, and 502 in 1923.

Trenton, the capital of New Jersey, is the home of the *Trenton Times*, an Allbritton newspaper, and the *Trentonian*, an Ingersoll paper. It is also the site of the great Trenton newspaper war, one of the last remaining head-to-head newspaper wars in America. In the 1970s, when the *Washington Post* owned the *Trenton Times*, it was a magnificent fight between two very different journalistic concepts. Today, with Allbritton-style "survival journalism" set against the tabloid *Trentonian*, the battle is far less interesting.

Fifteen miles south of Trenton lies Willingboro in Burlington County. In the late 1950s, when William J. Levitt began constructing a Levittown in what was then called Levittown Willingboro, the *Trenton Times* could have captured much of Burlington County. But the Calkins group, the publisher of the Bucks County *Courier Times*, acted first, creating what would become the *Burlington County Times*. While the Burlington paper sees itself as surrounded by competition—from Philadelphia, Camden, Trenton, and even New York—Levittown is peaceful compared to the newspaper battleground that is Trenton, New Jersey.

The Great Trenton Newspaper War

On Friday, October 30, 1981, a young, bearded man in shirt sleeves called for attention in the newsroom of the *Trenton Times*. Executive Editor Larry Kramer told the assembled staffers that the *Washington Post* had sold the Trenton newspaper to Joe L. Allbritton, the Texas millionaire who specialized in buying troubled properties. The price was somewhere between $10 million and $12 million, much less than the $16 million the *Washington Post* had paid in 1974.

Down the street in the offices of Trenton's tabloid newspaper, the *Trentonian*, it was a day of enormous satisfaction for Editor Emil Slaboda and Ingersoll Newspapers. The Washington Post Company had spent millions trying to dominate the Trenton market, and had failed in the most spectacular manner. The blue-collar *Trentonian* was now the circulation leader, and Katherine Graham, the head of the Post Company, had called the *Trenton Times* "my Vietnam."

The *Trentonian* was born out of the 1946 strike of the International Typographers Union against the *Evening Times*. The strikers started the *Trentonian* to pressure the *Times* into a settlement, but the Kerney family, then the owners of the *Times*, broke the strike instead. The union sold the *Trentonian* in 1949, and in 1961 it was purchased by Ingersoll Newspapers. From 1963 to 1974, the circulation of the morning *Trentonian* increased from 45,559 to 59,938, while the circulation of the evening *Trenton Times* actually decreased slightly from 73,053 to 72,750.

The $16 million price paid by the *Washington Post* surprised some New Jersey publishers, but the *Post* had purchased a respected newspaper with a heritage dating back to publisher James Kerney's close association with

Woodrow Wilson. The Sunday *Times-Advertiser* was thriving, with a circulation that had grown from 77,505 to 99,231 during the 1963-74 period. And the rich Post Company regarded its New Jersey venture as simply the first in a series of acquisitions of regional newspapers.

Richard Harwood, the *Post*'s national news editor, was sent to Trenton to take over the *Times*. This was considered a major promotion for the tough, talented newsman. The *Post* also sent in Joel Garreau to take charge of the *Times*' expanded soft-news operation, with great emphasis to be placed on entertainment, arts, business, leisure, and style.

Reporters from all over the country applied for jobs on the *Times*, which they regarded as the *Post*'s Triple-A farm club. The *Times*' news hole was enlarged, and new presses were being installed. Harwood intended to make the *Times* the most important newspaper in New Jersey—not a statewide newspaper, but the successor to the *Newark News* as the journal of impact and influence, hard-charging, a prize winner. "This is like having your own candy store," Harwood said in those early days. His first order of business was to dispose of the *Trentonian*. The city was just not big enough to support two daily newspapers.

The *Trentonian*, at that time, was a brash, breezy paper distinguished by Editor Gil Spencer's lively editorials. Published six days a week, it had a monopoly of the market on Saturdays, just as the *Times* had a Sunday monopoly. Much of the *Trentonian*'s success was attributed to Spencer, who was putting out an exciting little newspaper with a staff of only 40, less than half the size of the *Times* contingent. Spencer won a Pulitzer Prize in 1974 for his editorials, but soon after the *Post*'s takeover of the *Times*, he moved to the Philadelphia *Daily News*. (In 1984 he would be named editor of the New York *Daily News*.) The vacuum was filled by Slaboda, who moved up from managing editor.

Harwood's first push against the *Trentonian* was to begin publishing a Saturday edition. The new Saturday *Times* was a large, four-section newspaper with a soft-news emphasis. The *Trentonian* countered, introducing a Sunday edition. By the end of 1975, the two newspapers were competing seven days a week.

Harwood's *Trenton Times* was a first-rate regional newspaper. Full of news, full of good writing, hard-hitting, critical, and skeptical, it satisfied many of the ideals of professional journalism. The reporting staff was excellent, including Madeleine Blais, who later won a Pulitzer with the *Miami Herald*, and T.R. Reid, now Denver bureau chief for the *Washington Post*. The editors were undistinguished but competent.

Yet the *Trenton Times* never took off. Something failed to jell. Perhaps the paper was too impertinent. Perhaps Harwood's combative personality of infighting among editors affected the newsroom. A great deal of money was spent on the news operation, but sometimes the staff was improperly deployed (19 reporters were sent to New York for the 1976 Democratic convention). Although the newsroom contained many local journalists, the newspaper did not seem to have a clear understanding of the Trenton area. There was not enough local coverage. Wilson Barto, then the *Times*' ombudsman, urged Harwood to cover more local events, which Harwood dismissed as "covering chicken dinners."

Harwood's *Trenton Times* would have pleased a reader of the *Washington Post*, but it did not attract any *Trentonian* readers. Disappointed, Harwood returned to the *Post* in 1976. His successor at the *Times* was one of his assistants, Herb Wolfe, a former investigative reporter and assistant city editor who had served as Gov. Brendan Byrne's press secretary. Garreau also returned to the *Post*, and without his spark the *Times*' soft news pages would lose their brilliance.

The 1977 *Trenton Times* was no longer a journalist's dream. While it carried more advertising than the *Trentonian*, its news hole was actually smaller (even after adjusting for the difference in page sizes). According to the content analysis conducted by David Sachsman, it tied for 10th in the state for its total number of stories, while the *Trentonian* ranked fifth. It was fourth in state coverage, just behind the *Trentonian*, and seventh in the number of national stories, where the *Trentonian* was third. It ranked 11th for the number of longer stories, supposedly its strong suit, while the *Trentonian* ranked eighth. It tied for 15th in the number of photographs, where the tabloid finished fourth, and ranked 22nd in local coverage, compared to the *Trentonian*'s 18th place. While the 1977 *Trenton Times* was a bigger and better newspaper than it was before the *Post* took over, it surpassed the 1977 *Trentonian* in only two categories: the number of international stories and the number of locally originated stories. On weekdays at least, the *Trentonian* had passed the *Times* in sheer quantitative terms, and had become an impressive 74-page tabloid.

As the great Trenton newspaper war continued through the 1970s, the *Trentonian* clung to its blue-collar readership by increasingly accenting the local, while the *Trenton Times* became more and more obsessed with the war itself. When Larry Kramer took over in 1980, he found the *Times* in a chaotic condition. Various editors had pulled the newspaper in several directions. Circulation had dropped, and the publisher had tried to cut costs, even removing multiline telephones. "The paper was a physical disaster," Kramer recalled. "It had changed so many times that people did not know what to expect. The staff was in panic, afraid that the *Times* was about to abandon serious journalism."

Kramer found that the *Times* had begun printing two newspapers each day. A morning "blue-collar" paper was being produced for the sake of 4,000 street sales. Its aim was to hurt the *Trentonian*'s circulation figures. At least one-third of the reporters were working on something that had already been done in the other paper, Kramer said. To put out these two different newspapers, the *Times* news staff had grown to 118 people—nearly three times the number employed by the competition.

Kramer promptly ended the two-paper *Trenton Times*, saving money right from the start. He then decreased the staff by 25 percent, all by attrition. The statehouse contingent was reduced by half, from four to two. "We feel that no better than a thousand readers are all that interested in so much statehouse coverage," Kramer said at the time. "Just because we happen to be located in the capital doesn't make it necessary for us to devote enormous resources to it."

The 29-year-old former business reporter believed that he was improving the product. He was proud of the paper's soft news offerings, including *The Magazine*, the Sunday magazine section containing arts, entertainment, and travel. The business staff, with four members, was one of the biggest in the state. And good writing continued to be a goal.

"We will play a story on page one because it's interesting and readable," Managing Editor Rem Rieder said at the time. "Even with a smaller staff we continue to stress enterprise stories and investigative stories. The people have delivered beautifully." The push for good writing, Rieder said, extended to an increased emphasis in sports, with the *Times* "looking for an interesting and provocative sports story every day."

Local coverage did not improve. "We don't want this very talented reporter covering 23 meetings a week," said Rieder. "If we have rent control ordinances pending in three different towns, we want to do a story about all of them, so as not to get snowed under in minutiae."

"It's too thin," said John Kolesar about Kramer's *Trenton Times*. "They're living on reporters who were attracted there by the *Post* reputation. Coverage is very spotty and slender. People are covering five or six towns. Furthermore, they don't have the space. The paper must get bigger because to keep aggressive reporting you have to have room for it."

Kolesar, who had worked for the *Times* before moving to the *Record* of Hackensack, felt that the *Times* management was "too frightened." He argued that the circulation of the *Times* had not suffered any worse than various other afternoon newspapers around the state.

The *Trenton Times*' weekday circulation had held constant through most of the 1970s, but had begun dipping near the end of the decade. By the end of 1980, it was 67,480, down about 6,000 from its 1977 figure. The Saturday *Times* was in much greater trouble. It had lost 12,000 readers between 1977 and 1980, and with a circulation of 59,626, it had become a financial drag. Kramer called the decision to publish on Saturdays "the biggest mistake we ever made." The *Sunday Times-Advertiser* was still a prime moneymaker, but it had suffered badly in competition with the Sunday *Trentonian*. Where Mrs. Graham had once purchased a monopoly Sunday newspaper with a circulation of 99,231, in 1980 she owned a competing newspaper with 77,793 readers. The *Times* still led the *Trentonian* on weekdays and Sundays, but the tabloid was catching up quickly. In 1981, the *Trentonian* would hang a banner across its front page announcing that it had passed the *Times* in weekday circulation.

How did the *Trentonian* catch the *Times*?

"I think the big thing is we're a hell of a lot closer to the people than the *Times* is," said Frank Herrick, a *Trentonian* columnist. "I was born and raised here. Our publisher is local. Emil Slaboda is local. When I first started reporting, the cops all knew my father. Later they were kids I graduated with. Most of our people are from around here."

The *Trentonian*'s local flavor is exemplified by *Neighbors*, a Sunday magazine section that runs photographs—supplied by the parents—of children celebrating birthdays. "*Neighbors* is the one all the professionals laugh at," said Wilson Barto, the *Trentonian* city editor who had been the *Times* ombudsman. "When your kid's birthday picture is in the paper, you buy it. Your uncles and aunts buy it. There are 100 birthday pictures in there every week, and this has boosted circulation quite a bit."

The newspaper's accent on the local was Editor Slaboda's idea. "There was a lot of opposition from the staff when we started it," said Slaboda. "They thought it was hokey, doing what the weeklies do. Everybody laughed at us. Now they're all doing it. Hardly a week goes by that we don't get inquiries about our magazine."

Neighbors has contributed to the success of the Sunday *Trentonian*, which now boasts a circulation of more than 62,000. "The Sunday *Trentonian* is probably the biggest factor in getting the *Times*," said Slaboda.

The *Trenton Times* tried to fight the *Trentonian* on its own ground. It instituted a daily page of highly localized news called "Making the Rounds," a daily police blotter, and a public meeting list. It even tried serial fiction with a local flavor. Statehouse reporter Matt Purdy, using a pen name, wrote "The Capital Affair," a continuing story set in the Trenton area. The series was highly promoted—with a poster asking "Who Killed Senator Mastrano?"— and the promotion, itself, won a national award.

The *Times* also changed its circulation pattern, delivering a steadily increasing number of newspapers in the morning. This was to be a first step in converting the newspaper. "We've never been fairly compared with the *Trentonian*," Kramer said at the time. "If we go head-to-head, there's a good chance only one paper will survive. As quickly as possible we intend to invite the comparison. I can't help but think all their growth is due to the morning advantage and that when we've converted to mornings we'll have to pick up."

On December 21, 1981, the *Trenton Times* became a morning newspaper, but by then it was owned by Joe L. Allbritton, and a number of other changes had already been made. The new president of the *Times* was William Dean Singleton, Allbritton's right-hand man, and the new editor was Thomas Curran, former day news editor of the New York *News*. On the Monday following the takeover, Curran had fired 24 members of the news department, part of a reduction in the number of employees from 373 to 313. By March 1982, the *Times* would be down to 259 employees, including a news staff of 56.

Singleton called the firings painful and disagreeable, but said that the paper had been overstaffed and had to be pared down to restore profits.

"The *Trenton Times* was a journalist's dream," Singleton said. "It had good long stories, interpretive pieces. I thought it was a hell of a paper. But they'd spend days and days preparing some interpretive piece and let Hamilton Township and Mercer County go untouched. If you wanted to know what was happening here, it wasn't in the paper. They neglected to cover breaking news."

Although it was good journalism, he said, ultimately it failed. Letters to the editor showed an undercurrent of resentment against the "*Washington Post North*." But he said the *Times* would not become another *Trentonian*. "We are going to do interpretive reporting. We are not going to run pictures of pet dogs. We are not going to emphasize crime, with blazing headlines about rapes. We are not going to be so hokey that people are turned off by it. I'm not running their newspaper down. For their readers, it may be right. But we're going to do news about people."

Many of the newsroom staffers who had survived the cuts were wary of the new ownership. Allbritton's reputation among New Jersey journalists was that of a specialist in "survival journalism." At his other two New Jersey dailies, the *Paterson News* and the Hudson *Dispatch*, newsroom budgets had been cut to the bone to keep the papers operational. Some *Times* reporters were beginning to get the impression that their value to the enterprise was being measured by the number of stories they turned in. Messages went out to "keep it short." Specialties were downgraded, and the entire business news department evaporated.

"The Allbritton people keep talking about local news as the antithesis of in-depth reporting," said former staffer Diana Henriques. "The antithesis is short, superficial stories, not local news. They're cheap: they don't cost much to gather. Call up the cops and get the blotter from them; a good reporter can get one together in 20 minutes. But that gives the impression that crime is the only thing going on in Trenton. Good reporting is more expensive."

"The first week everybody started looking for jobs," said John Mintz, who eventually left for the *Record* of Hackensack. "We'd be running into each other at other newspaper offices." But even reporters like Mintz still held hope for the *Times*. Rem Rieder and Metro Editor Rick Levinson, holdovers from the *Washington Post* era, still commanded influence in the newsroom and seemed able to sway Curran, who was seen as a good journalist despite his perceived role as an Allbritton emissary.

The situation changed as the result of a single galvanizing incident. On January 25, 1982, John Chester began his first day as a full-time writer for the *Times* as the newspaper's only business reporter. That afternoon he tried to determine whether United Department Stores was filing under Chapter 11 of the Bankruptcy Code. This was an important story because United is the parent company of Dunham's, which has five stores in the Trenton area including the only remaining department store in Trenton's deteriorating downtown.

Dunham's also is a major advertiser in both the *Times* and the *Trentonian*. That same afternoon, Harold Kaslow, the president of Dunham's, called the two newspapers asking that they run a press release announcing the financial reorganization of United. At the *Times*, the call was taken by General Manager James Bennett, who after talking with Curran, called Kaslow back to say that the release would be run verbatim. The *Trentonian*, in fact, published the story in the exact words supplied by the company.

It was late in the day when Curran gave the release to Chester, telling him to punch it into the video display terminal verbatim and without any additions. Following the general newsroom rule that press releases should be checked for facts and clarified to increase reader understanding, Chester used some of the information he had come up with that afternoon, including phrases mentioning Chapter 11 and the Bankruptcy Code.

After the story appeared in the *Times*, the 23-year-old reporter was fired for "insubordination." The newsroom was in turmoil, and the relationship between the *Times* and its advertisers would soon become public knowledge.

Linda Cunningham, who had been overseeing Allbritton's two North Jersey dailies, was brought in as the executive editor of all three papers, relegating Curran to the number two spot in the news department.

Rieder was fired, and went public, saying: "There is obviously a great sensitivity now to please advertisers."

Singleton also spoke publicly, denying that advertisers determined coverage, but stating that at Allbritton newspapers "we don't have a situation where the newsroom is autonomous."

Within a few weeks after the firing of Rieder, the core of the newsroom was gone, including Metro Editor Levinson, Night Managing Editor Jack Steele, and statehouse reporter Purdy. Altogether there were about a dozen resignations.

On March 7, Allbritton, himself, tried to put the pieces back together with a signed editorial titled "A Matter of Integrity." In it, he said that the management decision to agree to publish a release verbatim was wrong: "It is not now nor has it ever been the policy of Allbritton Communications Company to allow the interests of our advertisers to influence the news or how the news is printed." But he also said the reporter had been wrong to act "contrary to firm instructions." Chester would not be rehired.

Singleton now said: "We blew it. This should have been a staff-written story, not a press release. We have taken strong measures to see that it will not happen again."

Cunningham intelligently stayed above the fray. In a memo issued when she took over, she made it clear that the *Times* would emphasize local coverage, including "everything from chicken dinners to corruption," and that she expected "at least one solid municipal story, one reader interest story, and a third story" from each reporter every day. "We will still do the investigative pieces, but no reporter will be able to take time from his regular coverage unless we have hashed out the subject and all are agreed it is worth the time."

Cunningham is a master of the Allbritton style, which is not all that different from the kind of journalism practiced by the *Trentonian*, where editors direct the staff to write short news stories, and lengthy ones are sent back for pruning. But while crime stories and human interest features now can be found regularly on the front page of the *Times*, the newspaper cannot match the *Trentonian*'s cozy, homey approach to news. The tabloid likes columns, all highly colloquial, on such subjects as family life, the good old days, and gossip. And its sports staff numbers 11, almost 25 percent of its newsroom strength.

Cunningham came through the difficult year of 1982 with flying colors, consistently arguing that the *Times* was a solid newspaper. She concentrated her energies on the *Times* editorial product, and was even able to add a few staffers. When the New Jersey Press Association awards were announced a year later, she felt she had proved her point. The *Times* had won eight state awards for work done in 1982. The list was impressive: three photography awards; first place for front page layout; first place for family section layout and content; and third place awards for editorial comment, business writing, and enterprise reporting.

The news department of the *Times*, with 60 staffers in 1983, still outnumbered the *Trentonian* contingent of 46, but both were clearly understaffed. "That's pretty lean for what we're trying to do," said Barto of the *Trentonian*. Given the limited number of reporters, the tabloid's approach is to "jump on the main story every day," he said. Both newspapers make up for their undersized staffs by publishing a considerable amount of wire material and syndicated features.

The *Trenton Times* in 1983 was showing a profit—the result of the Allbritton brand of survival journalism. There will be no more expensive attempts to blow the *Trentonian* out of the water. "Nobody wants to see somebody else

The Trenton Times

25 CENTS • FINAL • TRENTON, N.J., FRIDAY, SEPTEMBER 28, 1984 • 4 SECTIONS 82 PAGES

School board chief rips administration

By GIDEON GIL
Staff Writer

Top Trenton school administrators, including the superintendent, lied to school board members during the summer to keep them from learning about computer problems that fouled up the class schedules of hundreds of high school students, board president Nathaniel Walker and vice president Virginia Conti charged yesterday.

"As chairman of the (board's) Data Processing Steering Committee, I think I have been shamed," Walker said. "I think I've been told less than the truth." When asked whether administrators lied to him, Walker replied, "Absolutely."

The board president said the administrators' disregard for the data processing committee that has prompted him to abolish the advisory body.

'Those students are going to be behind. I am not so sure they are going to be able to get students to give the time. You can't make up three weeks in an hour.'

— board member Jo Carolyn Dent

In a letter to be delivered to board members and Superintendent Crosby Copeland today, Walker wrote that he abolished the committee because "it is apparent that the administration is more responsive to the board as a whole."

Although computer scheduling soft-

ware and computer terminals for the high school were delivered late — the terminals arrived in August — administrators told the data processing committee in June and July that "they were on target," Walker said.

At those meetings, Walker said, Robert Lawrence, director of computer services, "assured us everything was okay." The board president said Lawrence spoke for Copeland and assistant superintendent Thomas W.

Mitchell, who were both present at the meetings and heard Lawrence's comments.

"I call it a snow job," said Mrs. Conti, who was a member of the data processing committee. "They assured us everything was all right." She said Lawrence told the committee and full board in late August that "99 percent of the kids would start school with no

• continued on A16, column 3

Mathesius asks OK for fewer freeholders

By JoANN MOSLOCK
Staff Writer

Mercer County Executive Bill Mathesius yesterday called for a public referendum to change the structure of the county legislative branch and said he believes the majority of voters would opt for fewer freeholders.

"Nobody knows who they are. Nobody knows what they do. Nobody knows where they're from," Mathesius said of Mercer's seven freeholders.

But the board's alleged anonymity is not what has Mathesius thinking about a change.

"There's a nucleus of negativism on the board that has brought responsible government to a halt," Mathesius declared. While the county executive will admit that some of his major initiatives have been blocked by the freeholders, he complained that the freeholders make county government "look foolish."

THE PROPOSAL for a referendum, however, was not warmly embraced by at least two freeholders, who claimed Mathesius is just letter because the freeholders exercise and defend their right to second-guess the administration.

"If the county executive understood what legislative oversight is, perhaps the level of tension would be re-

• continued on A16, column 5

ITS DANCER —Barbara Gallup (left) and Sarah Gove put the finishing touches on one of the topiary reindeer which will go on display at the World Trade Center's Christmas Show. The displays, made of moss attached to wire, will include 3 reindeer and 3 bears. Story, A3.

Staff photo by Herman Lasher

Hamilton halts squads serving Trenton calls

By JO ASTRID GLADING
Staff Writer

HAMILTON — The township's three volunteer emergency squads are refusing to send their rigs into Trenton, a move the director of the city's ambulance squad said is placing more strain on Trenton's already reduced emergency services.

The drastic move by the three township squads will mean longer response times and "could mean the difference between life and death" for a city resident, according to Lynne Peck, director of Trenton Emergency Medical Services.

Representatives of the three Hamilton squads told the city this week that because of recent budget cutbacks to TEMS, too much demand was being made upon the Nottingham Ambulance Squad, Rusling Hose Co. and Yardville First Aid Squad.

CONTINUING TO HELP out TEMS would place "an unacceptable burden on our squads

and would be depleting our own resources," the captains of the three squads wrote in a letter sent to city officials this week. The letter is dated Sept. 12 and Peck said the township's boycott of city calls began then.

The letter states that since July 28, when TEMS cut back to only one ambulance at night, calls asking the assistance of ther Hamilton squads have gone far beyond "mutual aid" and are at or close to "actual coverage levels." On one afternoon, the township's squads were dispatched into the city five times, the letter states.

The squad leaders said, however, that they would still be available "during a multi-casualty or disaster situation in the area." They said Trenton should provide a minimum of three ambulances on a 24-hour basis and should meet with its two volunteer squads to better coordinate resources.

Peck charged the Hamilton squads with employing a harmful tack to prove a futile point.

• continued on A16, column 1

Gromyko rebuffs Reagan in speech at United Nations

UNITED NATIONS (AP) — Foreign Minister Andrei Gromyko of the Soviet Union delivered a stinging public retort yesterday to President Reagan's conciliatory overtures, calling for "concrete deeds rather than verbal assurances" from the White House.

Gromyko, who is to meet with Reagan at the White House on Friday, devoted most of his 75-minute speech before the United Nations General Assembly to sharp attacks on "repeated" American policies increasing the threat of war.

However, he left the door open for improved relations.

"The Soviet Union believes it is precisely concrete deeds rather than verbal assurances

that can lead to normalizing the situation in our relations with the U.S. The U.S.S.R. will not be found wanting. Every American, every American family should know that the Soviet Union wants peace and only peace with the U.S.," the 75-year-old foreign minister said.

He spoke in Russian and the Soviet U.N. Mission issued a 20-page English translation. As Gromyko spoke, the speech was simultaneously translated into the U.N.'s five working languages — English, French, Chinese, Spanish and Arabic.

Secretary of State George P. Shultz, who listened impassively from the second-row bank of seats assigned to the U.S. delegation, said as he left the hall that he did not like the speech.

• continued on A16, column 1

Five-month suburban drug probe nets 23 suspects

By SUE LANDRY
Staff Writer

EAST WINDSOR — A methamphetamine (speed) operation that reached into three counties was broken yesterday with the early-morning arrests of 23 men and women, most in their early 20s, East Windsor Township Police Chief Joseph Micinisky and Mercer County Prosecutor Philip S. Carchman announced.

The five-month probe was the "largest drug investigation in the history of East Windsor Township," and included a wiretap this month on the phone of the alleged main figure in the drug ring, Carchman said.

Yesterday's raids at individual homes in several Mercer County communities were the latest in the county prosecutor's proclaimed "suburban drug offensive."

More than 60 law enforcement officers from the prosecutor's offices

Student teaching tiff at Princeton

Associated Press

Princeton University's small education program fails to comply with new state regulations, prompting a dispute between New Jersey's two top education officials over the Ivy League school's request for an exemption.

Princeton has proposed only eight weeks of student teaching for its undergraduate candidates for degrees in education, while the new regulations require a full semester of student teaching, said Martin Friedman, director of the office of teacher education in the Department of Higher Education.

Officials at the prestigious university contend that having a senior

bullied," Singleton observed. "That turns people off and they will root for the underdog."

The Allbritton management views the readership of the *Times* as loyal and upscale, distinctly different from the *Trentonian*'s equally loyal, working-class readers, and believes the area can support two newspapers. Singleton argued that because there is no local commercial television station or strong regional radio, the newspapers get advertising that in other markets normally goes to broadcasters.

Many outside observers question whether the advertising base in the Trenton area is really large enough to sustain two competing newspapers. They argue that whenever one newspaper in a competitive situation appears to get the upper hand, the other generally loses advertising and eventually becomes unprofitable. The long list of newspapers that were unable to survive such competitive pressures includes the *Washington Star*, once owned by Joe L. Allbritton.

As of 1983 neither Trenton newspaper appeared to have the upper hand. But the issue was clouded by a *Trentonian* challenge of the *Times*' circulation figures. The *Trentonian* led the *Times* on weekdays, 66,477 to 65,047, in the calculations for 1982. The best available figures showed increases for both papers in Saturday readership, with the *Times* leading 65,691 to 64,706. The *Times* Sunday circulation was listed as 79,966 in 1982, compared to the Sunday *Trentonian*'s 62,491. The delicate balance of advertising also remained stable, with the *Times* leading on weekdays, according to Singleton, and far ahead on Sundays.

At the 1983 *Trenton Times*, virtually nothing was left of the *Washington Post* influence. "We do not feel an obligation to print what we think readers ought to know, but what they want to read," Singleton said, remembering the arguments he used to have with Jack Steele before the editor left the paper. "Steele would say, 'Let's lead with a story on the Middle East because the public needs to know about it.' Some people think a newspaper is a hallowed institution. A newspaper is a product, like a candy bar. You have to package it to be attractive to the reader. You have to put in the ingredients they want. You have to market it properly."

Singleton resigned from Allbritton Communications at the end of 1983 to form a corporation with Richard Scudder (former publisher of the *Newark News* and founder of the Garden State Paper Company) and purchase the *Gloucester County Times*. Taking his place as head of the Allbritton newspaper division and president of the company's New Jersey newspapers was Michael Moore, an executive at Allbritton-owned banks with no previous newspaper experience. Early in 1984, Richard Bilotti, who had been president and publisher of the *Gloucester County Times*, was named publisher of the *Trenton Times*. Bilotti, an experienced journalist who had worked for the

Cleveland *Plain Dealer*, the Associated Press, the *Newark News*, and the *Star-Ledger*, told *Jersey Publisher* in March 1984 that he planned no major changes in the direction of the *Times*.

The great Trenton newspaper war was once a battle between two very different journalistic concepts, with the *Washington Post* set against a brash tabloid. In the process, the *Trentonian* actually gained in stature, improving its product to combat the enemy. It was a magnificent fight, and the readers were the winners. The Trenton newspaper war continues, but there is no longer anything great about it.

The *Burlington County Times*: Growing Up in Levittown

William J. Levitt had the bright idea of building whole towns of identical, low-cost, single-family homes in suburbia. The first Levittown—on Long Island—was an immediate success. The residents loved it, and so did the publishers of *Newsday*, the newspaper that was to become the quintessential suburban daily.

When Levitt started building his second Levittown in the early 1950s in Bucks County, Pa., just 10 miles from Trenton, the *Trenton Times* should have taken advantage of the windfall. But the *Times* chose not to expand, leaving a clear field for the publishers of the tiny Bristol, Pa. *Courier* to start a new paper, the Levittown *Times*. Today the Bucks County *Courier Times* has a daily circulation of 66,000, about the same as the *Trenton Times*, and the publishers of the once-tiny paper call themselves Calkins Newspapers, since they now own six dailies and two weeklies—including the *Burlington County Times*.

In the late 1950s, the Calkins group was riding the wind, and when Levitt began constructing a Levittown in Burlington County, 15 miles south of Trenton and east of Philadelphia, a new Levittown *Times* was born. Levittown Willingboro would become simply Willingboro, and the newspaper would become the *Burlington County Times*. Once again, the *Trenton Times* could have made inroads, but the Calkins group acted first, and today the *Burlington County Times* has a circulation of more than 43,000 daily and more than 45,000 on Sundays.

Local coverage is the key to the newspaper's success, along with extensive use of wire service and syndicated material. This combination of local and wire stories fills a large news hole, giving the *Burlington County Times* weight as well as balance, and making it a complete newspaper.

The study of 1974 New Jersey newspapers conducted by the Center for Analysis of Public Issues found that the *Burlington County Times* had an unusually large news hole for a paper with 38,000 readers daily. Its 18 pages of news ranked sixth in the state, while its 23 pages of ads ranked 11th. The *Times* was third best in the quantity of national news, fifth in foreign news, eighth in local coverage, and 15th in state coverage. The quality of its local reporting was judged third best in the state by the survey of editors and reporters taken in the same year.

The content analysis of 1977 New Jersey newspapers conducted by David Sachsman found the evening *Times* to have a 20-page news hole (tied for seventh place), and 32 pages of advertising (fifth best in the state). Daily circulation was up slightly to almost 40,000. The *Times* ranked sixth in the total number of news and feature stories, tied for third place in international news, and tied for fourth in national news. It tied for second for its use of wire service and syndicated stories, tied for eighth for its use of photographs, and tied for 13th in state news. The study found the *Times* to be low in locally originated stories (tied for 15th) and local coverage (tied for 20th), but this proved to be the result of the newspaper's system of replating.

The *Times* publishes three editions daily, replating three to nine pages for each edition. The first edition goes to press at 11:30 a.m. and is distributed to Mount Holly and the eastern and northern sections of the county. The 12:15 p.m. edition goes to the southern portion of the county, bordering the Delaware River, the Camden County line, and the Pinelands. The third edition, published at 1:15 p.m., stays close to home: Willingboro, the Burlingtons, Edgewater Park, etc. Since the *Times* often replates local stories, the amount of local coverage in any single edition is bound to appear low compared to other papers. "We're putting out practically three different newspapers a day," said Executive Editor Daniel Eisenhuth.

The *Times* sees itself as surrounded by competition. "You can have six daily newspapers delivered to your front door," Eisenhuth said. "We've got the *Inquirer*, the *Courier-Post*, the *Trenton Times*, the *Trentonian*, us, and of course you can get the *New York Times* here." The death of the Philadelphia *Bulletin* resulted in a circulation gain of about 3,000 daily and 4,000 on Sundays for the Burlington County newspaper.

The *Times*' news staff of about 48, including part-timers, is principally devoted to local coverage. "We give each reporter anything from one to four townships and make them geographically contiguous so the reporters are not running all over the county," said Eisenhuth. "The reporters are responsible for anything at all that happens in those townships. We try not to shuffle

Burlington County Times

Burlington County's newspaper

Tuesday, October 2, 1984

C   25 cents

Sugar, spice and spikes

Times staff photo by Nancy Rokos

Everyone knows that a football team fields 11 men...well, almost every football team. The Pemberton Area Athletic League 116-pound Junior Midget team's defensive alignment consists of 10 boys and one girl. Lynn Stanwood, number 72, is an 11-year-old first-string tackle on the Burlington County Conference team. Story on Page 15.

Labor chief angered by 'inquisition'

Associated Press

WASHINGTON — Labor Secretary Raymond Donovan, his term in the Reagan Cabinet plagued by allegations of past wrongdoing, is fighting to hold onto his job in the face of a grand jury indictment he says "is not worth the paper it's written on."

Donovan, a onetime New Jersey construction executive who survived investigations by a Senate committee and an independent special prosecutor in 1982, announced late yesterday that he is taking an unpaid leave of absence.

Deputy White House press secretary Larry Speakes said President Reagan approved the leave. "The president is comfortable with the precedent of innocent until proven guilty," Speakes said as he accompanied Reagan on a campaign trip in Mississippi.

Donovan said he was "outraged and disgusted by the obviously partisan timing" of the indictment, which came from a Bronx, N.Y., grand jury investigating allegations that he once took part in a scheme to misrepresent the work of a minority subcontractor on a New York subway project.

Explaining why he volunteered to step aside, the blunt-spoken Donovan said: "My concerns are that my family has to endure this mindless inquisition and that this not reflect negatively upon the president."

During the 1982 investigation, some Senate Democrats called for Donovan's resignation and several White House aides, including Chief of Staff James A. Baker III, reportedly have urged that Reagan relieve his labor secretary of his duties. Reagan steadfastly has refused.

Donovan, a part-owner and former executive vice president of Schiavone Construction Co. of Secaucus, N.J., was being arraigned in New York today along with company president Ronald Schiavone and six other officers.

Although Donovan volunteered to step down temporarily "to assure that this matter does not become a part of the current election campaign," he also declared:

"I fully expect to resume my duties just as soon as this injustice has been dealt with."

Donovan, who testified before the county grand jury on Sept. 24, accused Bronx County District Attorney Mario Merola, a Democrat, of having political motivations. The 54-year-old secretary said he had passed a polygraph test taken at his request "with flying colors" and voiced confidence of "ending once and for all this witch hunt."

Ford B. Ford, undersecretary of Labor, the No. 2 department officer

Raymond J. Donovan
...takes leave of absence

(Continued on Page 11, Col 1)

Electric rates drop for winter

Associated Press

NEWARK — Electricity prices for more than 2 million customers served by two New Jersey utilities will begin the winter billing period for the utilities began.

Barbara A. Curran, president of the Board of Public Utilities, said the billing system for the utilities was switched to winter rates a month earlier than in previous years "to better reflect the actual winter electric rates."

The summer heating season now will be four months long rather than five months for Public Service Electric & Gas Co. and Jersey Central Power & Light Co.

Gene Murphy, a spokesman for PSE&G, the state's largest utility with 1.7 million customers, said the utility was prepared for the change and had no objection to it.

Under the winter rates, a monthly electricity bill for a typical residential customer is $51.97 for PSE&G, a drop of $8.73, or 15.4 percent, and $56.10 for customers of JCP&L, a drop of $3.94 or 6.6 percent.

Rates go up at the end of May because the demand increases when customers turn on their air conditioners, said Murphy.

BPU spokesman George Dawson said price reductions for commercial customers were comparable, but he could not provide a detailed breakdown.

Ms. Curran said the electric utility firms have used seasonal pricing rates for more than 10 years. The higher summer rates, she added, are aimed at encouraging conservation, "thereby saving on the need for new generation plant construction."

Atlantic City Electric Co. and Rockland Electric Co., the two other privately owned electric companies in New Jersey, begin their winter billing periods in November.

Residents denied say on porn

By Gail C. Lerner
Times staff writer

BURLINGTON TOWNSHIP — Because there is not enough time to get four questions dealing with pornography on the November ballot, residents will be informally polled on the subject.

Township solicitor Thomas Foy said a minimum of 60 days is needed to place a referendum on the ballot, so township officials will opt for a house-to-house survey instead. Foy said the poll could be taken at minimum expense.

If residents register their opposition to locating pornographic businesses in the township, it "would be evidence to establish what we believe is the community's standards regarding obscenity," Foy said.

However, he added, the questions probably will be placed on the ballot in November of 1985.

The questions to be asked of residents are whether they want massage parlors, adult bookstores, nude or filmed entertainment and X-rated movies and videotapes banned from the community. According to Foy, the questions are patterned after state statutes which govern obscenity.

In their continuing fight against pornography, township officials will appeal directly to local merchants and ask that they stop the open display of adult books and magazines, Foy said.

Also, township officials plan to meet with county prosecutor Stephen Raymond to seek his help in taking legal action against merchants who refuse to remove

X-rated books from public view.

"We need his support to bring action against the merchants under state obscenity laws," Foy said. "State law preempts local enforcement of state statutes."

Those who plan to meet with Raymond are Mayor Joseph Foy, township public safety director Walter Corter and township solicitors Foy and Ronald Bookbinder.

The township has been trying to ban all businesses dealing with pornography since last June, when a Camden County man tried to open an adult entertainment store on Route 130 which would feature live peep shows and sell X-rated books.

When residents learned of the proposal, they stormed council meetings and presented a petition signed by hundreds who opposed

the idea. Council acted quickly to pass five new ordinances prohibiting such businesses.

And solicitor Foy, who is also a state assemblyman, introduced state legislation which would allow local municipalities to "make, regulate, amend, repeal, enforce and license anyone involved in live nude entertainment."

Meanwhile, the planning board revoked its prior approval of the new adult store after they learned no agreement of sale had been obtained from the owner of the building where the adult entertainment store was to open. The board ruled that Saverio Garofalo, who was seeking to open the establishment, had no authority to present his plans to the board.

1,000 county welfare checks lost in mail

By Pete Perrotta
Times staff writer

As many as 1,000 monthly public assistance checks sent out by the county Welfare Board apparently have been lost in the mail.

Welfare spokesman Kenneth Wendel reported today that the checks were mailed Friday morning but got lost somewhere between the Mount Holly Post Office and the

U.S. Postal regional headquarters in Bellmawr, Camden County.

The checks were destined for post offices in Beverly, Mount Holly, Moorestown, Riverton, Riverside, Burlington City, Maple Shade, Palmyra, Edgewater Park, Cinnaminson, Burlington Township, Lumberton and Eastampton.

A Beverly woman who receives assistance checks said she called the

county welfare board when her checks did not arrive as usual — on Saturday or Monday.

"They told me to try and borrow some money," said the woman, who identified herself only as Mary. "They said they didn't know where the checks were and they would get back to me."

"But I've got PSE&G on my back, and other bills to pay," she

said.

Wendel said his agency mails monthly checks through the Mount Holly Post Office, which in turn sends them to Bellmawr where they are sorted and mailed to the individual townships.

He said the checks should have arrived there by yesterday at the latest.

"We have received about 125

complaints already on this," Wendel said.

Mary Lucas, administrative supervisor for the welfare board, said this morning that those who haven't received a check can come to the county welfare office at the Lumberton Plaza to be issued an emergency check.

Ms. Lucas said the agency will issue stop payments on lost checks.

IN THE TIMES

Machine is star
of hospital lab

p3

reporters around too much so they get to know the towns that they're covering and know what to look for." Stringers help out with night meetings.

Newsroom specialists include an entertainment editor, a travel writer, two reporters who cover the county complex in Mount Holly, and three general assignment reporters, one of whom used to cover the statehouse. "We had both UPI and AP, which were doing a good job of covering the statehouse, and we thought it was triplication of effort to have a person in there," Eisenhuth said. Although the *Times* relies primarily on the wire services, the paper occasionally sends a reporter to Trenton to cover legislation judged important to the county.

The sports department consists of an editor, an assistant editor, four full-time reporters, and three part-time writers. It shares coverage of Philadelphia professional sports with other Calkins newspapers in the area. A *Times* reporter, for example, writes about the 76ers basketball team for four Calkins newspapers, and the *Times* shares coverage of the Flyers hockey team with the Bucks County *Courier Times.*

The Burlington County newspaper has a Wednesday food page, a Thursday consumer page called "Money," and a 24-page Friday entertainment guide called "What's Happening." National and international news from the wires is used to lead off one section of the paper every day. Continuing concerns at the newspaper include toxic wastes and the Pinelands. "We consider ourselves the newspaper of record for what happens in the Pinelands," said Eisenhuth.

The *Burlington County Times* has created a niche for itself by emphasizing local coverage and carrying pages and pages of wire news, a reasonable mix for a suburban newspaper with a circulation that is less than 50,000.

6

The Jersey Shore . . . and Points South

There is a joke told in Atlantic City that goes something like this:

> Where are you from?
> New Jersey.
> What exit?

From an Atlantic City perspective (or anywhere else on the Jersey shore), everyone in New Jersey lives just off an exit of the Garden State Parkway.

The parkway has transformed the Jersey shore from a strip of summer colonies to a year-round suburban sprawl. It is filled with commuters heading north every morning, and gamblers heading south to Atlantic City.

The Jersey shore is the home of the *Asbury Park Press* and the *Atlantic City Press*, the third and fifth largest newspapers in the state. Living in their shadows are the *Daily Register* of Shrewsbury, the Toms River *Ocean County Times-Observer*, and the three small dailies of South Jersey's sparsely populated Cumberland County, the *Bridgeton Evening News*, the Vineland *Times Journal*, and the *Millville Daily*.

South Jersey is also the world of the fourth largest newspaper in the state, the Camden *Courier-Post*, whose circulation area stretches as far north as Burlington County and as far south as Cape May. The *Gloucester County Times* lies within that area, as does *Today's Sunbeam* in Salem County.

Living in the Shadow of the *Asbury Park Press*: The *Daily Register* and the *Ocean County Times-Observer*

The completion of the Garden State Parkway opened the shore communities of Monmouth and Ocean counties to development and turned the *Asbury Park Press* into a gold mine. It also spurred the growth of three small newspapers: the *Red Bank Register*, the Lakewood *Ocean County Times*, and the Brick Town *Ocean County Observer*.

The *Red Bank Register* was a successful 80-page weekly newspaper with about 18,000 readers when it converted to daily publication in 1959. "We were one of the biggest weeklies in the country at that time," said Editor Arthur Z. Kamin, "and it was a good base with which to start a daily. We knew that if we didn't do it, probably somebody else would."

The weekly readers bought the new evening newspaper, and with the growth in population in Monmouth County, the *Register*'s circulation reached 32,000 by the early 1970s. But while the competing *Asbury Park Press* continued to grow, the *Register*'s daily circulation stagnated. It was 32,238 in 1982, and 30,137 in 1983. Blocked on weekdays by the *Press* and the Woodbridge *News Tribune* (to the north), the *Register* began Sunday publication in 1976. The Sunday edition was successful almost immediately due to the *Register*'s loyal readership and the growth in retailing in the area. Its circulation reached 33,282 in 1982 but slipped to 31,122 in 1983.

The *Daily Register*, as it is now called, is a good newspaper for its size, and its quality is due at least partly to the intense competition in Monmouth County. "The readers really are the ones who benefit because we are competitive here," Kamin declared. "We are aggressive, we take pride in what we do, and the exclusive story is still important to us. I can't speak for the *Press*, but I think we sharpen them and they sharpen us."

The *Daily Register*'s news staff size runs between 35 and 40 people. Most of the news reporters cover municipalities, but the newspaper encourages them to develop specialty sidelines. Two reporters cover the Monmouth County offices in Freehold, one in the courts and the other reporting on county government, and the paper maintains a one-member statehouse bureau in Trenton. There is also a business writer since, as Kamin noted, brokerage houses have been proliferating in the area and many corporate executives live in the northern Monmouth communities.

The sports staff specializes in local coverage such as thoroughbred racing in Monmouth Park and ocean sports, but it also covers the New York and New Jersey professional teams.

The paper uses color extensively, especially for the front page and for food news. "Our circulation people seem to think it has a positive effect on the newsstand," Kamin said.

The *Daily Register* demonstrates its community involvement, Kamin said, sponsoring art shows, photography shows, magic shows, an "Afternoon with the Authors" program at the county library, and such special events as a "Holocaust Seminar" at Brookdale Community College, where prizes were presented to school children for essays written on the Nazi persecution of the Jews. Kamin said the newspaper has established links to the black and Hispanic communities: "We want both groups to know that the *Register* will print their news, their concerns, and I think we've succeeded." He noted that a continuing program called "Coffee with the Editor" keeps the paper in touch with a wide range of local concerns.

Major local issues such as ocean dumping, toxic wastes, and orderly growth in Monmouth County receive solid coverage from the *Register*, but the meat and potatoes of the newspaper is its coverage of individual municipalities. "We cover municipalities in the same way that the *Washington Post* covers Capitol Hill, the Supreme Court, and the President," said Kamin. "We cover zoning boards, planning boards, sewer commissions. We really put strong emphasis on local government and local education. We want our reporters to do enterprise, feature, and investigative writing, but right now I think that municipal government and board of education coverage has a strong place, and I think we're coming back to it—the regional papers, medium-sized papers, and even some of the larger papers too."

The *Daily Register*'s emphasis on local coverage is nothing new. In the content analysis of 1977 newspapers conducted for this project, the *Register* ranked third in the number of local stories. Furthermore, it was fifth in the number of longer stories, tied for fifth in the number of longer stories, tied for fifth in state coverage, tied for sixth in both locally originated stories and the use of photographs, and ranked ninth in the total number of news and feature articles—a very strong showing for a small-circulation newspaper.

The *Register* moved from Red Bank to nearby New Shrewsbury following a fire in its offices in 1970. Kamin gives credit for the paper's survival to the *Asbury Park Press*, which made its production facilities available to the

Register for several months. The paper built a new plant with modern facilities.

The *Daily Register* is a two-edition newspaper, with a 6 a.m. press time for the early edition, which goes to the central and northern portions of the county, and a 6:45 a.m. press run for the western Monmouth edition. On Mondays, the paper emphasizes sports; on Tuesdays, it features newsmakers, with a page of articles on local people; Wednesday is food day; Thursday is business; and Friday is weekend entertainment.

Evening newspapers with early morning deadlines often are forced to carry stories a day late. An important announcement released at 10 a.m. cannot be published until the next day. Aware of this problem, *Register* editors are particularly vigilant in the middle of the night, when it is still possible to make the 6 a.m. deadline.

Night Editor Russel P. Rauch was listening to a police radio scanner at 4 a.m. on Jan. 10, 1981 when he picked up part of a message concerning a rest home. Because he had not heard the details, he assigned a reporter to call the police. The police line was busy, and so Rauch decided to go with his hunch, dispatching two reporters to the scene. It was the Beachview Rest Home fire, the worst boarding home fire in New Jersey history, and the *Register* was the first newspaper on the newsstands with the story.

The *Register* was sold in 1982 by Block Newspapers to another newspaper chain, Capital Cities Communications, but Kamin stayed as editor (until early 1985), and the paper remained solid.

While the *Register* was growing and prospering on the northern flank of the *Asbury Park Press*, two tiny newspapers were nipping away on the southern flank. The weekly Brick Town *Ocean County Observer* became a daily newspaper in 1964, moved to Toms River in 1973, started a Sunday paper in 1976, and by the end of that year had a circulation of 23,000 on weekdays and 20,000 on Sundays. In 1976, the *Observer* was sold to Ingersoll Newspapers, the owner of the *Trentonian*.

The Lakewood *Ocean County Times* increased its daily circulation from 4,000 in 1964 to 7,400 in the mid-1970s, but was struggling. In 1977, Ingersoll bought the *Times*, which it soon merged with the *Observer*. (Ingersoll also owns three weeklies in the area.)

Today's *Ocean County Times-Observer* apparently is having some trouble keeping up its circulation. While its 1981 readership was 26,356 on weekdays and 25,215 on Sundays, its 1982 figures dipped to 23,172 on weekdays and 22,653 on Sundays. Though the numbers increased in 1983 to 23,948 daily and 23,704 on Sundays, the competition from the *Asbury Park Press* is tough.

The *Times-Observer* is a morning newspaper with a news deadline of 11:30 p.m. It covers all of Ocean County with a news staff of 21 full-time employees and a number of part-timers. "I'm preaching local copy all the time," said

Getting even

Lacey avenged an early season loss yesterday by shutting out Point Boro in field hockey. Meanwhile, Pinelands remained undefeated.

Sports, Page 15

On the move

Success is no surprise to 9-year-old David Conway of Manchester who will appear in a TV special. He says he's a "natural."

Life Today, Page 18

OCEAN COUNTY
Observer

SINCE 1850

'ALL THE DAILY NEWSPAPER YOU NEED'

VOL. 132 NO. 239

FRIDAY
OCTOBER 5
1984
TOMS RIVER, N.J.

25¢

Is Marshall murder linked to theft ring?

By Anthony A. Gallotto
Staff Writer

TOMS RIVER — New Jersey and Louisiana authorities are closer today to unsnarling a web of southern bank burglaries and at least two murders somehow connected to the "contract killing" of Maria P. Marshall.

Suspects in the Sept. 7 shooting death of Mrs. Marshall are believed to be tied to "a string of bank burglaries" in Louisiana, Texas, and Arkansas," a spokesman for Caddo Parish Sheriff Donald Hathaway confirmed last night.

About 13 Shreveport, La., banks and six other banking institutions in eastern Texas and southern Arkansas were the victims of burglars who have managed to steal over $1.5 million by breaking into night deposit boxes.

In several cases, the deposit boxes were ripped from the banks' walls. The burglaries began Aug. 2, 1982 and the last one occurred in May 1983, one week before a federal grand jury convened in Shreveport to hear evidence on the break-ins.

The bank burglary probe was handled by Louisiana law enforcement officials until the grand jury convened. The Federal Bureau of Investigation is now in charge of the probe. At least five Louisiana men, thought to have played a role in Mrs. Marshall's shooting, are also linked to the bank burglaries, according to law enforcement sources.

Mrs. Marshall was shot in the chest with a .45-caliber gun after her husband, Robert O. Marshall, 44, drove into the Oyster Creek picnic area off the Garden State Parkway to change what he thought was a flat

Continued on Page 4

Officer pleads guilty

By Eugene Kiely
Staff Writer

TOMS RIVER — A 25-year-old suspended Lavallette police officer pleaded guilty yesterday to lewdness and official misconduct for stopping a Seaside Heights woman on a motor vehicle violation and following her to her apartment, where the woman said she was sexually attacked.

Anthony Baccello, 2019 Pine Meadow Ave., Toms River, pleaded guilty to the lesser charges at the conference he faced two counts each of criminal sexual contact and official misconduct.

The charges stemmed from two separate incidents involving two different women. The first allegedly occurred in Dover Township on Feb. 6 and the second in Seaside Heights Feb. 15.

All counts involving the incident in Dover were dropped. The charge of criminal sexual contact in the Seaside Heights incident was dropped, with a complaint of lewdness being lodged against Baccello in its place.

Baccello, who faces a maximum sentence of five years in prison and $500 in fines, took the stand to enter a guilty plea on charges of official misconduct, a third degree offense, and lewdness.

He told Ocean County Superior Court Judge Mark Addison that he stopped the woman in Seaside Heights and followed her to her apartment, where he admitted to committing a lewd act.

Baccello, who was on duty at the

Continued on Page 5

Pole crash

An 81-year-old Point Pleasant man received minor injuries after his car hit a telephone pole on Hooper Avenue, one-half block south of Route 37, shortly after 3 p.m. in Toms River yesterday. Ernest W. Ludwig was treated at Community Memorial Hospital. No other cars were involved in the mishap.

Photo by Jon Hurd

Arson claim argued during murder trial

By Eugene Kiely
Staff Writer

TOMS RIVER — A retired arson investigator for the Essex County Prosecutor's Office yesterday disputed the testimony of a state expert who said the blaze which killed David Schumm "was set."

James P. Graham, who for the first time in his lengthy career was testifying for the defense, said he "would be afraid to" conclude the fire was arson. He said there was not enough physical evidence, particularly samples of the couch material, to estimate the time frame needed to determine an arson fire.

Graham testified on behalf of Loretta Ruvolo, 20, who is accused of murder, felony murder and aggravated arson for allegedly killing Schumm Dec. 23, 1982 by setting fire to the couch in the apartment she shared with him at James Towne Village.

"I couldn't give you an estimate of time," Graham said. "I don't believe anyone can. All materials burn differently."

The defense rested its case yesterday, with summations and deliberations expected to begin today.

Graham's testimony directly disputed that of a key state witness, James Dolan, a former Dover Township fire inspector, who took the stand for the prosecution Tuesday and Wednesday. Dolan, although admitting no tests ever were conducted to determine the contents of the couch material, said the material did not make a difference in an arson investigation.

On Tuesday, Dolan told the jury he first determined the fire was accidental and caused by "discarded cigarette materials." On Wednesday, he concluded his testimony by saying

he changed his opinion two months later and ruled the fire "was set."

Dolan said he reversed his opinion after learning Miss Ruvolo may not have been asleep at the apartment at 1 a.m., as she said, and instead may not have returned to the apartment until 3:30 or 4 a.m. He said the new time frame "ruled out all accidental possibilities."

Graham was one of several defense witnesses — including Horace Wilson, an investigator with the Ocean County Prosecutor's Office, and Paul Mercready, records supervisor for Dover Township Police Department — used to highlight what Judge Peter J

Continued on Page 5

Worlock lawyer: Client was 'sick'

By Don Bennett
Staff Writer

TOMS RIVER — Carl Worlock was insane when he gunned down two men in Jackson Township after an argument over his wallet which contained a picture of him in sado-masochistic garb, his attorney told a jury yesterday.

"He's a sick and troubled young man" Lawrence Ravitz insisted.

Two defense psychiatrists will tell the jury of the mental illness which made it impossible for Worlock to know what he was doing was wrong when he shot Gaetano Abrahamson, 20, and Shawn A. Marchysyhn, 18, at the Pennant Club apartments in Jackson Township June 28.

Worlock has admitted the killings, saying he was angry because Abrahamson had stolen his wallet.

Assistant Prosecutor William Cunningham told the jury Worlock, 22, of Castle Avenue, Jackson Township, wanted the wallet back not only because it contained about $130, but also because it had a picture of

him masked, wearing leather sado-masochistic garb.

Ravitz said Worlock is an admitted homosexual, who has twice been hospitalized at Marlboro State Hospital for mental illness.

In 1979, the attorney said, Worlock was diagnosed as being psychotic and suffering from drug use. The next time he was sent to Marlboro, doctors said he was schizophrenic.

In addition to being in the state hospital, Ravitz said Worlock had served time in the Yardville reformatory.

"He's not an angel. He's got a problem. He's sick. Does he know it? I don't know," Ravitz said.

He said Worlock intended to kill Abrahamson, who he called a "scum bag" who bullied Worlock. The killing of Marchysyhn, he said, was accidental.

Marchysyhn died after a single shot pierced his aorta, a main blood vessel from his heart.

Continued on Page 5

Congress lets the cash flow — for a day

WASHINGTON (UPI) — Congress approved a one-day stopgap measure yesterday to allow a half-billion idled federal workers to return to work and the Senate passed a $2 billion fiscal 1985 money bill, brightening hopes for adjournment.

"The president will sign the bill," a White House spokesman said. "Workers are to report back tomorrow (Friday)."

The stopgap measure, passed by voice vote in the House and Senate, was needed to give Congress time to resolve its differences over the catchall, year-long money bill needed to keep the government operating through fiscal 1985.

An hour earlier, the Senate — tacking on anti-crime measures — passed the $472 billion long-term money bill, but the promised speedy action came too late to keep

500,000 federal workers on the job.

The stopgap measure will provide the government with spending authority through 6 p.m. tonight.

Budget director David Stockman reiterated to Senate leaders the administration wants "a clean" spending bill without extraneous items attached.

And a S nate Republican leadership source put the chances of adjournment Friday at "one in five," adding that if work cannot be completed by Friday evening he expected the Senate to return Tuesday.

The joint conference committee

seeking to resolve differences on the larger bill met briefly late Thursday and planned to meet again through the night.

"We're very hopeful we can complete this conference expeditiously.

Continued on Page 5

Inside

My Pet Peeve

My pet peeve is taking a metal detector to the beach — hoping to find gold watches and diamond rings —

$1,000 a day fine

Lacey presses fuel rod fight

By David Sommer
Staff Writer

LACEY — The township's ban on importing nuclear waste, stuck down last month in federal district court but still the subject of ongoing appeals, was amended last night to in

Third Circuit Court of Appeals, the last step before the U.S. Supreme Court.

A motion to stay Bissell's decision is also pending in that court, and Lacey officials have vowed to continue the battle to stop the fuel rods

was passed.

He also disagreed that the rods have to be returned to Oyster Creek, the contention of the General Public Utilities Nuclear Corp. officials who operate the plant for JCP&L.

GPU Nuclear officials say that the

sites.

The committeeman said the company could store the used fuel at another nuclear site, such as their unusable Three Mile Island reactor, or else "put pressure on the feds to store it in their facilities."

Editor Robert Boyle. "It's what this paper should be, should have been, and hopes to be—the local news in depth." In the content analysis of 1977 newspapers, the *Observer* tied for eighth in local coverage.

The paper has few specialties beyond sports and lifestyle. One reporter writes a regular feature called the "The Neighbors," which Boyle describes as "chit-chat." Reporters are assigned to cover county government, the courts, and political news, and occasionally a reporter is sent to Trenton.

The *Ocean County Times-Observer* is the skeleton of a good newspaper waiting for growth. It cannot be compared with the *Daily Register*, which is already a good newspaper, let alone with the *Asbury Park Press*, one of the best newspapers in the state. Nevertheless, the *Times-Observer* has come a long way from the days of the weekly Brick Town *Observer* and the Lakewood *Times*.

The *Atlantic City Press* Bets on Casinos

Atlantic City was once the queen of the Jersey shore, with grand hotels catering to the finest clientele. But by the 1960s it was a resort in trouble. Its hotels were aged and threadbare, and poverty was taking the place of prosperity.

Vacation patterns had changed, explained Robert Ebener, managing editor of the *Atlantic City Press*. For those with money, it was the age of Miami, the Bahamas, and the Caribbean. When the 1964 Democratic National Convention was held in Atlantic City, a spotlight was thrown on the problems of the city. "There was no squalor then, but a growing shabbiness," said Ebener. "The city was on a balancing board."

The *Atlantic City Press* is a regional newspaper. Its motto is "Serving Southern New Jersey." Despite the decline of Atlantic City in the 1960s, the newspaper increased its circulation from 53,525 daily and 41,130 Sundays in 1963 to 70,209 daily and 67,076 Sundays in 1974. The newspaper became truly suburban in 1970 when it moved most of its operations from the city to nearby Pleasantville. The paper was attacked for its departure, and some city boosters actually went so far as to blame the decline of Atlantic City on the *Press*.

"We have been blamed for it," said Ebener, "because we pointed out the shortcomings of the political community, the business community, hotel operations, and the treatment of visitors. People came here and went away with the feeling that they were being taken, or ripped off. Hotel owners were milking their properties. We felt the city was in decline and wanted to get the

city out of it. We gave a voice to the black community and were highly
chastised by the establishment. They thought we were giving an outlet to
something that would just go away. The Miss America Pageant was disrupted
[by feminists]. Some people felt that everything would be all right if the lid was
kept on. The media became a scapegoat."

The election of Brendan T. Byrne as governor in 1973 quickened the pulse
of the dying city. Byrne reversed the policy of his predecessor and promised to
give Atlantic City a chance at the long-discussed innovation of casino gambling. A proposal for state-operated casinos, based on the Puerto Rican
model, was placed on the 1974 ballot but was defeated. Two years later, casino
proponents persuaded the state legislature to offer a referendum on a somewhat different proposal, privately owned gambling facilities regulated by the
state. The voters approved and in May 1978 Resorts International became the
first to open a hotel with gambling. By 1982 Atlantic City had nine casino
hotels.

The chairman of the pro-casino campaign for the 1974 referendum was
Robert Ford, the publisher of the *Atlantic City Press*. The newspaper had
joined the boosters.

"This wasn't a very good situation, to be honest with you," said his successor, Charles C. Reynolds. "We had a long talk about this strange form of
urban renewal. We agreed that it would be best that we try to cover all sides of
the campaign."

For the 1976 referendum, the pro-casino effort was professionally organized and heavily financed. The *Press* embraced the concept editorially, as did
the Philadelphia *Bulletin*, the Philadelphia *Inquirer*, the *New York Times*,
and the Passaic-Clifton *Herald-News*. Opponents included the *Record* of
Hackensack, the New Brunswick *Home News*, the *Asbury Park Press*, and the
Star-Ledger.

The *Press* backed up its editorial support, however, with cash, contributing
$45,000 to the campaign. Reynolds, who was now publisher of the *Press*,
agreed to serve on the Committee to Rebuild Atlantic City and soon found
himself a reluctant member of its executive committee. "It was a holy crusade
in this area," he said. "In Atlantic City it passed by a 10-to-1 margin. It was
hard to find anybody who would speak out against it."

Reynolds frankly admits that news coverage of the issue in the *Press* was
heavily weighted toward the pro-casino position, but he contends that this
coverage simply reflected the prevailing sentiment. Anti-casino speeches were
faithfuly covered, and opposition from communities within the *Press* circulation area, such as Wildwood, was reported. During the campaign, an interim
report of the National Commission on Gambling was released. It advised
against placing casinos in urban centers arguing that crowds could be more
easily policed in less accessible areas such as Las Vegas. The *Press* carried

news reports about the commission on the front page to the consternation of some members of the Committee to Rebuild Atlantic City, who wondered which side the newspaper was on.

"I never felt easy about my part in this," Reynolds said, "although there is nothing specific that I regret. And I have no regrets about the outcome. There are unsavory aspects of gambling, but the alternative would have been worse. Our only industry has been entertaining visitors; we had reached the point where nobody wanted to come here."

Reynolds acknowledges that the city's problems have not been solved, but he adds: "I'd hate to see what Atlantic City would be like without casinos. Of course we have slums, but we had them before."

Atlantic City, said Ebener, is "factionalized, almost in torment, crowded with political fortune seekers, which has made it impossible to get a sense of cohesiveness in the city government. It's a city that has not availed itself of the opportunities given it by the casinos."

Ebener believes that Atlantic City is still a good convention city, but he worries that the resort may not be able to keep up with the competition. In 1981, for example, the *Press* reported that the baking industry was ready to switch its $20 million 1985 exposition to Atlanta because plans for convention hall were falling short of realization. "Everybody is saying there won't be more casino investment until the convention hall is built," said Ebener. "Everything is on hold. It all has to come together. What if we get the center but don't have the hotel room? We're back to 1964 again."

Despite its support of casinos, the *Press* had editorialized against the proposal to keep them open around the clock. "If 24-hour gambling is approved," the *Press* said in 1981, "Atlantic City's 'clockless casinos' may become nothing more than gamblers' hangouts, dashing any hope of rebuilding the city as a quality resort with diversified attractions geared to the family trade."

The *Press* also makes it clear that it is not a public relations organ for the casinos. In 1981, the newspaper's statehouse reporter, Michael Diamond, came up with a devastating confidential state police report on the rise of crime in Atlantic City since the coming of casinos. The *Press* ran it on page one. And in the same year, the newspaper published a three-part series on the increasing number of derelicts in the city.

Before the casinos came to Atlantic City, the *Press* was not a very good paper. It was not ranked among the state's leaders in any category in the 1974 poll of reporters and editors conducted by the Center for Analysis of Public Issues. The center's study of 1974 newspapers found the *Press* to be a 33-page paper with 19 pages of ads and 14 pages of news. Thus it ranked 16th in advertising, and 19th in the size of its news hole. It was 13th in the quantity of national news, 15th in local coverage, tied for 15th in foreign news, and a lowly 22nd in state coverage.

The content analysis of 1977 daily papers conducted for this project shows a bigger newspaper significantly improved only in the area of local news coverage. The 1977 *Press'* 24 pages of ads ranked a strong seventh, and its 17-page news hole put it in a three-way tie for 12th. The increased number of local stories earned a tie for fourth place, but the *Press* tied for ninth in international coverage, tied for 17th in national news, and tied for 22nd in state coverage. Thus it ranked only 18th in the total number of news and feature stories. The *Press* tied for 11th in the number of locally originated stories, tied for 14th in the number of longer stories, and tied for 19th for its use of photographs.

Today's *Press* is on an upswing. Its circulation has been increasing steadily, if unspectacularly. It has the fifth largest circulation in the state (up from eighth place in 1977), with 1983 sales of 79,629 daily and 86,602 on Sundays. While the casinos have not brought prosperity to Atlantic City, there has been growth in the neighboring towns, and the very suburban *Atlantic City Press* has benefited significantly. The labor-intensive casinos have created roughly 30,000 jobs, and for the *Press* this has meant an increase in classified advertising, especially for help wanted and real estate. New jobs have been created at the *Press* as well, and the paper now has an impressive news staff of 94.

The coming of casinos has changed the newspaper content considerably. An entertainment writer works full-time covering casino performers, and there is a special entertainment section on Fridays. A reporter is permanently assigned to casino news. A labor reporter spends much of his time on casino issues, as does an organized crime reporter who explores possible mob infiltration. The statehouse reporter spends about half his time covering the Casino Control Commission, which usually meets in Trenton, and legislative issues involving gambling. Reynolds says, "The casinos have done wonders for the caliber of news we've had to report."

Casino coverage is local coverage for the *Press*, and local news is clearly the newspaper's strong suit. Two reporters cover city hall in Atlantic City on a full-time basis. The paper maintains a nine-member bureau in Vineland, six reporters in Wildwood, and three in Manahawkin. "We cover a huge area," said Ebener. "We try to cover at least every governing body meeting in the towns that we are in. If we don't, we try to determine in advance that we can skip it. If it's a polarized situation, we're there. We don't cover some outlying towns for sheer lack of manpower."

In addition to its home base of Atlantic County, the *Press* covers all of Cumberland and Cape May counties, the southern half of Ocean County, parts of Salem and Gloucester counties, and the eastern fringe of Burlington County—an ambitious assignment. Competition comes from several sources. Cumberland County has three daily newspapers. The *Asbury Park Press* dominates northern Ocean County, and the *Ocean County Times-Observer* is in Toms River. The Philadelphia *Inquirer* and the Camden *Courier-Post*

The ⟨NJ⟩ Press

Copyright 1984 South Jersey Publishing Company

Serving Southern New Jersey

Single Copy 25¢   Home Delivered/$1.50 Per Week   ATLANTIC CITY, N. J. THURSDAY, SEPTEMBER 27, 1984   *Cape May County Edition*

A.C. Court Backlog Blamed on Judge

Judge GENNARO CONSALVO
'Lack of responsibility' cited

By JOSEPH TANFANI
Press Staff Writer

ATLANTIC CITY — The city Municipal Court doesn't work efficiently mainly because Municipal Court Judge Gennaro Consalvo doesn't work enough, according to the area's supervising judge.

Assignment Judge Philip A. Gruccio, in a tough-worded introduction to a state study of the city's court, said Consalvo's record as Atlantic City judge is

marked by a consistent "lack of responsibility."

According to the study by the state Administrative Office of the Courts, Consalvo has persisted in his lackadaisical work habits since he was appointed in March 1980. He misses work entirely one day per week and spends only two-thirds of the required amount of time on the job, according to Gruccio and the AOC.

Consalvo repeatedly has been called onto the carpet by Gruccio and another judge and ordered to

The complaints of postponements, cancellations of court and of court never starting on time are unending,' Judge Philip Gruccio wrote.

devote at least 30 hours a week of bench time to his $57,200-a-year judgeship. Those orders have been ignored, Gruccio said; Consalvo instead works only about 20 hours a week, and spends a mere 11 hours on the bench hearing cases.

"The question must be asked,

'Why does the Municipal Court continue to be backlogged and incapable of maintaining any degree of efficiency?' " Gruccio wrote in a Sept. 18 letter to Mayor James Usry.

"The answer is provided consistently within the attached (report); the present judge is a 'full-

time' judge in the Atlantic City Municipal Court only in name," the letter reads.

Gruccio's letter to Usry is accompanied by an 18-page analysis of the resort's Municipal Court prepared by the Municipal Court.
(Continued on Page 3)

U.S.-Soviet Dialogue Resumes

Reagan's message: Uncle Sam has 'spine of steel' — Page 14

UNITED NATIONS (AP) — Secretary of State George P. Shultz and Soviet Foreign Minister Andrei A. Gromyko met for three hours Wednesday, making what one official described as "a good start" on improving frayed U.S.-Soviet relations.

The talks will continue Friday, when Gromyko journeys to Washington to meet with President Reagan at the White House.

A senior U.S. official, who spoke only on condition he not be identified, indicated that decisions for improving relations weren't made at the Shultz-Gromyko meeting but that the atmosphere was "calm and thoughtful" and that both sides had "a good give-and-take."

The two superpowers are "in the midst of a process of discussion" this week, the official said. "Today's discussions were a good start."

Shultz and Gromyko both were smiling and relaxed after the meeting at the U.S. Mission to the United Nations. Gromyko joked that while he couldn't answer any questions until after his meeting with Reagan, reporters could ask him "a thousand questions" then.

The Soviet minister said that he and Shultz discussed a wide range of topics but that "the discussions were not concluded, not full" and would be continued in Washington.

The U.S. official who briefed reporters indicated that Shultz had raised Reagan's proposals for improved relations with Moscow, including the president's suggestion for regular Cabinet-level meetings.

He declined to characterize
(Continued on Page 14)

Local 54 Leaders Win Stay

By DANIEL HENEGHAN
Press Staff Writer

An appeals court ruled Wednesday that the president and another official or an Atlantic City union will not have to resign by Friday as ordered by the Casino Control Commission.

The Appellate Division of Superior Court panel issued a stay of the commission's order that President Frank Gerace and executive board member Frank Materio resign their posts with Local 54 of the Hotel and Restaurant Employees and Bartenders International by Friday. The casino commission had ordered the men to resign because of their associations with Nicodemo "Little Nicky" Scarfo, the reputed head of organized crime operations in Atlantic City and Philadelphia.

The union represents approximately 12,000 non-casino employees in Atlantic City's 10 casino hotels as well as approximately 2,000 workers in non-casino hotels and motels.

The appeals court ruling came within hours after the casino commission refused to issue a similar stay. It also rejected a request from the union and three of its officials to reopen a hearing that was concluded in September 1982.

Attorneys for the casino commission and the Division of Gaming Enforcement indicated they are considering appealing the de-

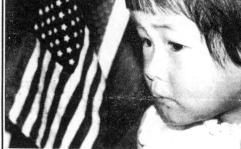

THE NEWEST AMERICAN — Clutching her American flag, Korean native Christin Roesler, 2, of Egg Harbor City, looks somber as she and 18 others become U.S. citizens during

naturalization ceremonies in the Atlantic County Courthouse in Mays Landing on Wednesday. (Story, more photos on Page 32.)

Staff photo by Walter O'Brien

Wildwood Worker Is Indicted

By WILLIAM J. WATSON
Press Staff Writer

WILDWOOD — Sanitation foreman Edward Williams filed false information in order to get Civil Service hiring preference, according to an indictment handed up by a Cape May County grand jury Tuesday.

Williams has been suspended

by City Personnel Director Kevin Yecco "in accordance with city policy." Yecco said a departmental hearing would be held after court proceedings against Williams are concluded.

According to the indictment, Williams, the center of controversy in Wildwood for months, falsified a job application in 1982 "by knowingly altering the discharge

date on his report of honorable discharge from the United States Air Force."

That, the indictment charges, gave Williams an "unlawful hiring preference."

Williams faces up to 18 months in jail and fines of up to $7,500 if convicted.

The indictment comes one week before City Council opens

hearings into how Williams was hired. The Press has learned that the allegedly false discharge date is only one "discrepancy" City Council noted in reviewing Williams' personnel file.

The hearings will open Tuesday as scheduled.

Williams' existence as a city
(Continued on Page 14)

Broadcaster John Facenda, 72, Dies

PHILADELPHIA (AP) — John Facenda, the dramatic voice of National Football League highlight films and a pioneer broadcaster credited with originating late-night television newscasts, died Wednesday. He was 72.

Facenda's rich baritone was recognized by millions and his smooth, evenly paced style earned praise from broadcasters throughout his 51-year career in

Award ceremonies less than two weeks ago but unable to attend, died at 8:45 a.m. in Fitzgerald Mercy Hospital in nearby Darby, a spokeswoman said. His colleagues said he had been suffering from cancer.

"His marvelous voice and unique delivery will always be an important part of the history of the National Football League," said NFL Commissioner Pete Rozelle. "All football people and

executive vice president of NFL Films Inc., of Mount Laurel, N.J., which hired Facenda to narrate its weekly highlights show in 1962. His last work for the company involved highlights of this year's Super Bowl.

"He had a voice that could make a laundry list sound dramatic. Somebody once said he could make the coin toss sound like Armageddon. I called it his

for 25 years at WCAU-TV where, in 1948, he convinced management to broadcast an 11 p.m. news show, the first of its kind in the country, according to the station.

Called "Here at the 11th Hour," the show debuted in September 1948 on a weekly basis and had become a daily fixture by 1952, when Facenda joined the station full time after 17 years on radio

reach into many *Press* areas. Pleasantville has a strong weekly paper, and the weeklies in Cape May County are competitive.

The shore communities are particularly concerned with the problems of toxic wastes and offshore dumping, and the *Press* takes environmental coverage seriously. The paper has a full-time energy and environment reporter, and the statehouse reporter pays close attention to the Department of Environmental Protection.

Seven staffers are assigned to sports, covering local events and Philadelphia professional teams, but other areas of coverage receive little emphasis. The paper does not have a full-time business reporter, and there is little business news other than that supplied as part of casino coverage. State, national, and international stories provided by the Associated Press, United Press International, States News Service, and the Los Angeles Times/Washington Post News Service are run on the second and third pages of the newspaper, which are left free of advertising. But even in its selection of wire-service news, the *Press* demonstrates its basic concerns, giving prominent display to stories involving casino gambling.

Abarta, Inc., the family-controlled corporation that owns the *Press*, the Bethlehem (Pa.) *Globe-Times*, and a number of Coca-Cola bottling plants, has been both wise and lucky. It moved the *Press* to Pleasantville and avoided the crush of casino traffic that came nearly a decade later. It installed video display terminals and modern production facilities in 1975, just in time to handle its growing needs. And it put money in its news operation in line with the newspaper's expansion.

"I think we have a higher quality staff than we had years ago," said Ebener. "This is partly due to better salaries. Also a lot of people are knocking on our doors, and at other papers like ours. Once it was such an employee's market that if some high school student said he wanted to write, we'd train him."

The *Atlantic City Press* still has too many holes (in its state, national, and business coverage) to be considered a very good newspaper. But it now has a large, qualified staff, and its local reporting, already solid, appears to be steadily improving. Many suburban newspapers emphasize local and regional news and pay little attention to other coverage areas. Such unbalanced coverage is often a necessity for small papers with limited resources. The *Press* is now a major regional newspaper, and it is time for it to offer substantial reporting in all significant coverage areas.

Cumberland County's Three Dailies

South Jersey's sparsely populated Cumberland County is the only county in the state with three daily newspapers. For many years they were all locally owned: the Johnson family owned the *Millville Daily*, the Leuchter family had the Vineland *Times Journal*, and the Schofields controlled the *Bridgeton Evening News*.

"My dad used to talk to the Johnsons and the Leuchters about the savings that could be effected if we all got together with a central printing plant," recalled John Schofield, the publisher of the Bridgeton paper. "But he could never get them to go along."

The country-squire atmosphere disappeared from publishing in Cumberland County when the Detroit *News*' corporation, the Evening News Association, first bought the Vineland daily, and then the Millville paper. The company also purchased three area weeklies, the *Hammonton News*, the Egg Harbor *News*, and the *Atlantic County Record*, and has a large commercial printing subsidiary in Vineland.

The *Bridgeton Evening News* remains a distinctly local operation. Schofield's son Dean serves as managing editor, nephew Edwin Schofield is vice president, and nephew James Homan is advertising director. Schofield's son John runs the computer facilities.

Published in the county seat, the 12,419-circulation *Evening News* covers much of Cumberland and a small portion of Salem County with a newsroom staff of 11 people. Schofield said he had no thought of switching the weekday paper to morning publication, although the Saturday edition is distributed, for the most part, on Saturday morning. None of the three Cumberland dailies publishes a Sunday edition, and none has changed to mornings.

The study of 1977 New Jersey newspapers found the Bridgeton *News* to be somewhat better than its small circulation would suggest. Although it was very weak in state coverage and in the use of longer stories and photographs, its news hole tied for 15th, and the paper ranked 16th in national news. It ranked 17th in local news and tied for 18th in locally originated stories.

The Bridgeton newspaper continues to be a modest operation, with little in the way of specialties except for sportswriters and "women's page" writers. It publishes a business page on Tuesdays and an enlarged section of "women's" material on Wednesdays. It gets its statehouse news from the UPI service.

The *Millville Daily*, with nine on its news staff, and the Vineland *Times Journal*, with 20, are combining many of their operations. "For a while the two papers were kept separate because it was feared that people would resent a combination," said Ben Burns, then the publisher of both newspapers. "But it was silly to see two reporters covering the same event for the two papers. We

Showers
Details on page 2

Vineland Times Journal

Saturday
September 15, 1984
Twenty Cents

Delsea Teachers Protest

By FRAN SHEEHAN
Staff Writer

FRANKLINVILLE — Delsea Regional High School teachers, frustrated over delays in settling their contract, picketed in front of the school Friday to make their complaints public.

Representatives of the Delsea Education Association and Delsea Regional School Board are expected to meet at a collective bargaining session 7:30 p.m. Sunday to discuss salary, benefits and working conditions.

Teachers have already voted to strike if talks reach an impasse.

The parties failed to reach a settlement during a negotiation session at the high school Thursday evening which continued into the early morning hours of Friday.

"One of the primary concerns is a change in working conditions this year," said protester Eileen Master, an English teacher for 13 years. "Last year, for example, we worked from 7:30 a.m. to 12:30 p.m. without a break. This year, we work from 7:30 to 1:20 and get no break. I mean, six hours without one ten-minute break to go to the lavatory? We're talking about basic human needs here."

The teachers' schedule was changed from last year because

(Continued on Page 2)

Staff photo/James Ballerie

Teachers walked a picket line outside Delsea Regional High School Friday to protest a delay in the settlement of their work contract. Negotiators will meet Sunday night to continue to hash out an agreement between the school board and teacher representatives on salary and work schedules.

Pres. Reagan To Campaign In Hammonton

By JEFF DAVIS
Staff Writer

HAMMONTON — President Reagan is planning a brief campaign stop here next week which will include entertainment from the award-winning Vineland High School Marching Clan, officials confirmed Friday.

The President's advance team has been in Hammonton for several days preparing the area for the Wednesday visit which is expected to include a brief campaign address from Reagan during an outdoor rally.

Members of the Vineland band were told Friday afternoon that they were invited to entertain the President in Hammonton. They will spend the next few days getting ready for the late-afternoon performance under the direction of band advisor John Parks.

The Marching Clan will perform with bands from Hammonton High School and Oak Crest High School.

The campaign stop is expected to last about an hour, with the President heading to Connecticut to campaign later in the day, officials said.

Hammonton's main street, Bellevue Avenue, will be blocked off and a stage set up for Reagan's address. He is expected to arrive in Hammonton at 5 p.m. accompanied by Gov. Thomas Kean and Senator William Gormley, R-Atlantic.

Hammonton Mayor George Mortellite is expected to address the crowd.

"This is the biggest thing we've ever had," said Mortellite, whose farming community is well known for its blueberry production. "We're very enthused about this."

Mortellite said that even though Hammonton has a population of 12,500, he expected 15,000 to 20,000 people to attend the rally.

"He has a great deal of support here," said Mortellite. "The people love him here. He's a Republican, and people here are Republican. People think he's done an excellent job."

Mortellite said he believed his town was chosen for the visit because of the enthusiastic welcome local residents gave Kean when he visited for the community's Feast of Our Lady of Mt. Carmel celebration last July 16.

Judge OK's Hearing In Davis Case

By JACK CHIELLI
Staff Writer

MAYS LANDING — A Superior Court Judge ruled Friday to hold a special hearing to determine in advance of the sentencing trial of confessed murderer Stephen Raymond Davis if testimony by an expert witness is admissible.

Judge Manuel Greenberg agreed with Atlantic County Chief Assistant Prosecutor Lloyd Levenson that the admissibility of noted criminologist Dr. Marvin Wolfgang's testimony should be decided at a pre-trial hearing rather than during the course of the trial, which is the standard procedure.

Davis shuffled into the courtroom cuffed and belted and sat quietly listening to the court proceedings.

The 27-year-old painter from Buena pleaded guilty last fall to the murder of Barbara Blomberg. He is the first murderer in the state to plead guilty to a capital offense knowing he could face death by lethal injection.

Blomberg, 24, was found in the bedroom of her Minotola apartment on Jan. 17, 1983, strangled and stabbed 48 times.

The question of whether Wolfgang's testimony was admissible was ruled on by the state supreme court in June.

The court ruled statistical evidence showing someone's personal background can be heard.

Wolfgang is expected to testify that national statistics support the defense's contention Davis can be successfully rehabilitated in 30 years and pose no threat to society.

Levenson contends Wolfgang's testimony doesn't distinguish Davis from the mass of society.

Greenberg said he never had a request for a pre-trial hearing to determine whether a witness's testimony was admissible or not.

"In light of the supreme

Taxpayers Won't Foot Demolition Bill

By JEFF DAVIS
Staff Writer

The run-down and controversial property at the corner of Fourth and Wood streets will be torn down by its owner later this fall and not with taxpayers' money, Vineland Mayor Joseph Romano said Friday.

Romano said he met Wednesday with Bernard Brown, owner of the property, and was told the three houses and former laundry building will be torn down in November.

The announcement ends speculation that the city was going to tear down the property at the expense of the public.

The mayor's announcement also may prompt the council to find another use for the approximately $250,000 left over from a $1.7 million grant the city received from the U.S. Department of Housing and Urban Development in 1982.

"Bernie Brown decided he didn't want to be obligated to the city, and he didn't want any problems," Romano said, adding that he was angered by recent accusations that a "deal" was being worked out between Brown and the city.

"There were no 'deals' made, and there never will be any

'deals' made by Joe Romano," the mayor said.

"This administration has always been concerned with that area and now something is going to be done about it," Romano said. "It's not going to stay like that for four years."

Brown, chairman of the board of National Freight Inc., could not be reached Friday for details on his plans for the property.

Romano said plans for the property were discussed at a recent closed session of the city council.

The abandoned houses and old laundry were the center of several controversies during the past few years after it was suggested the grant money be used to tear down Brown's buildings.

One side — headed by former City Council President Carlo Costantino — argued the funds should be used for downtown sidewalk and curb improvements, rather than bailing out property owners who neglect their land.

The other side — including Council President Si Solazzo and

then-councilman Romano — argued that since the money was targeted for downtown improvements it would best be used at the dilapidated Fourth and Wood site.

Part of the $1.7 million grant was used in 1983 when several buildings — including the MIT Apartments and Sam's Bar — were purchased at their assessed value and torn down. New sidewalks downtown were also partially funded through the federal program.

Tax Board Nominee's Confirmation Expected

Vineland insurance executive M. Jay Einstein is expected to be confirmed by the New Jersey Senate as the newest member of the Cumberland County Board of Taxation.

The 36-year-old Republican committeeman was nominated for a seat on the board by Gov. Thomas Kean. He will replace Vinelander Victor LaTorre at $8,000 a year post.

Einstein, a Certified Life Underwriter, (CLU) is a partner with his father in Einstein Associates, a Vineland insurance firm. He ran for city council on the Republican ticket in 1976 and in 1980, making the runoff election twice.

The board of taxation hears tax appeal cases from all municipalities in the county. Cases that cannot be resolved before the board

(Continued on Page 3)

M. Jay Einstein

Amusement Park Indicted In 8 Deaths

TOMS RIVER (AP) — A Jackson Township amusement park and two executives were charged in an indictment unsealed Friday with manslaughter in the deaths of eight teen-agers trapped when a "haunted house" erupted into flames four months ago.

(Continued on Page 3)

Don't Wait for Disaster to Strike To Discover Red Cross Programs

By MALINDA REINKE
Staff Writer

The problem with the Red Cross, she said, is that people don't usually give it much thought unless they're in a fire or a flood.

In less troubled times, it keeps a very low profile.

Marian Ricci, head of the local chapter, and her assistant, Monica Billings, sat at a table in the Vineland Red Cross office on East Avenue and talked about all the good things their organization does in town and all the things it would like to do — if only people would take advantage.

"The Red Cross is a fine organization," Ricci said. "It's good for Vineland, especially since we're in an economically poor area.

"There are people without food and housing here. We rarely turn anyone away. There's usually something we can do, even if it's just a referral.

"Talk like this — tooting-its-own-horn-talk — is not the Red Cross style in Vineland. But once in a

Vineland United Way and the Vineland Police — local senior citizens, handicapped and homebound can receive help if they're in trouble.

If a poorman finds a person's mail has not been removed from the box the following day, he will notify the Red Cross. A Red Cross worker and a police officer will check the home.

So far only eight people are taking advantage of this new service. Red Cross workers ask anyone interested in participating to contact the office.

"This community really needs the Red Cross," Ricci said. "But unless you're a serviceman or you give blood on a regular basis, you just don't think about us at all."

The Vineland Red Cross helped Clarence and Lois Prince contact their serviceman son, Gregory, last October during the trouble in Lebanon. Gregory was stationed in Beirut at the time the U.S. Marine barracks was destroyed. They wanted to know if he was OK.

Another time the chapter funded a trip to Germany for the parents of a local soldier who was

just don't have that much manpower that we can afford to waste it. Now we have one person covering the court house in Bridgeton for both newspapers."

The first step in the consolidation was the closing of the Millville printing press. Both papers are printed at the Vineland plant. "The papers will never have the same local news content," said Burns, who was an assistant managing editor at the Detroit *News*. "*Millville* runs a regional wrap-up, for example, and may use a digest of copy from the Vineland paper, but not the same stories."

Many other features are being combined, such as the comics page. Identical national and international news stories are being used in the two newspapers. The photographic staffs are being combined, along with the photographic services of the three weeklies the company owns in the area.

The study of 1977 New Jersey newspapers rated the *Millville Daily* the weakest newspaper in the state. The then 7,126-circulation paper finished at the bottom or near the bottom in every category. The 1977 Vineland *Times Journal*, with a circulation of 17,032, carried three more pages of news than the Millville paper, but five less than the Bridgeton *News*. While its local and state coverage were respectable, it finished near the bottom in virtually every other category, and among the state's lowest-rated newspapers overall.

Burns intended to publish "an all-purpose newspaper, so that readers, if they want to read one paper, can get everything in ours." Nevertheless, the 17,441-circulation *Times Journal* and 6,915-circulation *Millville Daily* had no newsroom specialists except for sports and home economics writers, and continued to rely on the AP for state new coverage.

Competition from outside Cumberland County comes from Philadelphia, Camden, and Atlantic City, with the *Atlantic City Press* maintaining a large bureau in Vineland.

The *Gloucester County Times* Goes Local

Just south of Philadelphia and Camden lies Woodbury, N.J., the home of the *Gloucester County Times*. Once known as the *Woodbury Daily Times*, the newspaper was locally owned until 1972, when it was purchased by Harte-Hanks Communications, a daily and weekly newspaper chain based in San Antonio, Texas.

In December 1983 Harte-Hanks announced that it was selling the evening newspaper to William Dean Singleton, who as an executive of Allbritton Newspapers served as president of three New Jersey newspapers, and Richard Scudder, former publisher of the *Newark News* and the founder of the Garden

State Paper Company. The sale was to take place early in 1984, and Singleton was to leave Allbritton Newspapers to become publisher of the Woodbury paper.

In the mid-1970s Harte-Hanks dropped the newspaper's Saturday edition and added a Sunday edition. According to Publisher Richard Bilotti (who would leave Woodbury in 1984 to become publisher of the *Trenton Times*), the company at that time stressed the paper's all-purpose quality, rather than emphasizing local coverage.

"I think it was a very dumb idea," said Bilotti, a former *Newark News* reporter who served as Sunday magazine editor for the Cleveland *Plain Dealer* before becoming editor in Woodbury in 1979. "Now it is a local paper. About 80 percent of what's in it is locally produced here by the staff. We do have national and world news, and state and regional news, but our strong point is local news." The mistake, he said, was to try to compete as a world and national newspaper against the Philadelphia *Inquirer*, which he described as "one of the best if not the best newspaper in the country."

"We're not going to compete with that," he said. "We know that people locally are interested in their tax rates, who is going to pick up the leaves, who is stealing money from the county government, and how we're going to get rid of the gypsy moths—and there's nobody else around to give them that kind of news. So we cover Gloucester County like the *Washington Post* covers the United States government. We'll go to bat for people and take on crusades. All of our editorials are locally produced about local topics. We take stands on stoplights and on anything."

Bilotti as editor worked hard to de-emphasize meeting stories and make the newspaper people-oriented. But since he moved up to publisher in 1981, "it has floated back the other way a little bit," he said. "I think what you have to do is find out what's happening at the municipal meetings and develop trend stories." Bilotti's approach was to cover municipal meetings with stringers, augmented by full-time people.

The contént of the newspaper showed the Bilotti influence: local people-oriented feature columns, and a weekly insert called "Our Town." "In that little weekly newspaper," Bilotti said, "we have made it possible for a local advertiser that is only interested in people in Woodbury to afford advertising. And we've also given ourselves more news hole to run things about the local school board, the chicken dinner kind of news." By 1983 a number of different versions of the "Our Town" insert were being produced.

The *Times* has a newsroom complement of 25 full-time people and eight to 15 part-timers and stringers. Ten to 12 reporters cover municipalities, four or five people compose the feature department, and about the same number put together the Living section for Sunday. Specialized reporting includes police, county government, the county court house, transportation, business, entertainment, consumer news, and statehouse coverage in Trenton. The newspaper has a Sports Monday page, a Wednesday food page, consumer news on Thursday, and a Friday entertainment section called "Breakaway." A five-member staff covers sports, including the home games of Philadelphia professional teams.

The *Times'* circulation at the end of 1983 was 28,234 daily and 30,062 on Sundays, up from 26,134 daily and 26,606 Sundays in 1980, and 24,663 daily and 23,990 Sundays in 1976. The paper publishes a single edition with a 10:30 a.m. press time, and competes with the Camden *Courier-Post*, the Philadelphia *Daily News*, and a number of weeklies, in addition to the *Inquirer*.

The 1983 *Gloucester County Times* was a very different newspaper from the one analyzed in the study of 1977 New Jersey papers. The 1977 *Times* was 10th in national news and tied for 13th in international news, while tying for 13th in local news, tying for 15th in locally originated stories, and tying for 16th in state news. The 1983 *Times* was much more local, and it appeared to be a better newspaper overall.

Today's Sunbeam Serves Salem

The newest daily in the state, *Today's Sunbeam*, was created out of five weeklies in 1972. Located on the southwestern edge of New Jersey, just across the Delaware River from Wilmington, *Today's Sunbeam* covers Salem County and little else, with heavier coverage along the riverfront than in the eastern part of the county.

It is a very small newspaper (22 pages) with a very small circulation (10,685) that shows no sign of growth. Its newsroom staff numbers only 15, including two photographers, two sports editors, and a Family Living writer. Its news reporters are assigned to local geographic beats.

Considering its size, *Today's Sunbeam* made quite a respectable showing in the study of 1977 New Jersey newspapers conducted for this project. Although 23rd in national news and tied for 24th in state news, it tied for 13th in local and international coverage and for the number of locally originated stories, tied for 14th for the number of longer stories, and ranked an amazing fifth for its use of photographs. Not bad for a newspaper with a 12-page news hole.

Today's Sunbeam is a one-edition morning Monday-to-Friday paper, with a 1 a.m. press time. There is no serious talk about Saturday or Sunday publication. "We're quite happy just publishing five days a week," said then Editor Eugene Laning. The paper has no chief competitor, Laning said, but the competition is nonetheless real for that. To the east there are small New

Jersey newspapers, to the west there is Wilmington, and in the north lies Camden and Philadelphia.

When *Today's Sunbeam* was created, the new daily kept the same staff as had worked on the weeklies, and the same presses. The *Penns Grove Record*, a weekly acquired in 1979, operates out of the *Sunbeam* newsroom with its own reporters, but sharing some functions.

The *Sunbeam* news content sometimes makes it appear as if the paper were still in the process of converting from weekly publication. One issue in 1981 included a five-paragraph item detailing where a Pedricktown family took visitors on the various days of their stay—including the homes in which they had dinner. Another story devoted three paragraphs to the birthday party of a 4-year-old Woodstown girl, describing the cake and the Bugs Bunny theme. But the paper does provide substantial coverage of the major issues in the area, such as the problems involving the nuclear generating plants, Salem 1 and Salem 2.

In October 1984, the *Sunbeam* was sold to William Dean Singleton and Richard Scudder, who had earlier acquired the *Gloucester County Times*.

Postscript

New Jersey's 26 daily newspapers differ widely in size, scope, ability, and technology—ranging from grand, fullcolor, regional dailies to small, struggling, local papers. Nevertheless, it is possible to make some generalizations about them, and about the press and the suburbs.

First, the general level of the state's daily newspapers appears to be fairly good. This impression is based on interviews and discussions with a variety of peripatetic reporters and editors who have worked for papers throughout the country. New Jerseyans tend to underestimate their newspapers because they compare them to the giants of New York and Philadelphia and not to dailies of comparable size and resources.

The American press, like professional baseball, has a number of different levels. New Jersey journalism is comparable to Triple-A baseball—full of good players waiting to be called up to the big leagues, the nation's major metropolitan dailies. For one thing, most New Jersey newspapers do not pay enough to keep their best talent. But more importantly, many young journalists view the state as a place to learn their trade—a stepping stone to greater glories elsewhere. Their role models are the former New Jersey reporters who

147

have gone on to fame and fortune, people like political writer Richard Reeves and Carl Bernstein of Woodward and Bernstein. Someday, perhaps, New Jersey journalism—and suburban journalism in general—will be seen as a place to stay and become famous, but today it is still one step short of the big leagues.

Second, the general level of the state's daily newspapers is better than it was a generation ago. This is not unique to New Jersey, but part of a national trend. Most newspapers today top their performances of 20 or 30 years ago because of an increasing professionalism in the ranks, but New Jersey papers may have improved more than the average. For one thing, their news holes have increased considerably. A Thursday *Star-Ledger* in 1984 is just about as big as a Sunday *Newark News* was in 1964. And together with this added space, many of the state's dailies now carry science writers, consumer writers, movie critics, and other specialties that were rarely found on New Jersey dailies a generation ago.

Suburbanization is directly related to this trend. In response to increases in circulation and advertising, many suburban newspapers have transformed themselves from small-time dailies or even weeklies into solid, regional papers. Although they are moderate in size and scope compared to major metropolitan dailies, the degree of change in the suburbs has been extraordinary.

Finally, the successful New Jersey newspapers have responded flexibly to the changes in their environment to the point where New Jersey journalism and suburban journalism are now virtually synonymous. These papers have adjusted to the new economic base, which can be characterized as the "shopping-centerization" of America, and the new demographic base of suburbs that have become bigger than some center cities. To symbolize this change, many of them have dropped the old city names from their titles, and a good number have completely moved their plants to the suburbs.

One practical outcome of suburbanization is that despite the increase in specialties, most New Jersey reporters cover beats defined by geography. In urban journalism, reporters are assigned to cover specific political or social structures; one covers hospitals, another covers the transit system, and a third covers the city council. In suburban journalism, most reporters cover geography: East Atherton Township, West Atherton Township, and Bickerton. Like other suburbanites, they must own cars, and they spend a good deal of their time in them. Suburban reporters drive from one township and borough to another, from one meeting to another, from one police station to the next, in a fast-paced effort to keep up with what is happening—or to come up with the night's quota of stories.

Suburban journalism is usually defined as local, local, local. Many consider this local emphasis the key to the success of suburban newspapers. The best suburban dailies define local coverage in terms of their entire circulation area, and cover critical issues such as housing, transportation, education, and the environment from a regional perspective. But all too many suburban newspapers define local coverage in the strictest terms, rarely giving reporters assigned to geographic beats the extra time needed to venture beyond them. Parochialism is both the strength and the fundamental problem of suburban journalism.